NOTE FROM

On Friday, August 13, 2010, just as St. Martin's Press was readying its initial shipments of this book to be released from our warehouse, the Department of Defense contacted us to express its concern that our publication of *Operation Dark Heart* could cause damage to U.S. national security. This was unexpected, since we knew the author, Lieutenant Colonel Anthony Shaffer, had worked closely with the Department of the Army, and had made a number of changes to the text, after which it passed the Army's operational security review. However, the Department of Defense, and the Defense Intelligence Agency in particular, insisted that the Army review was insufficient. Thereafter, Lieutenant Colonel Shaffer worked with the Department of Defense, the Defense Intelligence Agency, and other interested U.S. intelligence agencies to review the changes that they demanded he make to his book. Because Lieutenant Colonel Shaffer is a security professional having some twenty-five years experience, we were confident then, as we are confident now, that he had not revealed anything in his book that could damage our national security, harm our troops, or harm U.S. military intelligence efforts or assets. However, based on the discussions our author had with the government he requested that we incorporate some of the government's changes into a revised edition of his book while redacting other text he was told was classified, though he disagreed with that assessment.

Because we support our author fully, we honored his request that we make those changes and redactions. The text that follows is the result of the extraordinary review of Lieutenant Colonel Shaffer's book by the Department of Defense, the Defense Intelligence Agency, and other U.S. intelligence agencies. We apologize for any frustration readers may encounter in reading *Operation Dark Heart* in this redacted form, but we are confident Lieutenant Colonel Shaffer's remarkable and vivid story will shine through nonetheless.

—Thomas Dunne

New York, September 8, 2010

OPERATION DARK HEART

SPYCRAFT AND SPECIAL OPS ON THE
FRONTLINES OF AFGHANISTAN—AND
THE PATH TO VICTORY

LT. COL. ANTHONY SHAFFER

THOMAS DUNNE BOOKS
ST. MARTIN'S GRIFFIN
NEW YORK

THOMAS DUNNE BOOKS.
An imprint of St. Martin's Press.

OPERATION DARK HEART. Copyright © 2010 by Lt. Col. Anthony Shaffer.
All rights reserved. Printed in the United States of America. For information,
address St. Martin's Press, 175 Fifth Avenue, New York, N.Y. 10010.

www.thomasdunnebooks.com
www.stmartins.com

Designed by Kelly S. Too

The Library of Congress has cataloged the hardcover edition as follows:

Shaffer, Anthony.
    Operation dark heart : spycraft and special ops on the frontlines of Afghanistan—and
the path to victory / Anthony Shaffer.—1st ed.
    p. cm.
    Includes bibliographical references and index.
    ISBN 978-0-312-60369-4
    1. Shaffer, Anthony.   2. Afghan War, 2001—Personal narratives, American.
3. Afghan War, 2001—Secret service—United States.   4. Afghan War, 2001—Military
intelligence.   5. Intelligence officers—United States—Biography. 6. United States.
Defense Intelligence Agency. 7. Espionage—Afghanistan.   8. Special operations
(Military science)—Afghanistan.   I. Title.
    DS371.413.S535 2010
    958.104'7—dc22   2010021685

ISBN 978-0-312-60691-6 (trade paperback)

First St. Martin's Griffin Edition: October 2011

D 10 9 8 7 6 5 4 3

✦

To my great-uncle, Joseph "Tony" Fernandez, who served in World War II, and dedicated his life to helping the family. If not for him, I would not have been able to do the things I've done. He died never knowing that I was an intelligence officer.

CONTENTS

ACKNOWLEDGMENTS

First—my colleagues and friends with whom I served in combat: Thanks to Col. (Ret.) Juan Negro, former director of the Leadership Targeting Cell, Bagram, Afghanistan; Commander (Ret.) David Christenson, Senior Naval Intelligence Officer; and Mr. John Hays, National Geospatial Intelligence Activity imagery analyst and all around brave guy; all contributed to this effort directly and it would not have been possible without them. This book would not have been possible without the support and encouragement of my colleagues who served with me in combat and in the real-world battles of trying to beat the bureaucracy and win the war.

Thanks to my FBI colleagues who served with me in Afghanistan—"M" and "D"—while I cannot mention your names, you both were outstanding officers in every way. I am proud to have served with you and would serve with you again, anytime, anywhere. So much for a "benign environment," to debrief a terrorist, eh?

Next—to three leaders who did more to help this country than anyone will ever know: For all the "prep" to push me forward, thanks to Lt. Gen. (Ret.) Pat Hughes, U.S. Army; Maj. Gen. (Ret.) Bob Harding, U.S. Army; and Col. (Ret.) Gerry York, U.S. Army, who all provided me guidance and mentoring, and allowed me the extraordinary privilege of being allowed to run real operations with freedom, resources (most of the time), and the opportunity to work for, and learn from, men of intellectual courage and character.

Thanks to my fellow "Jedi Knight"—Sean, who is even now out on the battlefield fighting the forces of darkness, and that darkness is all too often not al Qaeda, but our own bloated bureaucracy of meandering nabobs of criticism and ignorance. God bless ya, brother!

Thanks to Col. David Strickland, USAR, Assistant Division Commander, 94th Division, for being smarter and wiser than most colonels in the army today—and my gratitude to him for helping make this book possible.

Thanks to my support team, Jacqueline Salmon, who offered invaluable advice and assistance in the project, and my agent, Deborah Grosvenor, who served as a wonderful advisor—without their hard work none of this would be real.

Last but not least, my thanks to Col. (Ret.) John Tempone, USMC, who is himself portrayed in another book, *Cook, Baker, Candlestick Maker* for his heroic exploits in Lebanon, who was also my class leader at "the Farm." He encouraged me to endure, to never give up or accept mediocrity or defeat, and to always, no matter what, do "the next right thing." Semper Fi!

AUTHOR'S NOTE

This book is based on my recollections, and the recollections of other members of the Leadership Targeting Cell in Afghanistan, who graciously agreed to collaborate with me in this effort. I also drew on a journal that I kept at the time. While memory is never 100 percent accurate, I've done my best, with the help of others, to tell the story truthfully.

Names have been changed in a number of cases. Some people are still undercover, while others, for any number of reasons, chose not to have their real name published.

The views expressed in my writing do not necessarily represent the views of the U. S. Army or the United States.

GLOSSARY

ACM—Anti-Coalition Militia

ADVON—Advanced Operations

AFB—Air Force Base

AFG—Air Force Group

AFSAC—Air Force Special Activities Center

AMF—Afghan Militia Forces

ANA—Afghan National Army

BCP—Bagram Collection Point

BDU—battle-dress uniform

CENTCOM—U.S. Central Command

CH-47—Chinook heavy-lift helicopter

CJSOTF—Combined Joint Special Operations Task Force

CJTF—Combined Joint Task Force

CONOP—Concept of Operations

CSAR—Combat Search and Rescue

DCI—Director of the Central Intelligence Agency

DCU—desert camouflage uniform

DIA—Defense Intelligence Agency

DOCEX—Document Exploitation

EBO—Effects Based operation

Farm—CIA training Facility

FLIR—Thermal imaging, forward looking infrared camera

FOB—Forward Operating Base

FRAGO—fragmentary order

G2—army director of intelligence

HESCO—a modern gabion made of wire mesh containers lined with heavy fabric and filled with dirt and rocks.

HIG—Hezb-e-Islami Gulbuddin—terrorist group founded by Gulbuddin Hekmatyar

HOC—HUMINT Operations Center

HQ—Headquarters

HSD—HUMINT Support Detachment

HSE—HUMINT Support Element

HUMINT—Human Intelligence

HVT—High Value Target

ID—identification; identify

IG—Inspector General

INSCOM—Army Intelligence and Security Command

ISAF—International Security Assistance Force

ISI—Pakistani Directorate for Inter-Services Intelligence

J2—senior intelligence officer, joint staff

J3—director for operations, joint staff

JDAMs—Joint direct attack munition

JSOC—Joint Special Operations Command

JSOTF—Joint Special Operations Task Force

JSTAR—airborne surveillance and target attack radar sytem

LIWA—Army's Land Information Warfare Activity

LTC—Leadership Targeting Cell

LZ—Landing Zone

MIDB—Military Intelligence Database

MP—military police

MRE—meal ready to eat

NCO—noncommissioned officer

NFN—National File Number

NIMA—National Imagery and Mapping Agency

NSA—National Security Agency

NVGs—Night-Vision Goggles

OIC—Officer in Charge

ROE—Rules of Engagement

RPG—rocket-propelled grenade

SA-7—Soviet-made SAM (surface to air missile) a.k.a. GRAIL or Strela-2

SAW—Squad Automatic Weapon

SCIF—Sensitive Compartmented Information Facility

SF—Special Forces

████████████████████

SOCOM—U.S. Special Operations Command

██

████████████████████████

TOC—Tactical Operations Center

██

██████

VTC—video teleconferencing center in SCIF

OPERATION DARK HEART

◆ 1 ◆

THE USUAL SUSPECTS

"War is for the participants a test of character: it makes bad men worse and good men better." —JOSHUA LAWRENCE CHAMBERLAIN

IT'S damned hard to sleep with your head propped up on the butt end of an M-4.

After your body is soaked by months of exhaustion, however, sleep comes fast—even when you're aboard an MH-47 Chinook chopper, subfreezing wind blowing through, as it thumps through the thin air of the Afghan mountains headed for trouble.

First stop: a rendezvous with my team of operators in the field, who were going to be thoroughly pissed off with the orders I was bringing them for our new mission. Second stop: An assault with the U.S. Rangers on a northern Afghan village that the CIA claimed housed senior al Qaeda leadership.

I was jostled awake when the 47's momentum shifted as it turned right to follow the valley. Out of the right-side gunner position, I caught a glimpse of a tall, rugged, gray mountain towering over the aircraft, silhouetted by the mid-November full moon. Christ. We were at 10,000 feet, and these mountains go up another 3,000 feet easy. *No wonder the Muj could take Russian choppers down in this area during the occupation.* We were sitting ducks to any sheepherder with a Red Rider BB gun and careful aim.

The MH-47s are giant copters used for Special Operations. I was flying on the 47 CSAR bird—Combat Search and Rescue—the medical and recovery chopper. I'd only had thirty minutes to prepare for this ride. No time to get on any combat gear. It had been come as you are: long-sleeved T-shirt, khaki pants, leather boots, black fleece jacket, and my thirteen-round M-11 handgun. I'd just been able to grab my M-4 out from under my cot, along with my gray ammo vest that contained six magazines and my body armor—but no helmet. So I'd kept on my Operation Enduring Freedom baseball cap. It did have a nice American flag on it.

Whole lotta help it would be if we got stuck in a firefight.

The crew chief had given me the only seat they had—a standard folding chair that you'd find in any church or school auditorium. Looking at the fresh-faced crew from my chair, I suddenly felt my age. At forty-one, I was old enough to be these guys' dad.

Here I was in Afghanistan, ▮▮▮▮▮▮▮▮▮▮▮▮▮▮▮▮▮▮▮▮▮▮▮ ▮▮▮▮▮▮▮▮▮▮▮▮▮▮▮▮▮▮ My job: to run the Defense Intelligence Agency's operations out of ▮▮▮▮▮▮▮▮ the hub for U.S. operations in country. It was late October 2003, and I had arrived in early July for what ultimately, after extensions, would be six months of duty.

It was to be the longest, strangest period of my life when, despite the best efforts of myself, my team, and some of my commanding officers, the United States squandered the momentum it had after defeating the Taliban in Afghanistan after the September 11 attacks. Official timidity, bureaucratic foot-dragging, overanalysis—I saw it leading up to the September 11 attacks, I saw it in Afghanistan while I served there, and I still see it today.

We were headed to a staging area set up in the mountains by the Ranger assault team. There we were to pick up 10th Mountain troops, who were going to join with the Rangers in sweeping through a village near Asadabad that the CIA guys had assured them held Gulbuddin Hekmatyar's lieutenants. Hekmatyar was one of the key warlords who'd left the back door open to let bin Laden escape Tora Bora. The plan was for me to rendezvous with my team at the staging area. They were in the area guiding the Rangers to the high-value targets, using Afghan spies or, as we called them, assets.

It was a hot landing zone (LZ), the Rangers had warned. They'd observed random gunfire, and a rocket-propelled grenade (RPG) had been fired at the troops earlier that day. Accompanying the Ranger assault team on this flight meant that I would also be along for their assault on the village that supposedly held the bad guys.

███

███

███

███

████████████████ The new orders, handwritten by the Ranger G2— the military intelligence officer—were neatly folded and sitting in the warmth of my black fleece jacket.

My team was gonna take to it like an eight-year-old to asparagus. We'd ████████ recruited a scout to help smooth our way with the villagers, but the CIA had maneuvered him out of the picture. Now we were going to be on our own without a native guide.

Freakin' CIA.

With a slight shudder, our chopper moved forward in formation with four other MH-47s, accompanied by five Black Hawk attack helicopters, toward the northeastern mountains of Afghanistan. In the bright moonlight, I could clearly see the desert terrain, a cool, pale, whitish blue. Following the curves and bumps of the terrain— the "nap of the earth"—we passed over it at 150 knots per hour. The two gunners' doors were open, and the icy nighttime air swirled in. I was cold—as cold as I ever remember being in my life.

About fifteen minutes into the flight, the door gunners test fired their Gatling-style miniguns, and I jumped when the loud *rip* of the burst let loose. I could see the tracers arcing down toward the desert floor, and hear the sister helicopters follow suit and test theirs.

As the crow flies, the distance from Bagram Air Base (the U.S. base

40 miles north of Kabul) to the staging area was only about an hour and a half, but the route this night was in and out of numerous valleys. I felt a push on my shoulders as the helicopter pulled up to clear a ridge-line, then, quickly, my stomach rose toward my throat as it nosed back down. The cycle was repeated over and over for the next three hours.

As we approached the LZ, the crew chief stood in the center of the helicopter and held up his hands, fingers spread.

Ten minutes out.

Shortly after that, one hand. Five minutes away.

Two fingers. We were about to arrive.

As we slowed, I could make out the tiered, plowed fields, like pancakes stacked slightly offset from each other.

The crew chief caught me as I stood up to walk out. "Sir—don't forget—ten minutes. We can't stay," he yelled into my ear.

"Got it," I yelled back.

As the MH-47 landed and the rear ramp was lowered, I put my rifle on semiauto and moved out to two o'clock from the bird while half the team went out to establish security around the helo. At first, the exhaust from the two jet motors of the 47 washed over me like a tropical breeze. The heat was a welcome surprise.

I was next to an irrigation ditch that, I quickly found out after putting my foot into it, was full of cold water. I moved out of the ditch and went down on one knee. The noise from the bird was thunderous. I had ten minutes to meet with my guys, give them their new mission, and pass along the gear while the 10th Mountain guys loaded into the empty Chinooks. More than ten minutes, and the CSAR would take off without me and I would be left here with no winter gear, no additional weaponry, no extra ammo.

Feeling the cold ground on my knee through my pants, I watched the horizon for either the silhouette of an enemy troop moving forward with an AK-47 or one of our officers approaching me to make contact.

I flashed my blue signal light in one-second bursts, every 45 degrees into the darkness until I'd covered a full 360 degrees to ID my position to our guys. I moved a few meters from the spot where I'd shown the light just in case the bad guys had decided to take a potshot. I waited a few seconds, showed the light again, and moved once more. Because of the noise of the helicopters, short of bullets hitting the ground near me or slamming (hopefully) into the ceramic plate of my body armor, I wouldn't have known if I was being shot at.

Soon I saw the dark outlines of the 10th Mountain soldiers loading onto the other Chinooks.

One of my team showed up—it was Mr. White, the forward officer in charge. It was then that I heard the faint sound of gunfire and a sound like a fast-flying bug not far above my head.

We stooped and ran toward a mud hut about 200 meters away so we'd have some cover from the gunfire. I wasn't used to the altitude, and I gasped in the thin air. I was in good shape, but the 50 pounds in body armor and ammo weighed me down, and I struggled the last 100 meters. It felt like my lungs had shut down.

Now that I was away from the copter, the full-on cold mountain air hit my face. I heard the faint, harsh cough of the Kalashnikovs.

The other members of my team were at the hut, and we squatted in a loose circle. They'd been out for several days in the high mountains, and they were bleary-eyed. They looked like crap.

For operational security when we spoke on phones, we had selected color-coded nicknames. I was Mr. Gray.

Just to my back, I heard the increase of the torque on the rotors of the helicopters. One by one, the noisy beasts lumbered off the LZ and into the air. Only the CSAR remained behind for me.

The clock was ticking.

"Gentlemen—I've got the new mission with me," I said, handing over the cash. Mr. Red and Mr. Pink rifled through it. The guys glanced at each other and leaned toward me.

"Tony, we want to come out—all of us—now," said Mr. White. "There's nothing we can do here of use. You know we don't have access to our other guys who could give us intel on ███████. We've lost our source and we don't have any way to contact our other assets."

"That's not going to happen," I told him. ██████████████
██

████████ I ran them through the details of the new assignment. They weren't happy.

Mr. Blue, our native ████████████████ started, "This won't work. Without our guy, we're limited in our ability to guide our guys through these villages. ██████████████████████████████████████

██████████████████████████

"I agree," I said, "but Keller is determined that you all remain with the Rangers. Part of this is political."

"Tony this is shit," said Mr. Pink. His eyes glowed with anger in the moonlight. "It makes no sense."

The gunfire was getting closer as our voices rose.

This is insane, I thought. We're in the middle of a field being shot at. We might as well have just painted targets on our asses.

"Sonsabitches . . ." one of the guys muttered to no one in particular.

Behind us was another crack of an AK-47.

Two minutes left. I had to convince these guys to accept the mission and then get my ass back on the chopper.

"Look, this is the deal." I spoke rapidly. "I agree. This is a waste. We need to get you guys out. Just help me justify your reassignment."

"The SEALs are going into the valleys 10 klicks from here later this week," Mr. Blue said. His voice was urgent. The gunfire was coming more rapidly. "Our teams can do the recon and prep them for their mission," he added.

"What is their target?" I asked, glancing over at the lone Chinook. It was starting to take fire, but the crew didn't return fire. They couldn't be sure where we were.

"One of the HIG's suspected safe havens. They've got good intel to get one of his lieutenants." He was referring to Hekmatyar's group.

"Got it," I said. "I give you my word I'll have you all out of here by tomorrow afternoon."

Or so I hoped. I figured with this information and a logical argument, I could overcome the politics. ██████████████████

"Look, gentlemen, this is not my choice." I handed Mr. Pink the written instructions. "This is what we've been told to do."

One minute left, and I needed 30 seconds to make the run to the bird.

"I'll take one of you with me. You can come back and make the case to Keller and McChrystal. But the rest of you stay."

Mr. White was the man. He gave final instructions to Mr. Pink, and we were off, with me in the lead, running across the field. Hunched over, my ammunition vest slamming against my chest, I fought to catch a breath.

The options weren't good. Run or take the chance of getting aired out by a sniper.

By the time we hit the chopper, the rotors were screaming and the ramp was just barely kissing the ground. The crew wanted to get the hell out of there. Bullet holes spattered the hull, but the fire hadn't made it past the Kevlar lining within the airframe.

Even before we threw ourselves on the floor, I heard the whine of the motors increase, and the push on my shoulders as the copter lifted off.

Next stop was the assault. The 10th Mountain troops were going to set up blocking positions in and around the target village, and the Rangers would do the actual assault. The plan called for the CSAR to land to the south of the village, to stay out of firing range, and for the crew to move in on foot if a fight broke out and there were casualties. I'd stand by. Black Hawks would be overhead to protect us. Seemed simple.

Like hell.

THE "DARK SIDE"

I always wanted to be a spook. "Black ops"—the most top-secret class of clandestine operations—became my specialty for sixteen of my twenty-five years as an intelligence officer. ████████████████

████████████████████████████████
████████████████████████████████
████████████████████████████████
████████████████████████████████

I was part of the "dark side of the force"—the shadowy elements of the Department of Defense and the rest of the U.S. government that function outside the bounds of the normal system. Our job was to protect the country through subterfuge and deception. Hide the truth to get the truth, as we say.

It is effective, seductive—and dangerous to those who are a part of it. It is easy to exploit our methods and abilities to advance our own personal interests rather than use them for the greater good of the country. I have seen men lie, cheat, and manipulate others simply to advance their careers.

Looking back on my upbringing, I guess you could say it would have been easy for me to slip over onto that path.

I never knew my real dad. He left my mom before I was born and, while it may sound strange, I've never been curious as to who my dad was or what motivated him to not know me. I'm grateful just to be here.

After I was born, for the first seven years of my life, I spent a great deal of time with my relatives in Kansas—in a small town named Cherryvale. It was a simple and wonderful existence for a child.

My mom eventually married an Air Force captain and we moved to Wichita, Kansas. I was not happy about being pulled out of my comfortable life in a sleepy hamlet and I started to rebel.

I tended to stir up trouble everywhere I went, learning early how to survive and find my own path and—always—push the envelope.

On Clark Air Force Base in the Philippines in the 1970s, I bought World War II hand grenades—the explosives were mostly hollowed out—and old Japanese helmets from kids outside the fence. The Explosive Ordnance Disposal folks came out and confiscated the grenades. By the age of fourteen, when we were living in Lisbon, Portugal, I was bartending in the marine house for the embassy marine guard. I was drinking as much as I was serving. I went to the American international school, and on Friday evenings we'd go to the Bacaso bar in Cascais to have five shots—each—of Bagaso (Portuguese white lightning) with a beer chaser. Then we'd run two miles on the boardwalk to Estoril to go to a movie there, and whoever didn't throw up on the way got his movie paid for by the rest of the group.

Our school administrator called me the "happy-go-lucky rebel," and I lived up to the name.

Once, I found a key to the school chemistry lab and asked our chemistry teacher what was the most corrosive acid that could be made. He told me it was a combination of hydrochloric acid and sulfuric acid. So, during gym class when no one was around, I ducked into the chemistry lab and tried to mix them up. They blew up. Highly toxic plumes of smoke came from the beaker. I poured the brew out.

It ate through solid concrete. Fortunately, I had the brains to get the hell out of there before it killed me.

Maybe, if I was really smart, I wouldn't have tried the experiment the first time. Maybe.

I actually got the entire high school drunk when I was a sopho-more. The school was getting a tour of the Lancer's wine factory just outside Lisbon, and I talked a teacher into letting us buy wine to "take home to our parents." We all bought two bottles for $1 each and learned the art of punching corks in. Hank Sanders got so sick he threw up in the headmaster's car. Every kid's parents were called ex-cept mine. The next day, the headmaster called me in and asked me if I was responsible for what had happened. I was straight about it. "I gotta tell you, sir, I was." He never called my parents. He appreciated that I didn't lie, I guess, and I learned that telling the truth isn't that bad. It's a lesson I've applied many times in my life when something I did ran me into trouble.

I still have my high school yearbook. He wrote, "You have mucho talento. Use it wisely." I tried to keep that in mind, but I haven't al-ways been successful.

I may have been the happy-go-lucky rebel, but I was painfully shy around girls. Underneath the bravado, I was drinking because I thought it would make me feel more cool with them—but it didn't. So I drank more. I just didn't know what to say to women or how to act around them. I guess that's the reason I remained a virgin until I was twenty.

I had always wanted to become a spy—I just didn't know what that meant until I got to high school. In Lisbon, the American commu-nity was small, so everyone knew who the intelligence people were. I was periodically debriefed by the embassy attaché about the interna-tional students at school—what they were doing and saying. That's how I really became interested in the spy world. I saw all these games going on. Also, I wanted to help people. This may be the logic of a sixteen-year-old, but I figured a really good intelligence officer could save more lives than a doctor. If you were able to get information that could enable your side to save thousands of people, well, that was better than medicine.

I started at the bottom. When my family had moved to Ohio during my senior year in high school, I enlisted in the National Guard as a telecommunications center operator—basically a teletype operator for the army. I did my basic training at Fort Gordon, Georgia, where I was a super straight arrow—no drinking, no nothin'. I got several letters of commendation there and worked my way up to assistant platoon sergeant.

During my first year in the Guard, while I was a freshman at Wright State College, I started working with the recruiters who had recruited me. For every individual I recruited, I got an extra $25 (which in 1981 dollars wasn't bad), and I managed to land more than one hundred people. I also became public affairs director for the local Guard. Those activities got me inducted into the Ohio Army National Guard Recruiter Hall of Fame. Actually, I've never seen the Recruiter Hall of Fame and have no idea if it actually exists, but I have a plaque that says I'm in it.

Because of my work there, the commander of my unit—Col. Chuck Conner—told me that if I wanted to go into Officer Candidate School, he would give me any job in the command when I got back. I said I wanted the counterintelligence position he had open. He looked at me like I was crazy.

"I have an aviation slot I've kept open for you. You could become a pilot," he said.

I said, no, I appreciated that, but that I wanted to become an intelligence officer. It was a special agent billet and, technically, you had to be twenty-one to do it. I was only going to be nineteen when I graduated, but I got it anyway—Chuck had that much confidence in me.

While at Wright State, I took time off to get all the training to become an intelligence officer. My basic intelligence officer training was conducted at Fort Huachuca, Arizona, where I was the youngest person in my class. I resumed my mantle as the heavy-drinking, happy-go-lucky rebel. On Friday afternoons, three of my friends and I would hop in a car and drive the 100 miles to Tucson, drinking a fifth—or two—of vodka along the way.

Soon, I was working counterterrorism missions in the United States and Europe while still in the army reserves and having the time of my life. This was the height of the Cold War, and the military's entire DNA was built around opposing the Russians. I got involved in Return of Forces in Germany (REFORGER), which tested the military's ability to rapidly move massive amounts of troops and equipment over to Germany in case the Russians invaded. I started doing counterterrorism work on the ground there—what we call low-level source operations. These are cases where you go into a community undercover and set up nets of agents in local villages. I'd go talk to the burgermeister. I'd go into bars and restaurants and recruit. I'd ask people to call me if anything happens. Lotsa free beer there, too.

I loved that kind of work (not just the free beer). In the United States, I did an operational security survey of West Point in '85 to see how a terrorist might attack a target, and I was acting special agent in charge of the New York City Resident Office when we thought that Libya would attack the Statue of Liberty during its grand reopening in '86.

People were impressed with my efforts. I was invited into a course called Key Personnel Program that looks for talent in the reserves to bring into the army.

My drinking hadn't abated, though. I was guzzling booze like a freakin' fish. I thought my generation would die in a conflagration in Europe when the Russians swept through, so I figured I would be dead by the time I was twenty-nine. I lived life like that; it justified being wild. My motto was "live fast, die young, and wear clean underwear— or none at all."

Looking back on it, I don't know how I survived. I started having blackouts: I would start drinking in one place, wake up in another place, and not know how I got there. The "good" Tony, who was working hard and earning commendations and promotions, was starting to get further and further away from the "bad" Tony, who got drunk and said and did stupid things. I drank everything: pitchers of beer, Jack Daniel's with Heineken, Foster's Lager. I went through my white Zinfandel days, drinking a bottle a day. I kept a bottle of vodka in the freezer for times when nothing else was around. So far, at least, it didn't affect my job. In fact, some of my bosses drank as much as I did.

As I moved further into intelligence work, I recognized that a higher level of intelligence collection was being a spook—going undercover. There, I would be working to penetrate foreign governments, as well as terrorist groups, drug cartels, and other criminal organizations. I would identify, assess, and recruit foreign intelligence "assets" (the military's term for foreign informants who work full time for the U.S. government doing espionage work). As well, I would work in intelligence "technical collection"—that is, surveillance technology.

In all, these are the most protected programs in the U.S. government. It could be dangerous work—on many operations, I would need to hide my identity, my organization's identity, and many aspects of my background.

Moving to Washington, D.C., in November '87, I joined the ▮▮▮ ▮▮ ▮▮▮▮ I went through training at the "Farm" ▮▮▮▮▮▮▮▮▮—the six-month CIA course that turns you into an operative—and finished at the top of my class. While in Richmond, Virginia, doing surveillance training, we convinced the hotel staff that we were the advance team scouting locations for the TV show *Miami Vice*. One of my classmates was the producer, another came in as the lawyer. I was Don Johnson's driver's stunt double. People believed us—often because they *wanted* to believe us. We were also damned convincing.

Aside from those shenanigans, mentally and emotionally, it turned out to be the toughest six months I've ever spent. Right before you enter, the instructors call you into a room and tell you that if you want to quit now, this is your last chance because, after this, you will never look at people the same way again.

It was true. They teach you to detect, evaluate, and categorize the darkest components of human nature and manipulate them for the purposes of good—for intelligence collection. They teach you how to not only screw with people's minds, but also how to manipulate them so they will do things that are clearly dangerous for them and dangerous for their families.

I gotta tell you, when I got out and began using those skills, I found out they worked. I call them the Dark Arts. A group of us who were there at the time called ourselves the Jedi Knights—we still do. We tried to use the Dark Arts we had learned for the right reasons and vowed not to use our skills against our friends, families, or colleagues. Yeah, it sounds corny, but we recognized the danger of allowing those skills to go unchecked. Yet I know that a lot of other people spent their entire careers engaged in office politics, using their skills to better themselves to get to higher positions.

I came out with strong ratings, but I was so drunk at graduation I didn't even know who the graduation speaker was. It turned out to be Gen. Norman Schwarzkopf, who went on to command the coalition forces in the Gulf War of 1991.

I was young, and I was brash. I was the youngest person in my Officer Candidate School class in 1982, and I was also the youngest in my class at the Farm in 1988.

After the Farm, I worked for the air force ███████████ ████████████████████████████ as a civilian. █████████ ██ ██ ██ ██ ████ ███ ██ ██ ██ ████████

At the same time, I also served in the U.S. Army Reserve. (While

I was a civilian senior intelligence officer, we all had to maintain dual status as uniformed reservists—so we could go into combat if needed.) As one of my army reserve assignments, I went down to Alabama, assigned to a team with the FBI to monitor the Soviets who wanted to defect when they came here during negotiations to eliminate the Pershing missiles as part of the INF treaty in '89.

Since I was now an undercover agent, I could not be exposed to foreign nationals. As it happened, ███████████████████████████ ██ ████████████████████████████████ staying in the same hotel as the Soviets. There I was, helping out the stunt crew, drinking at the hotel bar, and keeping my ear to the ground, looking for Soviets who wanted to make a run for it.

Over the years, I did a lot of top-secret operations where I can reveal only a few details—the blackest of black. Counterterrorism, counterdrug, supersecret high-tech penetration of foreign nations. Some of my operations were so clandestine that I was only allowed to brief agency leadership verbally about them. They were too clandestine to be put into a memo or a database. No paper trail.

███ ███ ███████████ At one point, there were only eleven people in the Department of Defense who knew about it.

Other operations I handled myself by going undercover. ████████ ██ ██ ██ ███.

In another operation, ██████████████████████████████ ██ ████████████████████████████. Whatever they wanted, we got for them, but we were actually selling them stuff that we could use to spy on them—and it worked. We were able to penetrate a rogue nuclear-power country to the top leadership level.

All this time, though, I was drinking heavily. There were problems with my behavior, but not enough to revoke my security clearance. In fact, I was promoted. I moved from the air force to the army full time and, in the fall of '91, ████████████████████████████████████

████████████████████████████████

I hit bottom with my drinking in '92. It's a long story, but suffice it to say, I was living with one woman and sleeping with a colonel's secretary. Things got ugly—but they also got me sober, and I've stayed sober ever since. I got married and, in 1994, we had a son, Alexander.

██

████ in '95 when the Defense Intelligence Agency took over all clandestine human intelligence-collection assignments from the General Defense Intelligence Program. That resulted in the transfer of thousands of intelligence civilian billets to the Defense Intelligence Agency (DIA)—including the army human intelligence program that I headed.

It was a "hostile takeover," as it was described at the time, and I was one of the ones who was pretty vocal about it being a bad idea. The DIA is at heart an analytical organization, and its intellectual/ academia-rooted culture was never comfortable with the set of skills unique to operational intelligence on the battlefield. Those skills were radically different from those required to either count Soviet missiles or for military attachés to function in their duties in embassies in urban settings under peacetime conditions. Those of us who came in as part of the takeover were not liked. We were seen as dangerous men—knuckle draggers who shouldn't be in the intellectual mecca that was the DIA.

Guys like me who came out of the army, who understood the army and who were trained to lie, cheat, and steal for Uncle Sam, were the least popular within DIA. Its leaders didn't like clandestine HUMINT—and tactical HUMINT missions they liked even less.

All too often, the most important operations, in my view, were viewed by career bureaucrats as too dangerous for their careers—or dead ends, since you could be tied to them permanently with no potential to become a senior executive. I had no such fear. Often, I took on operations that nobody else wanted.

I took risks, but I subscribed to the philosophy that all army officers learned when they went through basic training. We were taught to take "reasonable risks." You didn't play it safe. You played it so you could win, and that meant taking some gambles. Now, you didn't take stupid risks and you didn't do stupid things, but you understood the situation, and you tried to calculate what would get you what you needed to achieve success.

Some people loved me, some people hated me. It's still that way. There was really no middle ground. Some people liked the fact that I could go in and find a way to get things done in very complex situations. Some people didn't. The truth was, I only did what I was permitted to do relating to the operation objectives that were approved at the highest level.

███ ███ ███████████████████████████████████████ ███ ███████████████████ We knew they contained significant information on individuals being trained in the terrorism camps—and, more importantly, their potential targets. My unit's mission, within the context of a much larger operation known as Able Danger, ███████████████████████████ ████████████████████████████ We were making progress—and had a pathway in—when things were shut down; a decision that was terribly flawed in retrospect.

███ ███ ███

Nevertheless, we faced constant resistance from the risk-averse DIA bureaucracy. My immediate bosses, who were nervous about these operations, sat on requests for equipment and travel and held up funding, despite the high-level support they were getting. I constantly had to fight to go around them.

At first, the unit did well—as did I—under DIA Director of Operations Maj. Gen. Robert (Bob) Harding and DIA Director Lt. Gen. Pat Hughes, who allowed me and my team to take "out of the box" ideas, and develop them into real intelligence operations. Their encouragement allowed for entrepreneurial concepts to develop. Although when General Harding left, his replacement, Maj. Gen. Rod Isler, seemed far more scared of risk. In fact, he opposed every sensitive operation that my unit, Stratus Ivy, was conducting. I battled constantly with bureaucrats like General Isler—at the same time winning awards for effectiveness. A commander once told me, "If you weren't the best damned intelligence officer, I'd fire you."

For example, in May 2001, I had to fight attempts by my boss at the time, Colonel Susan Cane, to get me removed as chief of Stratus Ivy and transferred to the Latin American desk after I asked her if I could get Able Danger going again.

A lot of folks at DIA felt that Tony Shaffer thought he could do whatever the hell he wanted. He was off the reservation. They never understood that I was doing things that were so secret that only a few knew about them. I was working in support of the most secret black operations run by DoD. They were operations that the most senior DIA leaders had no knowledge of. So, in the absence of direct knowledge, my co-workers' fertile minds filled with their own mythology about me.

After September 11, I was disgusted with the whole intelligence program. I believed—and still believe—that we had it within our means to prevent the 9/11 attacks. I volunteered for active duty and was assigned a position on DIA's Operating Base Alpha, soon taking over as commander. ███████████████████████████████
██
██
███████████ We knew that some of the terrorists would be headed toward Africa—Somalia, Liberia, and other countries south of Egypt.

The operation, which I supervised, was the first DIA covert action of the post–Cold War era, where my officers used an African national military proxy to hunt down and kill al Qaeda terrorists.

I became an intelligence planner for the DIA team that was planning the agency's support for the invasion of Iraq in 2003. ▮▮▮▮▮
▮▮▮
▮▮▮
▮▮▮▮▮▮▮▮▮▮▮▮▮▮▮▮▮▮▮▮▮▮▮▮▮ They would catch the Iraqis off guard by sending in a small contingent via helicopter to capture these sites. Great idea. Well executed.

Still, it yielded nothing. As we now know, no WMD were ever found.

I saw the Bush administration lunacy up close and personal. At one point, Col. John Sadler, executive officer to DIA deputy HUMINT director Bill Huntington, announced to the intelligence planners in a meeting that we had to start planning to put a defense attaché in the American Embassy in Baghdad since it would be open in a month.

Regardless of the fact that the invasion hadn't even happened yet.

We asked him to clarify his comment. Sadler glared at me (he was no Tony Shaffer fan) and said the Bush administration had information that divisions of Iraqi soldiers would surrender the moment hostilities started and that the U.S. armed forces would be "met with children throwing flowers at the feet of our soldiers."

I don't know about anybody else, but I never saw any friggin' flowers. Just a lot of grenades.

After only eighteen months, in early July 2003, I was forced to shut down Operating Base Alpha so that its resources could be used for the Iraq invasion. I was asked to take an overseas tour, so I volunteered to deploy to Afghanistan, where I figured the real war was being fought.

Just before my scheduled departure date, I took some leave and went down to Goshen Scout Reservation in southwestern Virginia as a parent assistant with my son Alexander, who would be spending two weeks at camp there with his Webelo troop.

This was a big transition for Alexander, a wonderful, hazel-eyed, nine-year-old, sandy brown-haired kid with a frame that was developing toward that of a football player. His mom, Karen, and I had gotten divorced back in 2001, and he had come through the transition fairly well. Karen and I were able to be adults about the whole thing—no lawyers. She and I decided to work things out with an eye on what was best for Alexander, and so it was as amicable a divorce as you could expect. Low on drama, high on cooperation.

Alexander had recently been promoted from Cub Scout to Webelo, and this was his first time at a camp—anywhere, really, by himself. I would be with him for three days, but then I had to leave for Afghanistan. I would be gone when he got home from camp.

The timing could not have been worse; he was not happy about my deployment, and no matter how much I assured him about how safe I'd be, he never seemed to believe me.

There were about five other parents along with me who were assistants to the troop, and we would go around doing the daily activities with the kids. Fun stuff: archery, pellet gun marksmanship, canoeing, rope tying, etc. Great character-building stuff . . . but the nights were going to be rough. I knew it just from Alexander's reaction the first two nights when he went off to his tent for bed.

The last night that I was at Goshen came. The kids knew I was an army guy so I took them on a night time patrol around the area and taught them some basic movement tactics. They ate it up and had a great time.

We all sat round the campfire that evening—Alex never left my side—and I knew it was time to talk.

I asked him to come sit with me on the hillside facing the north, away from the campfire glare; in an area where you could see the black sky and the bright stars very clearly.

He picked up a Capri Sun juice box from the cooler near the fire, walked with me to the overlook, and sat down beside me.

The air was still warm from the summer heat of the July day. The breeze didn't refresh, but it still felt good. I looked up into the sky and tried to contemplate what I could say to make the fear less and the pain go away. It was going to be tough.

I looked over at him and could only, barely, make out his silhouette and the slight sliver of the Mylar juice box he had close to his lips.

"Are you going to be OK?" I asked.

"No, Dad, I want to go back with you."

"Alex . . . you can't. I'm sorry. You have to stay."

"I don't want to . . . I want to be home with you."

I took a breath. I could tell by his voice that the tears were starting to well up.

"I'm not going to be home. I leave Monday for Afghanistan. So you need to help me. . . ."

His head turned to face me, and I could make out the flicker in his eyes from the ambient starlight.

"Help you—how?"

"Look, I need you to help your mom."

There was silence I interpreted as contemplation.

"How can I help by staying here?" he asked. Good question . . . I needed to think fast.

"You can show her you are growing up." I paused. "And, Alex, you are. I've been watching you. You are doing well here and having fun. You need to stay."

I got the sense that Alex was starting to understand that his role in life was changing—becoming bigger—and that was what I wanted.

"Will you be able to write me while you are gone?" he asked.

"Yep, I'm told that I will also be able to e-mail you often." I just left off the part, for now, that I'd be using the name Tony in my notes . . . did not want to add more stress at this point.

"And I can write back?" he asked with a bit more spirit in his tone.

"Yes."

I could sense he wanted to say something more and then, all of a sudden, the winds started to blow. First at the treetops and, quickly, down to ground level. I sat and looked up. The sky was still clear. What the heck was going on?

The wind had now become a gale, and I almost thought that there was a tornado; then I saw the first clouds begin to cover the stars as a violent summer thunderstorm came rolling in. I had never experienced anything like it—going from clear and calm conditions to a full-blown storm in less than five minutes. Just as my mind finished processing what had happened, the rain came whipping in like small bullets. Alexander and I ran for the tents—as did everyone else.

Alex was very frightened of thunder, and the booming sound started to roll over the hillside in waves. He climbed onto his cot as I sealed up his tent. He was still clutching the long empty Capri Sun container, holding it in his shaking hands just outside of his sleeping bag.

I took it from him.

"Dad . . . please don't go." His words came through chattering teeth just as a flash briefly brought daylight to the mountain, soon to be followed by a thunderclap.

I lay down next to his sleeping bag on the cot with him.

"It is going to be all right. I promise." It was the first thing I said all evening that I knew might not have been entirely correct. I was confident that, even through the now-torrential rains coming down on the outside of the tent, he and the camp would be fine. I didn't have the same confidence about the tour to Afghanistan.

The storm subsided after nearly a full hour of battering Goshen. I stayed close to Alex for another half hour to make sure he was asleep.

I sat across from him on the other cot in the tent and looked at him for a long time and wondered. What would he be like as a man . . . and would I be there to see him? I started to tear up thinking about how fortunate I had been, how by so many miracles God had somehow blessed me with continued existence and the gift of this wonderful young man. I said a small prayer, thanking Him for Alexander and asked Him to protect and preserve me to see my son again.

• 3 •

INTO AFGHANISTAN

JULY 11, 2003: I've ridden in a lot of C-130s before—and they never get any easier. The stiff nylon mesh seats are pressed up against the aluminum membrane of the plane; after five minutes of sitting upright, there is just no way to get comfortable. The constant vibration sinks into your bones. The earplugs expand to the size of marshmallows in your ears. The dry air also seems always either too hot or too cold. Nope. It never gets any better.

I was headed into my first war zone, so I wasn't exactly expecting an in-flight movie and a hot meal.

I was now ███████████████████████████ and I was packed in along with eighty others going forward into Afghanistan, headed to my new duties to run the Defense Intelligence Agency's operations on the ground. I had several titles, but in sum, my job involved overseeing human intelligence, case officers, interrogators, polygraphists, planners, the Document Exploitation (DOCEX) Detachment (document recovery team), and DIA's secret intelligence aviation equipment—among other responsibilities. Sort of a jack-of-all-trades. Master of some.

I would work as part of Operation Enduring Freedom, supporting the two primary U.S. fighting forces in Afghanistan at the time: Combined Joint Task Force 180 (the conventional forces) and Joint Task Force ████████████████ All told, the United States was operating in a country larger than Iraq with fewer than about 10,500 men on the ground—and fewer than 2,000 were actual combat forces.

The mission of the two task forces was: First, to conduct operations to destroy remaining al Qaeda and Taliban and its leadership; second, to provide command control and train the Afghan army; and third, to conduct civil/military operations and humanitarian assistance operations to stabilize Afghanistan and to establish conditions for economic success that would deter the reemergence of terrorism.

The stateside intro to my new job was minimal. No PowerPoint presentations or thick briefing books. Sure, I'd gotten training on off-road and high-speed driving—shooting out of cars and in shoot houses—and reaction drills in a live-fire environment. But DoD was just a little preoccupied with that *other* war underway, and the Afghanistan operation had seen a steady leakage of resources, personnel, and equipment over to Iraq.

In fact, Secretary of Defense Donald H. Rumsfeld had already declared in May 2003 that major combat activity in Afghanistan was over. He said during a visit to Kabul with Afghanistan President Hamid Karzai that we'd moved to "a period of stability and stabilization and reconstruction activities." Most of the country, he said, "is secure."

██
██
██
█████████████████ Even so, working on a clandestine computerized operation is different from actually being there. While I had done dangerous things my entire professional life, going into a war zone was a new experience for me.

I wasn't really scared. There was more of a feeling of emptiness. I was working to be very Zen about the whole thing; I had opened my mind to the new possibilities. No preconceived notions. Whatever was going to happen, would happen.

On the flight into Kabul, I ran back the tapes of my exit. I was still pissed off that Operating Base Alpha had been shut down because of the Iraq war, and I was sure my closing speech at the ceremony to case the colors of the unit did not win me any points with DIA leadership.

Then there was the sad and strange departure from Baltimore-Washington International Airport. My now ex-fiancée Rina and I had broken up just before we were supposed to get married—and I mean *just* before. Her family was driving up from Virginia Beach for the ceremony, and my best man, Lt. Col. Jim Brady, was at the house Rina and I owned when things came undone. Despite the drama and the stress, Rina had agreed to maintain my power of attorney and to take care of my bills while I was gone. She'd driven me to BWI for the flight out and actually came into the terminal with me. No matter what, we had started out as friends, and we were both determined to remain friends.

Rina helped me move my gear into the Military Airlift Command (MAC) terminal. We had agreed to sell the house when I got back, and we were clearly going in different directions, but we weren't bitter or even particularly angry at each other. We'd been through that. There was real sadness in our last kiss.

██
████████████████████████

After a charter flight to the U.S. base in Manas, Kyrgyzstan, I boarded the C-130 headed to Bagram Air Base after what felt like thirty nanoseconds on the ground. It was actually twelve hours, but there wasn't much in Manas to hang around for anyway.

I did run into spooks going elsewhere. I could tell by their bags. We all had exactly the same blue baggage, issued by DIA. Here we are, supposed to be undercover, and the DIA gives us all the same bags. Dumb. I made a note to myself: Never accept "official government issue" clandestine gear.

As I lugged the bags through Manas, I glanced down at my luggage tags, where I'd scrawled ████████████████████████ ███████████████████████ The blue ink was partially smeared.

██
██
██
██
██
██
██
██
██
██

I picked up the name ████ from a ██████████ movie, ████ ████████████ who molds his company into a combat-ready fighting machine. ████████████████████████████████████
██
██
██
██
██

███████████████████████████████████████

███████████████████████████████████████

███████ the unique chronicle, mostly in your head, which you maintain. Then you feel like Eleanor Rigby in that Beatles's song who keeps "her face in a jar by the door." We are taught that it's best to keep everything as close as possible to the real you so you won't trip yourself up.

My face prickled. I had grown a goatee at the recommendation of the folks who had already been to Afghanistan. Most men in Afghanistan wear beards, and facial hair can buy you time in a tense situation because you kind of blend in with the men there. The belief was that in that split second, as the bad guy tried to place you, you could escape. I'd never grown a beard before, so I wasn't used to the facial hair. Even though I'd spent much of my time in the military in undercover operations, where I could have had a beard since I didn't want to look like I worked for the government, I'd pretty much just gone with long hair. I had a ponytail during my years of running operations in support of DoD's counterdrug mission. I kinda missed it.

I wasn't expecting gunfire until we got to Bagram, but we got an early taste of it at a base in northern Afghanistan where we stopped to let some folks off before heading into Bagram. The back of the C-130 dropped down, and an air force enlisted guy on the ground drove up in an ATV and piled on some of their luggage. Small puffs of dust popped up around the ATV as he worked, but he coolly ignored it.

Somebody asked him if he was being shot at. "Yes, sir, they're shooting at us," he shouted over the roar of the propellers. As soon as those folks and their stuff were off, the pilot swung the plane around and we were outta there. No sense hanging around getting shot at, I guess he figured. I wasn't going to argue.

We flew the nap of the earth, following the land's contours for the next three hours into Bagram. We jerked and swayed in our seats as the plane skimmed over the mountainous Afghanistan terrain and miles and miles of desert.

To distract myself, I thought back to a conversation I'd had in May with Michael Hawk, my operations officer on Operating Base Alpha. In the process of closing it down, Michael had called me.

"They've been going through all your stuff since you've been in command," he told me, referring to the DIA bureaucrats—specifically a weasel of a man named Phil. Michael told me they were reviewing my financial records, my telephone logs—ripping through everything I'd done. They were going to push the DIA Inspector General Jimral for an investigation. "Don't worry about it," I told Michael. "I may have taken some shortcuts, but I didn't do anything wrong. I played it totally by the book. They can't get me on anything."

Michael gave a grim laugh. "C'mon, Tony. 'Don't worry about it?' They'll make something up if they don't find anything."

I put it out of my mind as I stared over my shoulder and out the porthole of the C-130. All I could see was tan desert and low mountains.

We'd come halfway around the world to deal with an enemy that cared about nothing but their narrow interpretation of God. They wanted to kill us simply because we did not think like they did. They could have continued to push the country even further backward in time had they had the sense to leave us alone. But they hadn't, and so, after 9/11, we'd gone after them.

The plane banked hard, and I gripped my bag tighter so it wouldn't slip away as we made our final turn to line up for landing on the Bagram Air Base runway. I could just make out the rows of CH-47s and Marine Corps Harrier AV-8 attack jets as we taxied to the terminal.

Tepid dishwater. That was my thought as I came out of the plane. Lukewarm, moist air, heavy with latent heat, with dirty brown drapes of dust that obscured the jagged mountains that surrounded Bagram for 360 degrees, literally making them shadows of their former selves. The dust just sat there, like a big damp blanket, waiting to be ripped away by the heat of the day. The kind of day that you'd just like to kick back, drive to the beach, and lay in the sun.

But no such luck. No beach here. Just a war.

In all, Bagram was serving as home to more than 7,000 U.S. and multinational armed servicemen. Used by the Soviet military during its doomed occupation of Afghanistan, the Americans and multinational armed services took over Bagram after the crap was beaten out of it during the country's civil war that raged after the Russians withdrew in 1989 and the fight waged by the United States and the Afghan Northern Alliance to oust the Taliban in 2001. We'd sunk a lot of change into fixing it up since then, but it still was no beauty. A beaten-up control tower. One patched runway. Smashed aircraft lying around. Hidden land mines. A number of newly erected structures on site but everything—and everybody—else were in tents.

As soon as I got off the plane into the 105-degree heat, my new boss, Bill Wilson, helped me load my luggage—two B-4 nylon bags full of military gear, two pelican cases, a field pack, body armor, and my bulletproof briefcase (Level IIA bulletproof inserts)—into the Toyota Tacoma ("surfs," they were called here). He took me over to my new offices, located in the heavily guarded SCIF (Sensitive Compartmented Information Facility) in the Combined Joint Task Force 180 compound.

CJTF 180 was a hybrid organization, consisting of 18th Airborne Corps staff, with combat power provided by the Army 10th Mountain Division and 82nd Airborne Division, and some special operations (Special Forces, Psychological Operations, and Civil Affairs) with some level of logistical backing from the 1st Corps Support Command.

Our facility was in a set of interconnected tents. The largest was the Joint Operations Center for CJTF 180. The SCIF—the most highly classified area—was attached to that.

The entire complex for CJTF 180 was surrounded by a twelve-foot wall—parts of it mud walls that had been on site and the rest constructed out of tall Hescos—wire mesh containers with heavy fabric liners filled with dirt and rocks similar to old-fashioned gabions. The entire wall was topped with triple concertina wire.

As we entered through the guarded entrance of the SCIF, we came into a large domed area, with huge mercury lights and dust dancing in their beams. There was a big, U-shaped conference table and various openings to other tents/offices off the main area.

The tents were insulated, air-conditioned, and heated, but still hot as hell in the summer and, I was to discover, damned cold in the winter. On windy days—which was most days in Bagram—the wind sucked and blew at the tent walls, flapping them with such force and volume that we often had to pause in meetings and wait for the gales to die down before resuming.

One of the first people we ran into was Lt. Gen. John Vines, commander of the U.S. and coalition forces in Afghanistan. Vines had assumed command of the Afghanistan operation in May, although he had been in country for nine months as commander of the 82nd Airborne Division. He was leaving the SCIF after his daily morning situation brief when Bill introduced us. Vines grabbed my hand for a swift, firm shake.

"Good to meet you, ███████████" he said. "Glad to have you here." My first impression was of a direct, no-nonsense leader.

Inside the SCIF, I started to meet members of the team I would be fighting this war with, starting with Navy Lt. Cmdr. David Christenson, a Senior Naval Intelligence Officer in Afghanistan.

"Welcome aboard, shipmate," he said, extending a hand. With satellites, bugs, receivers, antennas, and a bunch of other equipment ████████████████████████ Dave and his people kept an ear out for the bad guys from the air and from the ground. Lean and compact, blond and blue-eyed, Dave was the resident "lib" who became—despite his politics—one of my closest allies.

Because Dave had the appropriate clearances and background, I was able to tell him I'd worked with ████ on previous assignments, including a recent one in which ███████████ was embedded in my unit to ███████████ Dave looked impressed and said he wanted to learn more about that operation.

The human intelligence tent where I would be working had a kind of a submarine feel to it—long and narrow, with a plywood floor and computers slapped down on long tables along the perimeter. Dust was everywhere. Chairs were mostly the folding kind. Kind of primitive, I thought, but then this was a war zone. Just inside the entrance sat the 10th Mountain tactical human intelligence team. Bill introduced me all around, while I struggled to remember names. I was fighting fatigue and was still trying to get used to answering to the name of Tony.

They were all in uniform—a young-looking group. I got a quick handshake from everyone, but my attention was drawn briefly to the NCO in charge of the night shift. She reminded me of somebody I knew, or thought I had known. I searched my memory banks. That was it—she looked like Natalie Portman: high cheekbones, dark eyes, and the widest smile I'd ever seen. I glanced at her computer. There was a photo of her, smiling, hand in hand with a guy. She was wearing shorts. *Man*, I thought. *Gorgeous legs.*

Back to the task at hand, Tony, I told myself.

In the rear of the HUMINT tent, Bill grabbed a chair and motioned me to do the same. As my boss, Bill knew I was in alias and he knew my background.

"Tony, you've got a strong reputation, and I'm really going to need you to do a lot of the heavy lifting to get our mission focused with Task Force 180," he said as I sat down. "But, be aware, there is some kind of drama going on about you."

I rolled my eyes. "Look, Bill, I'm here to do my job. That's the only thing I want to do. I've done some very interesting ops and, for better or worse, I have a reputation for getting things done. I'm here to do that and to make sure the mission runs smoothly."

Bill ticked off my priorities. First, do a better job than my predecessor and repair DIA's relations with the other units. At one point, Bill said, our senior officer, Lt. Col. Ray Moretti in Kandahar, a city to the south that was the birthplace of the Taliban, had passed along to my predecessor great intel that Taliban leader Mullah Omar would be passing by a certain point. Well, my predecessor didn't bother to tell anyone until it was too late. Omar's entourage ended up beating up our Afghan informant, taking his phone, and driving away.

It was a low ebb in DIA's relationship with, well, just about every-body.

Second, since I was an army guy, Bill wanted me to get into the army planning process, because I was trained in it. Bill felt that we—as Defense HUMINT in DIA—were not playing a big enough role in the war and that our intelligence wasn't making it into the combat operations enough. Finally, Bill told me, I was to be DIA's representative to the Leadership Targeting Cell (LTC).

"I saw their tent here in the SCIF," I said. "What's their focus?"

As Bill explained it, the LTC was directly responsible for the coordination and prosecution of killing or capturing High Value Targets, or Tier 1 targets—like Osama bin Laden, his deputy Ayman al-Zawahiri, Mullah Omar, and others like them. The LTC was also responsible for Tier 2 targets, such as their lieutenants and their action guys.

Sitting on the LTC were representatives of Combined Joint Task Force 180 and other agencies—████████ the CIA, the FBI—as well as the National Imagery and Mapping Agency (NIMA; it's now called the National Geospatial-Intelligence Agency), the J2 (joint staff chief of intelligence), and other agencies in country. I would be the DIA representative. It was run by Col. Juan Negro, former Army Special Forces who had worked mostly in South America before joining the Special Forces Command in Tampa.

"Let's go over and meet him," Bill said, "but first, let's take care of your weapons."

He brought me back out into the main area of the SCIF and over to a large black foot locker near the video teleconferencing (VTC) room. With a quick twirl of the combination lock, he opened it up. It contained an array of M-4A3 assault rifles and M-11 (SIG SAUER P228) semiautomatic pistols and ammunition.

"Generally speaking, we issue M-4s when we go out on convoys or under enhanced threat conditions and carry M-11s when we're inside the perimeter," said Bill, giving me the combination of the locker. "We usually carry three magazines per M-11."

"The policy is you're supposed to keep the weapon unloaded while you're inside the perimeter," he added, "but, frankly, my weapon always has a round in the chamber."

"I got it," I said.

I picked out an M-11, racked it to make sure there were no stray shells in the chamber, slid the rack forward and slipped it into the holster on my right hip, then quickly scooped up three 13-round mags and a box of ammo. I loaded the bullets into the magazines and put the magazines onto the carrier on my left side. I slid a magazine into the gun but didn't chamber it until later.

"All set?" Bill said. "Let's go talk LTC."

In the LTC tent, it was cooler than the HUMINT tent, almost comfortable. Tim Loudermilk, Colonel Negro's operations officer, stood up and introduced himself, telling us that Colonel Negro would be back in a minute. In the meantime, I met John Hays, the rep from NIMA—lanky and sandy haired—who gave me a friendly greeting. John was in charge of pictures and maps and responsible for the toughest question of the day: figuring out where the ever-changing Afghan-Pakistan border was. Next up was FBI special agent John Kirkland, a big bear of a guy with a full beard and a massive grin, as well as Dan, another FBI agent.

John and I talked about my work on a project with the FBI— ██. He said the FBI's job in Afghanistan was to monitor the debriefings of detainees to look for information relating to domestic law enforcement and to look for leads on possible future attacks. It also did sensitive site exploitation.

"So anytime a major raid takes place, you guys go out and look at the scene?" I said.

"Yep," said John. "We try to evaluate anything they left behind—computers, books, notes, magazines—anything that might be useful to tip us off and help prevent a new attack."

I heard a shuffle behind me and turned around to face a calm-eyed colonel with a thick mustache, slightly taller than me, wearing DCUs with no markings other than the U.S. Army and his rank. "Sir," said Bill. This must be Colonel Negro. ███████████████ "He just arrived today. He's going to be our representative to the LTC."

For a moment, Negro stared at me, expressionless.

We sat down and talked about some of my predeployment training and about the LTC. I could sense some coolness toward me. He reminded me in some ways of Lieutenant Castillo from that '80s TV show, *Miami Vice*. Soft-spoken, quiet, but there was a lot going on behind those eyes.

Then Negro asked me about a particular case officer, and I said that I knew him.

"My dealings with him were never good," Colonel Negro said bluntly. Turns out the colonel had some run-ins with particular case officers and other undercover personnel, including this guy.

"My experience is that people with your background are prima donnas—high on talk and low on delivery," Negro continued.

Man. The guy sure could throw a punch.

Negro continued. He believed that DIA didn't participate enough in operations and didn't produce enough. Generally, we'd just phone it in and leave the difficult, mundane—but necessary—work to the white-world guys, and our clandestine operations didn't produce enough to justify the attitude or expense.

"Well, sir, I'm sorry you've had run-ins with some individuals," I said. "I've had problems with some of those individuals as well. I'd like to believe I'm not like them, and I'd like you to give me a chance to prove myself."

Negro nodded. "Clearly, you're going to have your chance to do that."

Wow, I thought, *he's gonna be a tough one.*

Afterward, back at the eight-man tent that I would be sharing with other members of the DIA team, I glanced warily at the barrier separating us from the ancient village of Bagram, home to several thousand Afghans. The wall was made up of Hescos about 15 meters from our tent. On the other side of the barrier were some people who seemed to have a problem with our presence here. They would chip explosives out of old Soviet mortars, I was told, insert them into cans or any other container, and wrap a bike chain around the whole package to serve as shrapnel. Voilà. Instant improvised explosive device (IED). Then they'd toss the thing over the barrier at us. Entertaining way to pass the time, I guessed. It made us real careful about getting too close to those Hescos.

Needless to say, for those reasons and plenty of others, security was extremely tight at Bagram. We had to carry our M-11 sidearms with us at all times. Even when sleeping or showering, we had to keep them within easy reach.

The showers were pretty good, I had been told, but the Porta-Johns were a long trudge from the tents, they cooked you in the heat—hitting 150 degrees in the summer—and froze your balls off in the winter. Dust and grit were everywhere from the ever-present wind that would die down to a slight breeze and then whip up to the speed and force of a freight train. It felt like a blast furnace in the summer and, I learned, an ice-covered knife in the winter. I'd been informed that the dust it carried contained high levels of fecal matter.

Great, I thought. *I'll be breathing shit for the next several months.*

◆ 4 ◆

THE BOY AND THE BOMB

SWEATING under my forty pounds of vest and ammo, I swung the M-4 up from my seat in the Toyota 4×4, thumbed the safety off, and aimed it through the windshield at the young boy. In the swirling dust and mayhem of Kabul, I had spotted him running full speed into the street, a metallic object in his hand, arm stretched out toward Dave Christenson's truck in front of ours.

A bomb.

We were near the end of a clandestine recon in Kabul, and everything was going to hell.

Moving like a blur, the kid tossed the metal item toward Dave's truck. My M-4 was up, now clearing the truck's firewall, barrel lined up, and I was just putting pressure on the trigger. Time seemed to go into slow motion.

I just got here, I thought, *and I'm gonna shoot a freakin' kid.*

◆ ◆ ◆

It had been a wild trip into Kabul from Bagram. Along the patched blacktop of the "new" Russian Road as it was called—one sorry excuse for a roadway that was barely two lanes wide—we roared into Kabul in a Toyota 4×4 at up to 100 miles per hour, airborne over the many bumps and bouncing over the potholes as we passed other U.S. and ISAF convoys of heavy military vehicles. Because we were in a soft-skinned vehicle, we were more vulnerable to grenades, RPGs, and IEDs than they were, and so we had to build survivability into our movements with speed and maneuverability.

To make ourselves an even tougher target, our driver, Sgt. Julie Tate, zigzagged down the road. She passed vans packed with people (some of whom were even hanging off the sides and clinging to the top), camels loaded down with all the worldly possessions of the no-madic tribes that roamed the Afghan mountains, military convoys, bicycles, herds of sheep—you name it. Shouting over the loud music she was playing and the road noise, she told me to watch for newly patched pavement—a sign of a possible IED. We also had to stay off the shoulders. There was a danger of IEDs, of course, but also, farm-ers often picked up unexploded ordnance from their fields (they were skilled at it), such as land mines left over from the Soviet occupation and unexploded cluster bombs from the Soviets and the Americans, and dropped them by the sides of the road. There, a fully loaded ve-hicle, like ours, could set them off.

"Don't worry, sir," Julie yelled. "I won't let you die."

I looked at her as we weaved down the road, the landscape flashing past. "Oh, *that* is very reassuring."

Much of the terrain between Bagram and Kabul was barren desert, a valley with a few settlements and compounds along the way. I could also see the occasional smoke-belching brick factory. Parts of it re-minded me of Arizona: small rises, dry river beds, all manner of shal-low ravines between the soaring mountain ranges. Brackish dust devils, tall as tornadoes, slowly waltzed across the valley in front of the far range of mountains. Harsh country, I thought, but with a subtle beauty.

The Russians had built the road in the 1980s after they got tired of getting blown up going through the villages connecting Bagram to Kabul to the east. The older route to the east was still open. It was shorter, but even more dangerous than this one.

We sped by Afghan army checkpoints—forlorn cement buildings in the middle of nowhere with the Afghan flag flying and a bed outside. Sometimes the road had speed bumps in front of the checkpoints, which we sailed over. Later, when I commanded convoys, I always told my drivers that if they didn't get airborne during the trip to and from Kabul, then they weren't driving fast enough.

As the landscape got more desolate, the foot traffic thinned out, but we occasionally saw people walking along the shoulder. Out in the middle of freakin' nowhere. God knows how they didn't get blown up by landmines. Maybe they did and we just hadn't seen it.

Dave had approached me the day I had arrived about conducting convoys with ███████████████████████ an Army unit that does intelligence collection to support ███████████████ mission. I used to work next to the chief of ███████ before I came to Afghanistan, so I was familiar with ███████ operations. Its people go out and collect intelligence that isn't available through ██████████ means, ████████████████████████████ ████ You can only get so much from far-off technical devices and if you need to be closer in to get information, you also need people—to take photographs, for example, ████████████████████ ███████████████████. That's what ███████████████ in close. As far as I was concerned, they were the unsung heroes of the intelligence community. Small in number, but creative and adaptive. In Bagram, ███████ only had a few people—at most three—so they depended on Washington and the DIA for mission support.

████████████ conducting covert missions around Afghanistan, although mostly in Kabul. To hide their missions, they would go in as part of convoys that ran regularly between Kabul and Bagram, break off in Kabul, do their job, and then join back up with the regular convoys to return to Bagram.

Dave had said he'd get me trained up to conduct missions with
█████ , but I hadn't expected to hit the road with the █████ crowd
one day after getting in. I was still punch drunk from the flight. After
the morning meetings, we suited up: body armor vests with Sapi
plates—small-arms protection inserts and Kevlar on the side, Velcro
strips holding it close to the body—and each of us grabbed an M-4.
We headed out in three vehicles, driving with about 100 yards between
trucks to assure that if an attack occurred, they couldn't get more
than one vehicle.

After a mountain pass on Russian Road, where we slowed down
slightly and passed a lumbering 10th Mountain convoy, we really hit
the gas as we headed downhill into Kabul. We then decelerated as we
entered the traffic bedlam of a city with about two million residents—
and only one working traffic light. Tightening our distance between
vehicles to 25 to 50 meters, Julie had me roll down my window, and I
rested my M-4 on the door, scanning the teeming crowds for threats.
Kabul was a chaotic ruin of a city that had been beaten down by outside
invaders and internal warlords. Because of the danger of attacks, we
still drove fast, weaving in and out of traffic and dodging pedestrians.
In the traffic circles that served as intersections, anything went, so you
just had to plunge in. With no traffic laws, everything spilled into
the streets: pedestrians, sheep, carts, bicycles, uniformed troops, etc.
The noise and heat were overwhelming. Most cargo was moved by
"jingle trucks," fully painted and decorated with names on the side like
HEAV-I or MR. MUSCLE. They had chains and other strips of metal attached to virtually every part of the frame—like dog chains cut into
8-inch lengths and welded along the sides and front of the vehicle.
When the jingle trucks moved, they sounded like a combination of
someone dumping out the silverware drawer in your kitchen and glass
shattering. The drivers stacked cargo on top, tied it down with ropes,
and piled passengers on top of that. It looked about as stable as it sounds.

Then there were the "Taliban taxis." About seven out of every ten
cars were yellow-and-white Toyota Corollas. When the Taliban were
in power, they declared that all vehicles in the country belonged to

them and that they would be taxis. They literally took all private vehicles and painted them white and yellow. Even though the vehicles had been privatized again, most owners hadn't repainted the cars.

Dazed by the heat and the ever-present dust and smog that was low to the ground, I struggled to focus on the blurry scene. What was I looking for? How would I know danger if I saw it?

The rules of engagement (ROE) at the time were if you believed that you were about to be engaged with deadly force by an adversary, you could engage that threat preemptively, but that meant you actually had to know what you were looking for.

No matter what, you kept going. That was the guidance given. Anywhere—on the left of vehicles, on the right, on the sidewalk, on the median—it didn't matter. If you got in an accident, you kept driving, faster than before because it might have been a setup for an assault. Even if you hit a pedestrian, you kept moving and notified the American Embassy later. We rode without seatbelts in the city. That way, if a bomb or hand grenade were thrown into our vehicle, we could bail out.

If one vehicle in the convoy was attacked, either in the city or on the open road, we were to circle around, provide covering fire, pull out survivors, and call for reinforcements.

Despite the dangers, on virtually every trip to Kabul, we stopped to shop (we are Americans, after all). It was part of our cover as non-military, which actually was fairly effective. In our civilian attire and vehicles, we tended to blend in with personnel from private relief organizations and the UN (even though they were unarmed), and with the private armed security forces that populated the city.

The best place to shop, everyone knew, was Chicken Street, Kabul's only Western tourist area. While you were there, the tradition was to hire child "bodyguards" that served as assistants. I always made a point of hiring girls. The Afghan men hanging around were obviously not happy about it and shot the girls dirty looks. Several boys tried to get me to fire the girls and to use a boy because being a bodyguard was men's work, but the girls and I always smiled and kept

going. I was pleased that the girls had the courage to stick to the job
in a culture that, under the Taliban, had treated women like cattle. I
always paid them $2 each (double the normal "rate") so they could
keep $1 for themselves after turning over $1 to their families.

This was my first trip, though, and it was all business. We headed
for the CIA station ███████████████████████████████████████
with thick concrete walls and several outbuildings ████████████
██
██
██
██
██████████████████████████

On the porch of the ██████, I ran into Jacob Walker, chief of station
in Afghanistan. With his gaunt face, deep-set eyes, and dark suit, he
reminded me of Peter Cushing, the actor who played Governor Tar-
kin, commander of the Death Star in *Star Wars*.

"Mr. Walker," I introduced myself. "I'm ██████████████████, the
new HUMINT operations chief here for DIA."

"██████████████, good to meet you," he said. "Are you an operator
or just another staff-type they've sent to the field to pretend they are
real operatives?"

The question caught me off guard. "No, sir, I went through the
Farm when Jim Fletcher was chief of base there." Jim was a well-
known internal CIA legend—one of those gallant officers from the
good old days at the CIA—and a name that Jacob knew well.

"Really?" he said with a bit of a shock. "Impressive. Have you
given any thought to joining us? If you're interested, I'd be happy to
bring you over."

The CIA, faced with a shortage of experienced officers, had been
frantically poaching officers from Defense since the start of the war.
At least two of my former DIA colleagues were now working for Jacob
but I had no interest. I'd seen too much of their bureaucracy and their
problems and, despite my problems with the DIA leadership, I knew
the grass wasn't always greener.

"I had a similar offer from your counterparts when I was in command ██ ███ cover operatives ████████████████████████.

The truth was, I'd tried to join the CIA when I was fresh out of college. I'd passed the interviews, the tests, and the psychological screening, and had gotten so far that they'd issued me a cover, but I was unable to pass the lie detector exam and didn't get hired.

Years later, the Defense Security Service showed me the results summary. According to the CIA polygraph examiner, I was "deception indicated" on criminal activity and illegal drug use. The funny thing was that the CIA polygraph examiner would not believe, no matter how many times I stated the truth, that I had never even tried drugs. He insisted that everyone in my generation had at least "experimented" with illegal drugs. Of course, I did some stupid things in my youth—bartending for the Marine Guard at their residence in Lisbon, and I'd been a drunken hellion in high school—but never any illegal drugs. Why bother when I had as much booze as I wanted?

Oh, yeah. When confronted with their allegations that I was "deception indicated" on criminal activity, I admitted on the polygraph that I had taken U.S. government Skilcraft pens from the American Embassy in Lisbon. Yeah. Just like John Dillinger.

After that experience, I knew never to believe the results of any polygraph exam. If they couldn't figure out I was telling the truth about drug use, then chances are they couldn't figure out who's telling the truth about anything else.

Looking back on it, though, God must have been smiling on me. The path I ended up on was far more interesting—and fun. I believe everything happens for a reason, and I just wasn't meant to work for the CIA. I'd moved past it years ago, and I shook off Walker's offer. "I'm pretty happy where I am," I told him, adding politely, "but I'll think about it."

In truth, my experiences with the CIA in Afghanistan would be less than happy. The CIA, it turned out, was running its own game, a game they didn't bother to coordinate with anyone on the Defense side of the house. At one point, I was to learn later, we had an ugly experience with a warlord who was on their payroll. It was not that they played against both sides. It was the fact that they did it so obviously and poorly that pissed all of us off.

Before we rolled out, Dave showed me the ███-bar" on the hotel's first floor, an honor bar ████████████ equipped with tables, chairs, and a few couches. You grabbed a cold beer or made yourself a drink, and tossed money into a box on the bar to pay for it. I always had tonic water or a Coke.

The white walls were covered with old, nonserviceable weapons, everything from Enfield rifles from the nineteenth century to Kalashnikovs captured from the Taliban during the 2001 invasion. Great quotes from spooks were scrawled on there as well, and, most poignantly, mementos of fallen comrades—scraps of clothing or pieces of *keffeyeh*, the distinctive black-and-white scarves that many wore to keep out the dust. The place had a great stereo system and a huge library of top-notch music CDs, left by departing spooks, which I later borrowed for convoy rides.

Those who had finished their tours of duty traditionally signed the wall, but only on your last day of duty. Signing any earlier was bad luck.

After, Dave briefed me on the ██████ mission. Among other tasks, we were headed for a destination away from central downtown. We were taking two vehicles. The first one was an equipment vehicle and the second was security. Our mission ███████ was classified, so I'll skip that part. Dave, as commander of the mission, drove the first vehicle.

"We're going to a part of town we've never been before," he told me. "I'd like you to stay with Julie in the second vehicle. Any questions?"

"No, I'm good," I said. Truth was, I was nervous as hell but working hard not to show it.

He stopped for a minute. "One other thing. Watch out for provocations. The Taliban has been training kids to do stuff. They've been throwing explosive devices at vehicles—hand grenades and IEDs. So be aware of what's going on."

I'd seen tons of kids today in the streets. Using them . . . I couldn't believe it.

We suited back up and rolled out again to do our business. Most of the areas we went to through the day were not market areas, but still heavily urban. Mainly mud huts and brick homes up to the crests of low hills that bordered the mountains surrounding Kabul.

After settling into the turbulent rhythm of the vehicle's movement, with Julie driving with expert abandon through the Kabul streets at an average speed of 60 miles an hour on the straightaways, I was almost enjoying the roller-coaster-like ride, watching the blur of people, men in their long pajamalike robes and women in their burkas. I was even getting used to the feeling of the drops of sweat condensing and trickling down from the top of my chest to my underarms. I let my weapon drop down toward my seat and contemplated pulling out the bag of lollipops Dave had given me to toss to the kids we were passing.

We hit a slight grade, slowing down a bit. Fully half the structures in the neighborhood we were passing through were bombed down to the foundations. Others had been rebuilt. I had to admire the fierce determination of a people who had been at war, some for their entire lifetimes.

Then I saw him emerge from the throng. The slightly built boy just ahead of us, running out of the crowd and toward Dave's vehicle, just about 50 meters in front of us, bomb in hand.

I instinctively swung up my M-4 from resting with the barrel down between the seam of the door and the dashboard, thumbed off the safety, and aimed.

Then, suddenly, out of the corner of my eye, I saw something. The shiny object fluttered in a sudden wind. *Bombs don't flutter.* I hesitated, my mind rocketing over the possibilities. The device the boy threw was blue and silver. Then I caught sight of a familiar logo.

It wasn't a bomb. It was a silver-and-blue Capri Sun juice container.

A freakin' *juice box*. Just like the ones my son drank when we were at Boy Scout camp together right before I left.

I lowered my rifle, slumped back in my seat, and let out my breath that I had instinctively held for the past few seconds. The kid was fading back into the crowd, but I caught his eye and stared at him. He looked to be about the same age as Alexander.

Clearly, he had been trained to pull that kind of stunt. The idea would be to create bad press if we shot him, or it would lower our threshold of concern so that after we had dealt with kids tossing juice boxes a few times, we would relax our vigilance. This kid didn't get it. He was being used and had almost ended up dead.

Only the wind gusting at that very second had saved this boy's life. I hoped he wouldn't try that again. *Inshallah.* God willing.

What a place. I thought back on my past training. I'd been schooled as a spy to take on a First World adversary, like the Russians or the Chinese. The way I had been trained, intelligence—even clandestine intelligence—was a gentleman's game. The idea of using a weapon or ending up in combat . . . well, we didn't go there. I'd been told by an old-school instructor at the Farm in one of my first training sessions that spies didn't need guns because if you couldn't talk your way out of a situation, then you weren't worth your salt.

Apparently, he'd never been in combat.

Even in the 1990s, the armed forces hadn't faced the fact that war had changed. Our enemies were just as deadly, but different. Now I was fighting an enemy that used children as a method of weapons delivery. This was alien.

Nevertheless we all had to damned well get used to it. We were facing an adversary that hid behind the innocent and targeted those who could not hope to defend themselves. I realized we had to get back on the offensive. George Patton's rule: The best defense is a good offense. We had to take the war to the enemy because if our adversaries were more worried about survival, about waking up to see the sun the next morning than about planning ops against us, they wouldn't have the will to attack us.

The realization was like a hard slap across the face.

I called the first vehicle on the Motorola gray brick.

"Did you see that?" I asked.

"Yeah . . . what the fuck! We had our hands on the door ready to bail! Did you see the kid?"

"Yeah," I answered back into the radio. "I saw him," and I glanced over to Julie, "and he nearly died." There would have been no way I would have missed at that range.

After another thirty minutes, we finished the mission and went back to the ███████ to collect the third vehicle. After we arrived, Dave and I were speechless. Dave, in particular, loved kids and, being a liberal in uniform, he in particular took to heart the plight of children in this environment. We just sat across from each other on the front stoop of the Ariana and stared out into space. I could see how the stress was going to add up quickly.

"We need to bring an extra vehicle back to Bagram," Dave broke the silence. "I'd like you to drive it."

"What?" I said. I'd had combat driving training back in the States, but this was taking some getting used to.

"I know how you're feeling," said Dave, now with some of his sense of humor and smile returning. "This is overwhelming, but I'm telling you it's not going to get any better by putting it off."

I figured there was no way out of it, so I focused on the mission. We went out to the parking lot, and Dave handed over the keys.

"Any questions?" asked Dave.

"Nope," I said. I looked at the dashboard. At least the truck had a cool stereo. This was starting to grow on me. Good music and a chance to drive like a bat out of hell.

"Where do you want me in order of march?" I asked him.

"Stay behind, you'll be fine." With that, Dave slapped me on the shoulder and walked to his vehicle.

As we pulled out past the guards and into the dusty sea of white and yellow Taliban taxis, animals, jingle trucks, and military vehicles, my senses were now hyperalert and focused. We cleared the last traffic circle of Kabul and headed north on the new Russian Road toward Bagram. It was late. The shadows had turned the light tans and browns of the dried mountain faces into muted grays and taupes, with growing blankets of purple.

As we hit 90 miles an hour, I punched my first song up. The Psychedelic Furs's "Love My Way":

> *There's an army*
> *On the dance floor . . .*

I was an experienced intelligence officer, but it was clear that Afghanistan was going to push me to the limits of my endurance— physically and emotionally. Just when I thought I'd reached my max, it would push me some more.

✦ 5 ✦

"WE WILL KILL THE INFIDELS"

"IS this the *Babylon 5* rerun?" I joked as I walked into the video conference tent in the SCIF. Dave Christensen and Tim Loudermilk, Colonel Negro's operations officer, were watching a grainy video on the plasma screen on the wall. Dave, as always, was scribbling notes on a yellow legal pad.

"Nope," said Tim. "We're watching the Taliban."

At the morning meeting, Maj. Ted Smith, one of my colleagues at DIA who ran the Document Exploitation Detachment, had announced that a video of a Taliban operation was available. It had been captured about three weeks earlier and after it had been translated, it was handed over to us. The videotape was the raw footage that the Taliban intended for recruiting and fund-raising—two critical tasks of any terrorist organization. The Taliban's targets for recruitment were young students in the Pakistan madrassas, religious schools across the border that had helped to spawn the Taliban movement. They were also using the videos to raise money from their partner, al Qaeda and from rich Arabs who sympathized with their cause. Our intel told us that al Qaeda was getting impatient with their partners-in-crime and wanted to see a little more action for the cash they were sinking into the movement.

"What are they doing now? Are they holding services?" I asked.

"Only for the guys they killed," Dave answered as he eyeballed the screen.

I settled in to watch, put my feet up on the table, and leaned back on two legs of the chair, taking out my notebook. Watching this clearly amateur video was a bit of a chore, but I had to admit that while it wasn't Hollywood, they knew what they were doing.

It had been shot with a small Sony camera in documentary style, with the constant movement of the camera and the subject to enhance the feeling of action. One guy had shot the footage and had narrated. Interesting. They made the sacrifice of an armed, able-bodied guerrilla just to play combat cameraman. If they could free up someone for that job, it meant they were thinking about information operations and how to use that against their adversary—us. That indicated a robust level of thinking and a complex concept of operations. One thing I'd learned about terrorists was that they are very adaptive. They aren't part of a large bureaucracy with a lot of rules and regulations. They don't have any oversight—or moral compass, for that matter.

These guys are changing and adapting, I thought, *learning to use propaganda and videos to find fresh recruits and raise money for their weapons and training bases.*

I grabbed a thick translation transcript.

Dave said the videotape had started in Pakistan in the training camps. A team of a dozen guys seemed to be in on this operation. We watched them take target practice with their AK-47s in a camp that appeared to hold maybe forty or fifty men. Smiling, they'd shoot off their Kalashnikovs into the air to celebrate. They talked to some elders—older men in black turbans—who were wishing them well. There were shots of them praying, probably to show off their Islamic devotion to their funders. As each Talib spoke into the camera, I skimmed the transcript. They were making some kind of religious statements or oaths: They were doing this for Allah. Should they die, they would go to heaven. This was to bring praise upon their family. The blood of the infidel will flow.

These guys were hams—but they were hams with guns.

In the bleak mountainous landscape—dusty, rocky, and brown, dotted with scrubby pine and some sorry-looking juniper—we watched as they moved across the mountains, over smugglers' trails into Afghanistan. They made camp, cooking food along the way. As they went, the narrator explained their mission: how important the war was, and how they planned to return Afghanistan to the Taliban, expel the infidels from the country, and give it to Allah. Conquering Kandahar was the first step in retaking Afghanistan. The fighters talked a lot of Mullah Omar. They wanted to take back the land for their brother Mulláh Omar, the one-eyed leader of the Taliban who had led them to dominance over the warring tribes in Afghanistan in 1995 and had eluded capture since then, so that he could walk freely and give them the benefit of his wisdom. They thanked Allah for their weapons and the good weather.

After twenty minutes of tape showing what appeared to be several days, they reached their quarry in the late afternoon: a small cement police station in a tiny village. An Afghan flag was fluttering above it. A dozen or so mud huts blended almost seamlessly into the surrounding landscape, with a thin, rocky road running through the settlement. From the looks of the terrain, they were near Khowst, a province on the border of Pakistan about 100 miles southeast of Kabul.

Outside the police station, in the sunshine of the waning day, two policemen in khaki uniforms and boxy caps were hanging around smoking, their AK-47s up against the building, under a worn poster of Ahmad Shah Massoud. Massoud—the "Lion of Panjshir"—was the leader of the Northern Alliance and fought the Soviets and then the Taliban, until the Taliban or al Qaeda finally succeeded in assassinating him on September 9, 2001. His poster was all over downtown Kabul, too, and at every AMF-controlled checkpoint I'd seen since I'd been in country. His leadership was greatly missed by Afghans, and frankly the more I learned about him, the more I recognized how much we'd screwed up by not supporting him during the dark post-Soviet-occupation days.

The filming was at a distance from the police station in the village, so the picture was shaky, but I could imagine that the policemen were talking about the day, going home to the wife—or wives—and kids, and so on. These police outposts were the closest thing to centralized government control that most Afghans ever saw—and the police were often as corrupt as *Casablanca*'s Captain Renault, also ill-trained. Still, they frequently were all that stood between the Taliban and central government control of a village and, in many instances, entire provinces.

In the video, the attackers moved closer and closer, scrambling down the mountainside, the narrator explaining in whispers. The transcript laid out in chilling detail their plan of attack. *We will kill the infidels. This will be part of a string of victories over them. Inshallah.*

They checked their weapons, then one guy gave the word and they moved down the hill, firing as they went, the camera bobbing as the video guy scrambled to keep up. Both policemen turned to look, expressions of shock on their faces. One tossed his cigarette aside and was shot and killed almost immediately. The other guy was hit and knocked down. The attackers were shouting and firing, the gunshot sounds distorted into something unrecognizable by the cheap microphone on the video camera.

The second policemen struggled to get to his feet, speaking pleadingly to the attackers. He tried to pull something from his breast pocket.

They shot him in the head.

I leaned forward. "Whoa," I said.

Not much of a fair fight—twelve to two in this encounter—and this sort of thing was being repeated dozens of times per week as the Taliban's ambitions became real and their minions were on the move.

After the murders, the attackers celebrated, mugging for the cameraman, smiling and dancing around, weapons above their heads. They rifled the pockets of the dead policemen.

If these deadly teams gained control of police stations, they pretty much had control of the village as long as they could cut a deal with the elders. The message to the elders was unequivocal: Play ball with us or die. A persuasive approach. It didn't take much in these remote areas to grab control over enough villages to give you effective control of the province. Newly elected president Karzai was weak—he was known sardonically in Afghanistan as the "mayor of Kabul"—with little control outside the capital. The Taliban were taking full advantage of that lack of strong central control.

They were also replacing their disorganized hit-and-run attacks against U.S. forces with better-coordinated assaults, and more sophisticated ambushes on softer targets: police officers, foreign and Afghan aid workers, and contractors.

The body count, as well as the intimidation, was rising.

In March 2003, an International Red Cross water engineer was grabbed by a member of the Taliban in Oruzgan Province in southern Afghanistan, the home province of Taliban chief Mullah Omar. The Talib who captured the engineer called up Taliban commander Mullah Dadullah and, on orders from Dadullah, shot him to death.

In May, two engineers working for a German aid agency were critically wounded by remote-controlled bombs that exploded near Jalalabad in eastern Afghanistan. Two members of a foreign ██████ team were also murdered that month when a suicide bomber in a car pulled up next to their bus as they were headed for Kabul Airport and then detonated himself. Dave was spared being caught in the blast, but came upon the scene just seconds later.

In June, four German peacekeepers were killed when a car bomb detonated in Kabul, and six guards working for a U.S. contractor overseeing the reconstruction of the road between Kabul and Kandahar were killed by gunmen in August.

Leaflets or "night letters" were also appearing in towns and villages.

They showed up more often than not nailed to a village's central "bulletin board," and where no board existed, they were nailed to schools, offices, and other community locations—all done under the cover of darkness. They'd creep into these villages overnight to prove the point of their invincibility. The night letters gave the Taliban credit for the attacks and called for jihad—or holy war—against the Americans and Karzai's new government. They compared the American "infidel" presence to the Soviet occupation in 1970s and '80s.

What was it that Rumsfeld had said a couple of months ago? War's over, boys. Major combat operations in Afghanistan were complete and the focus would now be on reconstruction. Right.

I'd once met the SecDef right after 9/11. I ran into him just outside the Pentagon at the end of a workout. He asked me why the highly accessible, unguarded "runner's entrance" to the Pentagon Athletic Club had been closed permanently. *Hmm*, I thought at the time, *this is a bad sign*. Pentagon attacked, security increased . . . and still the question about the entrance from the man who should know why it had been closed down. There was a pattern developing here.

Tim, Dave, and I watched the end of the video, as the Taliban celebrated the deaths of the police officers, in grim silence. "What does this mean?" I asked Dave.

He put down his pen. "Between their religious diatribes, they're giving indications of what they're up to and where they're going."

This was more than just a propaganda video. The info on the videotape fit into the intelligence Dave and his folks had been getting—that this operation was a small part of a much larger plan by the Taliban to retake Afghanistan. They had started by overrunning police outposts, but their ambitions were much, much larger. There were signs of coordination between the Taliban, al Qaeda, and the guerrilla group Hezb-e-Islami Gulbuddin, headed by Gulbuddin Hekmatyar, who was on the LTC's list. A Taliban rival in the 1990s, Hekmatyar had formed an alliance with them in recent years. One of our theories was that the HIG, as Hezb-e-Islami Gulbuddin was known, had become the de facto bodyguards of bin Laden when he was in

Afghanistan. If you could find the HIG, the thinking went, it could lead you to him.

Our sources indicated that more than 1,000 ACM (anticoalition militia) combat fighters were moving into Afghanistan, which meant you had thousands more on the Pak side helping plan, equip, train, and organize.

"In other words," I said, "they're coming back, and they have a very detailed plan on how to do it."

Dave nodded. "This isn't just about taking down checkpoints along the border." Intelligence pointed to a chilling goal: retake Kandahar—second largest city in Afghanistan with more than 300,000 residents—and the surrounding Kandahar province by Ramadan, two months from now. "They are very patient, and they know what they want to do."

"Can't we chase 'em back across the border into Pakistan and let the Paks deal with them?" I asked.

Dave shook his head impatiently. "Tony, you're naïve. You think that if we just do that, they're going to stay there."

"I understand that," I answered, "but my impression is that we are trying to seal off the border."

Dave rose and strode over to a wall-size map of Afghanistan and ran his hand along the bumpy eastern border with Pakistan—1,500 miles of mountains, canyons, caverns, and remote smugglers' trails. "Do you really believe we can close off that?" he asked.

"I guess not," I said. Not without the Pakistanis' help, and I was to learn that we couldn't rely on them. This was getting kind of alarming. "So what the hell do we do?"

Our combat forces were strung out all over a country the size of Texas. If these guys wanted to pour over the border, there wasn't a whole hell of a lot we could do to stop them just with conventional warfare. The intel was indicating that 1,000 battle-hardened Taliban insurgents, coming in from the Pakistani border towns of Wana and Quetta, were moving with haste into the interior of Afghanistan. The U.S. and Afghan forces couldn't shut down that entire border and, under agreements with the Paks, we couldn't pursue them into Pakistan. We had to be smarter, quicker, more cunning.

Dave leaned forward again. Clearly, he'd been thinking about this for a while. "I understand that we're focusing on leadership targeting, but I'd like us to work together to provide actionable intelligence to the 10th Mountain so they can more effectively counter the offensive."

"What do you have in mind?" I asked, now sitting with all four chair legs on the floor and paying close attention.

"I'd like us to combine intel for the effort," said Dave.

Whoa. This was radical. There are huge ownership issues over intel. Intelligence agencies like to keep their info in silos, send it in for analysis, and treat it as proprietary. In Washington ███████ ████████████████ analysts normally do triage and give you back what they think you need—and you never get everything.

"You want our raw source info?" I wanted to make sure I knew what he was requesting.

"Well," Dave said carefully, "it would be useful. We could infuse the data for any known terrorist, warlord, or enabler—anything you have."

I thought hard, putting my hand to my forehead. "I don't think the people in my organization are gonna like that very much." *No kidding,* I thought. *They'll go ballistic.*

Our reports were written without the exact source of the info to protect that source. We separated out the chaff and gave out just the kernel. However, the details related to sourcing were hugely important to understanding the big picture.

"It would have to stay within the holdings of the LTC. No foreigners" I said. Foreign troops were providing ███████████ as well as combat support, as part of the International Security Assistance Force (ISAF) troops in the country.

Dave nodded. "In exchange, I will make sure you get immediate coverage or answers we can pull directly from our data ███. We would use the combined data to put together a package on each guy. Then decisions could be made jointly." For Dave, that

meant details of what the bad guys were doing ████████████
██
██
████████████████, were hugely important to understanding the operational environment—the "spiderweb" of the terrorist infrastructure that we had to understand so we could act in a smart, cohesive fashion.

For Dave to offer to distribute raw data intelligence even though it would remain within the top secret security network, was also a radical move. Normally, Washington ████████████████████ gave people like Dave what they thought he needed in the form of finished or near finished reports, but Dave had cut a deal with them. He was getting everything so that his hybrid team of ████████████████ ████████ specialists could parse it and review it to establish their own intel. In promising me access to their data, Dave was stepping way, way, way out on a limb.

In my mind, I could just hear the screaming in Washington ████ ██ ████████████ if they knew about this level of information exchange.

"Where do you propose to keep it?" I asked. The fact was, our computer systems were incompatible, so we had no way to create a shared database. We would literally have to print out everything.

"I'm going to put them on my door," Dave said.

I rolled my eyes. "Oh, *that's* secure."

"We're in a SCIF. We're fine," Dave said, "and we need to have one central location that has one hard copy of all the information on any single target. When we decide to take action, we pull the target package down and we start looking at it as a team. Together, we make a decision on a course of action: kill, capture, or do nothing."

Kill, capture, or spy: that was the accepted equation of the new math that we dealt with every day. The temptation was always to kill, but actually it's better first to spy. ████████████████████ ████████████████████, so you had to perform a gain-loss evaluation of potentially losing that intel. If you spy on a bad guy and he gives you good intel, the benefit of having him out there telling you what's going on may be greater than the single victory of taking him out or bringing him in. So sometimes it's better to leave him hanging out there until he outlives his usefulness or it becomes clear he's planning some imminent action that could hurt somebody.

We would have to hold nothing back. I would even have to tell him who DIA's sources were, our subsources, how they were recruited, their tribal leanings—all the atmospherics in the ops traffic that often got scrubbed from reports. Then Washington could verify ▮▮▮▮▮

▮▮
▮▮
▮▮▮▮▮▮▮▮▮▮▮▮▮▮▮

"What do you think Colonel Negro, will think of this approach?" I asked Dave. We both looked at Tim Loudermilk.

"We haven't really come up with a methodology for the Tier 2 targets that will be of use in going after Tier 1," he said. "He could go for it. I think it'll help us on Tier 2 targets, which are mostly in Afghanistan and, when we focus on Tier 2, that will help us focus on operational objectives."

"You mean Mountain Viper?" asked Dave. That was CJTF 180's upcoming operation.

"Precisely," I said. I was ready to jump in.

"You've got my buy-in," I said. "We'll give you information from our sources in real time as it comes in."

Dave smiled. "That's great, shipmate. I really appreciate it. I think that will make us all more effective."

"We probably also need to get the buy-in of Colonel Boardman," I said.

We both looked at Tim.

Col. Robert Boardman was the senior intelligence officer (J2) of CTJF 180. He believed that all intelligence should be coming to him—not to the LTC—and that too much of the three-letter agencies' time and effort were going to support Colonel Negro and his folks rather than what Boardman thought was his job, which was to produce intelligence reports. Although we knew the intel would just sit on Boardman's desk.

There was a short silence.

"Why don't we just get Colonel Negro buy-in," Dave finally said. We knew Boardman would just hoard the information.

Later, after some raised eyebrows and a quick think, Negro did, indeed, buy in. So did my boss, Bill Wilson.

A showdown was brewing. I did sincerely believe our fighting forces were the best in the world, but after years of training for the Cold War "Fulda Gap Scenario"—where Russian troops were expected to flood through the Fulda Gap in Germany—I had my doubts. The Army, and really the whole of DoD, had trained to anticipate the expected force-on-force conflagration in central Europe in which a large Soviet combined-arms army would invade West Germany and push toward the Atlantic. The whole of U.S. military doctrine was based on training to counter and defeat the Soviet monolith, and things like Vietnam, Korea, etc. were nothing more than "proxy warfare"—with Vietnam being the most notable counterinsurgency we had faced . . . and lost.

In theory, small counterterrorism "mop-up" operations were all that would be needed to ensure favorable conditions for the Afghan people. This was an incorrect assumption by those rocket scientists at the Pentagon who would translate wishful thinking into policy.

General Vines had made it clear in his morning meetings that the war was not over, and it was his intent to take the war to the enemy. My kind of guy.

Despite that, the focus of the U.S. effort was 1,400 miles away in Iraq. Dave had even gotten a call from CENTCOM—U.S. Central Command that was responsible for Mideast and Central Asia. The essence of the message was: "Chill out. Why don't you guys just hold the line and not engage?" The funny thing was, there was no panic, no sense of doom, no concept in the Pentagon of how dire things were about to get here. Yet there was every indication that something wicked this way comes. Time to make some changes.

I got some pushback from my DIA staff, mostly from the reports officer, "Special Ed," who didn't see the benefit in sharing operational data.

"We have no process for transmitting that type of info to outside organizations," Special Ed said solemnly as we met in the SCIF to discuss the new arrangement. The source admin guy then chimed in to explain the proper procedure to report and forward source information.

"Yeah, so?" I said.

Ed added, "Well, Tony, it is a closed system—information goes in and we hold it."

I took a deep breath. As usual, process over progress.

"To quote a general I once worked for, 'Don't tell me how to suck eggs,'" I said. I looked over at Bill Wilson who was listening without emotion, propped up against the table next to the weapons locker.

"We need to do it," he snapped and got up and walked away.

I looked over at Ed. "Give me hard copy on Ray's net and speak to the Safe House about the sources they want to make sure do not get inadvertently whacked ███████████████████ " ██████████ ████████████████ and his "net" was his collection of Afghan agents and their informants.) ███████████████████████ ██ ██ █████████████████████████

Within the hour, Dave taped ten manila envelopes to his door, one for each of our top ten targets that we could stick our data in. He created unclassified code names for them, using the names of cities so we could refer to the targets on open lines and protect their true identity: OMAHA, MEDFORD, COLUMBUS, and so on. Then, if one of these guys was ████████████████████ and tracked down by one of our informants or linked to an event—a raid, a cross-border operation, a planning meeting that we found out about—we could just pull his file off the door. We could have a full eyeball on him, maybe send a JSTAR in for a real-time look at him. We would get the

LTC involved. Dave would talk to everyone, including the lawyers. Should we monitor? Disrupt? Capture? Kill? We were trying to make them uncomfortable, anticipate what they were doing, then degrade and disrupt their activities.

Our technique was a derivative of Information Operations known as Effects Based Operations (EBO). The idea behind EBO is to maximize your strengths and apply them directly to your adversary's weaknesses, monitor the effects of your effort and adjust accordingly to make sure you maintain the advantage. The trend in the army had been to establish standards, train to those standards, and conduct operations to meet those standards. The problem had become that achieving victory had been lost in the process—measures of performance became the measure to which one's military success was held. What got dropped was the focus on measures of effectiveness—or achieving victory. The military tends to worship mediocrity. Achieving and maintaining standards—even if those standards do not achieve victory—is the safest course of action. Follow process, no matter what.

EBO became the last and best option to ensure that the very limited combat forces in country would be used effectively. With a determined enemy who was learning how to retake lost ground, every efficiency we could find was needed.

Mountain Viper, the upcoming operation planned against the Taliban, would be a major test of the concept and its effectiveness. The limited number of 10th Mountain's troops would be the subjects of this test—with their objective to stymie the Taliban offensive.

Shortly after that meeting with Dave, our informants told us of a chilling development. Bearded men, riding on Honda motorcycles, carrying Kalashnikov rifles and satellite telephones, were driving along the trails of the deep, treeless valleys in Zabul province about 100 miles southwest of Bagram. They were on their way.

MOUNTAIN VIPER

THE Taliban were reinfesting southeastern Afghanistan, from the border province of Khowst, down through Paktika, Zabul, Ghazni, and Oruzgan provinces, and into Kandahar province—the heartland of the Taliban before they were ousted in 2001.

Armed with our intelligence and knowledge of HUMINT assets available to answer any intel gaps, I sat down with the 10th Mountain planners shortly after my meeting with Dave, in which we agreed to coordinate resources to conduct mission analysis and detailed planning. I wanted to interweave intelligence collected by our Afghan informants into the Mountain Viper Concept of Operations—the battle plan worked out by General Vines and his officers.

Majors Grubbs and Reichert, the 10th Mountain planners, were a little wary. "We've never had the Defense HUMINT guy sit down and talk to us about how we can prosecute a battle," Reichert said, eyeing me and my goatee skeptically.

Ordinarily, DIA people didn't play well with combat types. Somehow, DIA leadership—mostly the civilian executives—had come to feel that it was beneath them to conduct "field operations," but I didn't operate that way.

"C'mon, I'm army, just like you," I told them. "We've all gone through Huachuca. I just wear civilian clothes now."

They looked at me—then looked at each other—and with kind of a nod in each other's direction, they laid out a map and gave me a draft copy of the Operations Order, laying out the villages of interest.

The Taliban had done a good job of reconnaissance and preparation for their fall offensive. They appeared to have a firm understanding of where they would have to go and what they would have to do to regain control of Kandahar and the province. The fact is we were facing an elusive, lethal enemy that was readying itself to fight in a forbidding area of towering rocky mountains and steep valleys.

Their tactic was comprehensive attack. They had started by getting control of the police stations, as we had seen on the video, as a way to disrupt the central order of the country. If that strategy was successful, it wouldn't take long before they were aiming for Kandahar. We believed that Mullah Omar was making trips inside Pakistan to recruit fresh Taliban troops.

I looked over the plan. "Gentlemen, I'm going to take this to Randy, the head of our detachment ██████████████████████████
██
██

Despite themselves, Grubbs and Reichert were won over. ███████
██
██
██
██
████████████████████████████████

I had first encountered Ray while working in my office and watching a Steven Seagal movie (all his movies are the same but I like them anyway) on my computer about eight o'clock one night. A ton of movies had been loaded onto the secret-level network, and I took advantage of them because I disliked the stuffy, gritty hooch; I preferred to stay in the SCIF, and work.

An e-mail popped up.

"Activity reported on the border." It was the first I'd heard from Ray. Kandahar sat in between mountains and desert and was about a two-hour drive from the Pakistani border. Ray was referring to suspicious activity by the Taliban in an area I can't reveal. "Any interest in follow-up?" his e-mail asked.

I talked to Dave, who was eating tuna and crackers in his office with his headphones on.

"I just got this note from our guy, Ray, in Kandahar," I told Dave, holding out the printout. "He's asking me if we're interested in what's going on on the border." I named the location. "Are you guys?"

Dave immediately took off his headphones and read the e-mail. "We're very interested," he said. They had received several reports relating to the possible sighting of ████████ Mullah Omar. "Tell him we'd be interested in any observations of individuals or convoys of vehicles that match the profile of Omar and his entourage."

I got back to my office and back on the computer as fast as I could.

"Absolutely," I typed. "Our guys report this is a key location related to previously known Taliban activity possibly related to Mullah Omar. What do you have? V/R, Tony."

Almost immediately, my phone rang.

"Tony, why the hell you working this late?" I guessed it was Ray. He had a gruff voice, a broad New York accent, and a no-nonsense style.

"I'm always working," I said. "I never go back to the tent. Too many people. Too damned hot."

"Usually you guys shut down after five," he said.

"Not now," I said. "I'm usually here until eleven or twelve every night."

"That's great for me," Ray said. "I'm meetin' with my guys tonight. I need some things checked out. Can you take care of it?"

"Absolutely," I said.

An hour later, Ray sent me in a list of questions. "Can you see if there's anything on these guys here?"

"Are these guys the ones your assets are tracking?"

"Yeah," he said. There was a hesitation that I recognized as a half truth. "Sorta. I'm tryin' to sort through which of these guys are real targets and which ain't. Some of 'em come and go across the border a lot, and we can't figure out what's goin' on. Can you check 'em out?"

"You got it," I said. "Get back to you tomorrow morning."

The next morning, I briefed the LTC on Ray's report and gave them his questions. By the end of the morning, the two Marine Corps intelligence analysts had compiled the LTC's holdings of information on and about Ray's list of assets. They had provided new information and answers on 80 percent of the names. I e-mailed this info to Ray. For the most part, these names came up in relation to Mullah Omar. Some of them were known Taliban enablers, which I suggested to Ray should be our first focus for intelligence collection.

About midnight, I got a short e-mail. "Info I have from source is that enabler is going to meet tonight with his Taliban contact." Ray named the location coordinate. "Any interest?" Enablers were the dudes we kept a close eye on due to direct links to known bad guys. They were the arms dealers and the money men who kept the Taliban supplied with weapons and cash. Some were also emerging as significant players in the resurgent illegal drug trade. This enabler was a key part of the Taliban team we had detected preparing for combat operations, and Dave's folks had been focused on him for a while.

"Stand by, I'll get back to you," I wrote back.

I went over to Dave. "Here's what we got. What do you think?"

"This is perfect," said Dave. "This matches some of the intel we've got right now on this guy. Let's go talk to the operations chief to see if they want to do something."

Dave and I went to talk to Lt. Col. Raphael Torres, CJTF 180's chief of joint fires, who controlled the combat power: guns, missiles, and air power.

"Raphael, we have some info here. Other sources and mine have pinpointed an enabler." Dave laid out the situation.

Torres broke into a broad grin. He called in the lawyer, who questioned us and looked through the folder of intel for legal sufficiency to take him out.

"What is your consideration of collateral damage?" he asked.

"None," I replied. "According to our information, there appears to be only true believers present with the target."

"Go ahead," he replied.

Torres went over to the big board to talk to Colonel Robert Ault, the G3 (director for operations) of CJTF 180, in the open area while Dave and I consulted.

"Can you get additional info from Ray when he talks to his guys so we can focus ███████ on all the activities in the area?" Dave asked.

"Also," he added, "get me the information on all of Ray's guys so we don't inadvertently do something to them."

"Great idea," I said. In my office, I shot off an e-mail to Ray. "We're coordinating, but need the information on all your guys."

Torres came back. "Alt wants to bomb the meeting."

"Sounds great to us," I said.

"There's a B-1 loitering over the Gulf. We can put down JDAMs. ["Dumb bombs" outfitted with "smart bomb" technology.] We can probably put some iron on target in about a half hour."

"Good," said Dave.

I called Ray to let him know to get his guys' asses out of there for the bombing and then to get them back in there after the attack to verify who got whacked.

Sure enough, a short time later I got the confirming e-mail. ███

██

██

████████████████████████████

Man. This guy Ray was *gold*. Dave and I had already had our conversation about sharing intel and now it could begin to bear fruit.

Ray's intel on the Taliban began to pour in. He had nets of informants—Afghan nationals—all through the southern part of the country. Ray himself moved between a U.S. military installation in Kandahar and a Special Forces' forward operating base (FOB) in the mountains north of the city.

He could do things that nobody else could do—and he was fearless.

Ray reported to Randy, commander of our ███████ detachment, but because of Ray's location, seniority, experience, and independence, he was able to do his job without involvement from Randy. So Randy released Ray to work for me in the HUMINT Operations Center directly. It gave Ray the freedom to focus on the operational needs of ongoing combat operations and to perform intelligence collection for upcoming operations. It helped out in ways we never could have expected.

The 10th Mountain began deploying their troops in locations and CJTF 180 launched Mountain Viper on August 30 when coalition forces air assaulted into the mountains near Deh Chopan in the Zabul province to clear the area of Taliban forces.

We had plenty of logistical and manpower challenges. We couldn't go into Pakistan after the Taliban, so we had to wait for them to come into Afghanistan. Because of troop levels, though, the United States wasn't in a position to move rapidly and consolidate. We had to stay ahead of the Taliban, by thinking about where the enemy would be next.

It was going to be a giant chess game.

The 10th Mountain had a good concept. The strategy was defilade: get in front of the Taliban's avenues of approach and conceal themselves, taking advantage of the terrain so they wouldn't take enfilading fire or be outflanked.

What they needed from us, though, were crucial pieces of information: some of the locations where the Taliban would be doing resupply, major movements of troops, how the Taliban were being commanded, and where their command and control would be. We knew the Taliban had camps—training or staging locations—

operating near Kandahar, and in the Oruzgan province, site of the home village of Mullah Omar.

Working late into the night, Ray and I supplied intel to the planners, confirmed by Dave's information and John Hay's pictures to fill in the planners' intelligence gaps. Ray had informants watching the roads, trying to understand what was going on. His folks figured out that the enemy would use motorcycles for all phases of the operation: for command and control, for resupply, and for reinforcing numbers as people were killed. We learned to watch for the motorcycles; they were tippers for larger collection systems. When they showed up in a valley, we knew to start zeroing in on it.

We tried to cut the bureaucracy so that actionable information could be moved right from the point of conception to the people who could actually do something with it.

Then, out of the blue, we rolled up a female Pakistani intelligence agent. The 10th Mountain captured her in Khowst as part of a Taliban unit attacking a U.S. outpost there.

She was carrying Pakistani documents and tried to claim she was merely monitoring the situation in Afghanistan for her country. Monitoring, my ass. She was ISI—the Directorate for Inter-Services Intelligence; the Pakistani intelligence service. Nasty crew. They had a big hand in creating the Taliban, and we had no doubt that she was collecting intelligence for them. We already were aware that the ISI was giving the Taliban tips on how to better protect themselves from our surveillance systems.

She was transported back to the BCP. In interrogations, she refused to break, but we didn't need her to. We had the goods on her. Intelligence verified she was ISI ███████████████████ ██████████████████. Just as important, we now had clear and direct evidence that Paks were involved in the offensive. From that moment on, I considered anyone in a Pakistani uniform an adversary.

As I was working one night, Kate Reese came by. It was on her computer that I'd seen a glimpse of a pair of those nice-looking legs during my first day in the SCIF. She'd gotten in the habit of stopping back into my section of the tent in the evenings to say hello. The 10th Mountain had nets of low-level sources that sometimes intersected with ours, who were after the bigger guys. Her job was to consolidate intel overnight for a report for General Vines' briefing in the morning, look at the new info coming in, and put in the intelligence-collection requirements (what they needed to know and find) for the 10th Mountain intelligence-collection units in the field.

"I'm headed for the break tent for a cigar," she said. "Want one?"

I did a double take. "A cigar?" It's not often a woman asks you to share a cigar break with her. I was in the middle of an e-mail to Ray. "Let me finish this, and I'll come on back in about five minutes."

I had smoked cigars years ago, just after completing the Farm. I hadn't had one in a while, but the thought of one sounded good.

Kate had brought an extra one for me. They were small Partagas that took about twenty minutes to smoke. The conversation between us was easy. First it was intel issues, then movies, and then family. She was twenty-four and came from a remote Alaskan town where everything was a plane ride away. Besides Natalie Portman, she also reminded me of Hilary Swank in the movie *Insomnia*, where Swank played a fresh-faced local detective investigating a bizarre murder in an Alaskan town. There was the same no-nonsense style, but also the same brown eyes, cheekbones, and smile. Kate had joined the army when she was twenty. Like me, but two decades later, she'd gone through intelligence training at Fort Huachuca, and we traded stories about frustrations and experiences there.

It was nice to have a pleasant conversation in the midst of this mayhem. Plus, there was definitely an attraction between us. That was OK—she was separated from her husband, who was the guy in the photo on her computer—and my relationship had ended as well. Still, I was careful.

We got in the habit of taking a cigar break together once a night about midnight. She dropped by after her initial surge of work was done and sat on the desk near me with her feet in a chair while I worked and then we headed for the break area. She had a cigar humidor, and I bought Cuban cigars at the Italian PX in Kabul when I commanded convoys into town, and I donated them to the humidor. Soon, she was riding shotgun for me about once a week on convoys.

Those times with her were a small, though welcome, distraction from the overall mission against the Taliban offense.

Just after the kickoff of combat operations for Mountain Viper, Ray called me late at night. His voice was urgent.

"Tony, I've got indications we've got a company-size Taliban near this village." He named a grid coordinate—it was Deh Chopan, 100 miles northeast of Kandahar and one of the few villages in the rural Zabul province. One of his Afghan teams was in the area. It was in the heart of the Taliban activity. "We think they will overrun the place in the morning."

"Ask your guys if there are any Paks in the area," I told him. "I'll go talk to Dave and see what he can get ████████████

I went over to Dave's office. He was still working as well. "I just got this from Ray: a company-size Taliban element headed to Deh Chopan. What do you think?" I gave him the grid coordinates.

"Let me talk to Captain Knowles," he said and turned to our foreign analyst. They worked with Dave in the SCIF, ████████████ ████████████████████████████.

Capt. Mary Knowles looked up from her desk. "I've got indications of activity in the area."

Dave and I headed outside the SCIF to the fires area in the Operations Center and grabbed Torres.

"We've got a company-size element. There is activity according to my folks and his guys have got eyes on target. They're ready to take the village," Dave told him.

"You sure?" snapped Torres.

"Indications are that the village elder has been resisting their advances. He told 'em to take a hike so they're going to take it by force. Can we send anyone in to defend it?" asked Dave.

"Yeah, we got a company about 10 kilometers farther away in the mountains," said Torres. He was thinking out loud. "We might be able to get airlift in to move them closer. I'll have to check with aviation. Let's get together at oh two hundred and decide what to do next."

Torres gave an update to Ault and then to the aviation guys. Turns out a flight of Chinooks and Apaches was near one of the forward bases getting refueled. Torres gave him a verbal frago (fragmentary) order to change the existing order and then followed up a few minutes later with a written request.

About 0100, I got an e-mail from Ray. "Got a call from one of my guys. They're about one klick (kilometer) away from the Taliban position. The Taliban are dispersing," melting into the countryside to wait to launch an offensive soon on the village.

"Any indications of HVTs in the area?" I e-mailed back. HVTs are high-value targets like bin Laden, Hekmatyar, and Mullah Omar that the Leadership Targeting Cell was tasked to chase after.

"No."

That was too bad for the LTC, but it meant we could go in guns blazing.

"Will advise you in an hour," I typed back.

At 0200, we all gathered around the table in front of the big board in the SCIF.

"What do you got?" Torres asked.

"Indications are they're dispersing for the moment." The enemy knew the terrain. A lot of them were from the area, had been recruited, and had gone to Pakistan to train and had come back to try to retake these areas for the Taliban.

Torres nodded in satisfaction. "That's good news. I'm going to move the 10th Mountain guys into the village while they're still dispersed, and I'll send a squad around back—to the east of the village—to cut them off." We had to block off the road into Deh Chopan because we knew they were resupplying on motorcycles. We didn't want them to be reinforced from Pakistan.

Torres went over to the map. "Can you tell me how they're set up?"

I traced my hand along a ridgeline southeast of the village.

"They're along there. Indications are they're lying low and will attempt a dawn attack."

We disbanded, and I shot an e-mail back to Ray. "Make sure your guys know we have troops in the area."

"What do you need now?" he e-mailed back.

"Keep one of your guys on the road to watch them. Advise when they try to move out."

"Standing by," he e-mailed back.

Dave and I were out back talking to each other, plotting things out on a map. Torres let us know that the 10th Mountain guys were expected to be set up before dawn. They were coming in from the northwest so they could move in quietly.

I got back on the phone with Ray. "My guys tell me the ACM are starting to advance toward the village. They're coming from the east and the southeast."

This is what we had been waiting for. The Taliban were on the attack.

◆ 7 ◆

FORCE ON FORCE

IN the past five days, the small force of two reinforced companies of 10th Mountain soldiers and a handful of Special Forces soldiers, along with Afghan National Army help, had been humping up and down the freakin' mountains in continuous engagement with the ACM farther north of Deh Chopan. (ACMs were Anti-Coalition Militia . . . the Taliban to you or me.) This was officially a brigade combat team that, in reality, could not measure up to battalion strength. The fact that these kids could hang with this level of stress was a testament to their training and leadership.

At the SCIF, Torres had Colonel Ault issue the full range of orders to set into motion a movement of men, helicopters, and material to try to protect Deh Chopan. On Rob's satellite images, I inspected the thick-walled mud huts in the small village. They reminded me of Bedrock, the cartoon town that the Flintstones lived in. For a moment, it was interesting to contemplate the Taliban as a bunch of Fred Flintstones. Nah. I couldn't recall ever seeing a fat Taliban.

Dozens of DCU-clad officers sitting in the basketball court–sized operations tent, buffeted by periodic hurricanelike wind surges that rattled the tent down to the frame, began sending out information and orders to the commanders of the soldiers and aviators to choreograph the complex ballet of destruction.

With the detailed intelligence we had received from Ray's assets, and continuous confirmation from JSTARS orbiting just over the Indian Ocean, a major engagement was about to occur. We believed we had the upper hand. Then again, this was Afghanistan. We were up against a hardened force of suicidal fighters who knew the terrain better than we did.

Within minutes, electronic messages were sent to the aviation units from the desk officers in the Operations Center directing a flight of three CH-47s and two AH-64 Apaches to be prepared to securely pick up the two reinforced companies of infantry that would, hopefully, move approximately 60 miles in less than eight hours to catch the Taliban by surprise before they could infect another village. They would be picked up close to dawn, in rugged mountain terrain. The CH-47 pilots had learned, adapted, and become skilled at swinging the massive twin-rotor medium-lift helicopters around in that environment. In many ways, the CH-47 was proving to be a better combat helicopter in the mountains than the single-rotor UH-60 Black Hawk because of the inherently superior lift of two rotors.

At midnight, the company commanders and platoon leaders of the 10th Mountain Strike Brigade would be huddling in the frigid mountain air, receiving and discussing their new instructions. In small, temporary command posts, they would sit under a bluff, or in a small mud hut that they had found and occupied, using red lights and detailed maps to conduct hasty planning, and assessing the best approaches into Deh Chopan. The weather, the known and expected Taliban strength, the timeline, the number of MREs each man had to sustain himself during the assault, and, most important, which squads would conduct the assault/occupation and which would be designated to perform the "shaping attack" to cut off and block the Taliban from retreating back to Pakistan—all these were factors. They had to prevent reinforcement or resupply by the hundreds of motor-cycle couriers that the Taliban were now employing to support their invasion.

The young GIs must have thought Afghanistan would be a cake-walk, if they had believed the propaganda. The war here was over, right? It had been in all the newspapers. Rumsfeld had declared it. Taliban vanquished and al Qaeda but a whisper in the dark recesses of lost mountain villages.

Right.

Now, based on someone's idea of intelligence, these GIs were on the move. I sat at my desk and stared at my computer screen that night and thought about what was to come. These kids, no more than twenty years old for the most part, were taking it on faith that some-one out there (myself and the rest of the CJTF 180 intelligence team) knew what the hell we were doing.

At times, it was difficult for me to consider that my job—to task, collect, recover, and distribute intelligence, then recommend action—would mean life or death for these brave young men. It was tough to see the results of violence that I'd wrought in the form of a bombed-out ridge—or maybe even a body that was one of our own.

I had recently attended an Honor Review for a Navy SEAL. Everyone—and I mean everyone—in Bagram came to Disney Boule-vard (the paved road that ran through Bagram paralleling the air strip) and rendered honors as he passed. It was near sunset, and the road was lined with people standing shoulder to shoulder. There was an eerie calm, for Bagram, as the SEALs walked in formation behind him. In their civilian clothes and beards, the rugged operatives looked like a ragtag group of renegades, but they walked in formation with crispness and certainty in their steps. You just knew these guys were true warriors—true patriots—and that this death had affected them deeply.

In the SCIF that night, I contemplated my "weapons"—a computer, a phone, and my decades of experience in intelligence. My mission was to do the best damned job I could to help keep these GIs effective, deadly, and always in the right place at the right time.

I'd never felt my responsibility as heavily as I did that night.

The connection between action and reaction, decision and execution; intake and execution of concepts; this was the use of intelligence information in its purest form to affect the real battle.

This 10th Mountain band of brothers had been baptized in the ways of modern warfare by retaking the vital Moray mountain pass just days earlier, but there would be no time to celebrate or note the event by much more than a few scrawls in personal journals.

With orders issued by CJTF 180 that directed the soldiers to rally at the assembly area for pickup, the CH-47s were refueled and flying, and crews—ever watchful for the telltale glow of an SA-7 or Stinger missile rocketing up from the mountainside in the partial darkness of a half-moon night—choppered over the silent mountains en route to collecting the two companies of a very tired infantry.

On the leeward side of a plateau at just over 5,000 feet, a small landing zone was set up using chem lights that burned in the infrared spectrum so that anyone without night-vision goggles (NVGs) would not be able to see them, but they showed up clear and crisp to the aviators as they made their approach to the LZ. Two squads had been set up on and around the key compass points of the ridge to provide security and, if necessary, suppressive fire, should the Taliban attack during the consolidation of troops and load-up onto the choppers.

As dawn approached, with just a hint of color showing on the eastern horizon, the three CH-47s came lumbering into the rendezvous. In the shadows, watching the dark, whalelike shape approach, half the GIs would be longing for a cup of coffee, the others wishing for a smoke. All would be wondering if this would be the day that something bad would happen in a firefight.

As two goggle-eyed Apaches moved in slow circles around the LZ, pilots scrubbed the mountains for signs of Taliban by using the FLIR of their weapons systems. The typhoon gusts buffeted the soldiers now crouching in the shadows of the ridge, preparing for their rapid move into the relative warmth of the belly of the CH-47s. Hours of orders, preparation, and synchronization came down to this moment. Men and machine became one, lifted into the beginning of a late-summer Afghani dawn.

The sixty-mile movement to the LZ near Deh Chopan was swift, less than an hour from one LZ to another, even with a circuitous route designed to throw off anyone from knowing exactly where the assault force was headed.

A small Special Forces team prepared the LZ northwest of Deh Chopan, and readied to receive the inbound 10th Mountain troops. Dawn was an awkward time of day when night-vision goggles were not effective, and it was hard to distinguish anything more than gray and purple shapes. As the troops came off the Chinooks, they would be led into the short hills that lined the valley just to the northwest of Deh Chopan.

The three helicopters were on the ground for less than five minutes depositing the majority of the two companies. One lifted off still carrying a reinforced squad of soldiers that would be deposited near a blocking position, just to the east of the still sleeping village, to obstruct the road and the possible arrival of reinforcements.

The sky was almost a blue and burnt orange as the sun moved over the eastern mountains. The soldiers would have checked their weapons, conducted final rehearsals, and then found quiet places to break into groups and eat their MREs for breakfast. Officers and senior NCOs in their newly established makeshift command posts reviewed maps, now in the daylight, one last time, and finalized their attack plans and synchronized troop movements. Within an hour, the troops would be on the march toward the village in overwatch formation, with scouts and snipers a good half klick out ahead.

The stage was now set, and all indications were that the move had been made without observation by the Taliban. It appeared that the cavalry would at least be in the game. Now we'd see if they could get into town before the Taliban and avoid inadvertently killing Ray's guys, who were in town as well.

Young men, many of whom were playing Tom Clancy's Splinter Cell on their Xboxes twelve months ago, were now all grown up. In their new reality, many were set up as pickets all around the assault element or were moving with stealth a good half a kilometer out front, ahead of the force now preparing to sweep into Deh Chopan. All were facing the prospect of another armed clash with Taliban insurgents.

While we didn't know it at the time—but we sure suspected—scenes like this would play out again and again for the next six years. The same circumstances would reoccur: coalition and Afghan forces fighting to take ground in hundreds of villages like Deh Chopan throughout the region, holding it long enough to push out the Taliban, and then leaving, only to see the Taliban reemerge into the district unopposed.

Under the watchful eyes of Ray's nearly invisible spies, the 10th Mountain scout element, unopposed and unobserved by the Taliban, entered the village and secured its perimeter without incident. As these soldiers moved carefully into the village, consisting of a dozen or so mud brick buildings that were a slightly darker shade of tan than the Desert Combat Uniform pattern, the villagers, mostly men wearing the traditional hajji hats and flowing robes, watched them with knowing eyes, almost patient in their gaze.

While the 10th Mountain officers and noncommissioned officers did not trust the handful of Afghan National Army soldiers assigned to them as scouts, a mission that required a great deal of trust and autonomy, they did rely on them to be the spearhead of the main body moving in to occupy and secure the village. It was their territory, so it was only fair that they should go in first.

The late summer sun was now high in the blue sky and shadows were short as the two sides moved into this engagement—soldiers of the twenty-first century and civilized society versus warriors with a mentality similar to the tenth century, though using modern firearms to enhance their ancient warrant to kill the infidel.

The Taliban left no doubt that they were insurgents (a.k.a.

partisans, guerrillas, illegal soldiers, bandits, etc.). They did not wear any uniforms; they all looked just like any other Afghan national living in the mountains, but their weaponry and manner of movement gave sufficient justification for operating under the current rules of engagement. This was going to be a legal and honorable firefight.

While I wasn't there, I could picture from my seat in Bagram how it played out: Within five minutes the ANA soldiers would be in line, facing the Taliban as they slowly, and carelessly, moved toward the village. The remainder of the coalition combat forces would fall into a rough crescent running from the northwest to the southeast of the village, with its bulge at a northeastern point just outside the village.

Two Squad Automatic Weapons (SAWs) would be set up just to the right and left of the ANA soldiers, who were easily distinguished from U.S. troops by their woodland patterned battle-dress uniforms (BDUs). The SAWs would not only add fire support to the engagement but also set up a field of fire to the left and right of the primary ambush area to try to keep the enemy pinned down in the center.

I could just imagine that the first thirty seconds of the engagement were probably almost comical. A Taliban insurgent, now less than 50 meters from the first mud building, would glance at a low wall at the very end of the building. He would stare at the wall, while continuing to walk toward the village center. He would see the ANA solider in his defilade position—and they would stare at each other.

Perhaps it was disbelief that ANA soldiers could be at a village about to be occupied by the Taliban, perhaps it was sheer shock—but for whatever reason the Taliban and ANA solider would eyeball each other for another thirty seconds as the Taliban insurgent continued to walk forward with his buddies.

Finally, in what must have been a flash of realization, the Taliban insurgent would yell a warning to his comrades, now showing two dozen in strength and completely exposed.

All hell would break loose, and a wall of lead would welcome the insurgents. There would be shock and disbelief by the Taliban as most of them froze in place—the mind going into a "black" state where all fine motor skills go away, all primary body functions focus on preparing the body for a fight, and "tunnel vision" focuses the senses and slows down time.

Getting caught out in the open in a firefight is never a good thing, and within thirty seconds, half the Taliban would have been down, the others running for the ridge they had just come down, or toward a mountain range to the north of the ridge. Only a handful of Taliban managed to get off a few rounds from their AK-47s in the general direction of the village and the coalition forces within. All the bullets would be wild and wouldn't come remotely close to any of the ambushers.

The captain would call in a strike, his radio operator changing the frequency for him to speak directly to the B-1 aircraft now orbiting over the ocean, 500 miles from the village (a few minutes' flight for a B-1) at 40,000 feet, with a belly full of JDAM bombs.

The B-1's navigator/bombardier would program in the geocords (geographical coordinates) to the JDAMs in the bay as the B-1 moved onto an axis that would bring it within 25 miles of Deh Chopan.

By now the firefight would be less than twenty minutes old and already over. Yet the Taliban were about to get the second surprise of the morning.

In defiance, the escaped Taliban fighters would have shown themselves along the mountain ridge—taunting the coalition troops, hoping the soldiers would attempt to follow them up the ridgeline and into terrain of their choosing that would give them an advantage.

"Gecko, stand by" came the call in prep of the strike.

The targeting of the bombs took about five minutes—the solutions were plugged in, and the bomb bay opened as the B-1 reduced its speed from its ten-minute near-supersonic dash toward Afghanistan to a more reasonable 250 knots for the safe and effective release of the bombs.

"Weapons hot," stated the bombardier to the pilot, who had already opened the bay and was now checking the airspeed to make sure of the safe weapons release.

"Release," said the bombardier as six JDAMs rolled off the rotary bomb system into the thin, clear air.

In total silence to the troops below, large mushrooms of black and gray smoke would begin to blossom on the ridgeline directly north of Deh Chopan—followed in seconds by the sound (and force) of the shockwave.

So ended the battle for Deh Chopan. In less than thirty minutes, a force of 80 Taliban was reduced to fewer than a dozen able fighters, with nearly 40 killed, and nearly all others wounded in some way.

Ray's guys in the village reported on the success of both the firefight and of the JDAMs' devastation to the remaining Taliban on the ridgeline. Frankly, the body count was low because at least a dozen of the fighters were vaporized by near direct hits of the JDAMs—there was just nothing left of them to count.

This was touted as one of the first successful integrations of tactical clandestine human intelligence into a major combat engagement in Afghanistan. Skeptics of the "dark arts," like Colonel Negro and the CJTF 180 deputy commander, Brigadier General Bagby, who always thought that we spooks were not worth the trouble we brought, were seeing things differently. This was the good news, but from the good news came the reality that while we'd won this round, it was only the beginning.

Other crises were looming.

Kelly Broom, the civilian in the military affairs shop, came looking for me one day shortly after in the SCIF.

"Brother, we're in a world of hurt," he said in his down-home Texas accent.

"What's up?" I asked.

"We got a problem with Karzai, and he don't even know it."

"Didn't I hear he's out of the country right now at the UN?"

Kelly nodded. "Yep, that's right," he said, "and that's exactly the problem. Looks like one of his ministers is lookin' to take over."

"And that's a problem because . . . ?" I asked.

He grinned. "We ain't ready to change horses right now."

"OK, so what's going on?"

Kelly explained. Karzai's defense minister, Mohammad Qasim Fahim, who had been the military leader of the Afghan Northern Alliance that had defeated the Taliban in 2001, was planning a coup attempt against Karzai. The United States had known that Fahim had designs on the office, and it looked like he was now making his move. Fahim believed that the Afghanistan central government should be more effective at taking control of the countryside for Afghan citizens. He, like some of the other powerful warlords who had some sort of control over their own militias, believed Karzai was too weak. The attacks on the police stations were happening with impunity with no response from the central government. The Afghan government was in the midst of converting from the Afghan militia—the collection of warlords' armies that had banded together to defeat the Taliban—to the better-trained and better-equipped Afghan National Army. Fahim believed that he would be the better man to do that.

He had started by putting out feelers to the United States to take over bloodlessly while Karzai was visiting America, but the U.S. ambassador turned him down.

That didn't stop Fahim, who started staging his troops around Kabul.

Christ. A freakin' coup. We didn't need this right now. Our forces were either dispersed at border locations, at strongholds like Khowst and Kandahar, or were formed into small mobile teams located at Asadabad and ▮▮▮▮. The only combat power we had at Bagram was Special Forces guys and the military police (MP) who provided base security. Our intelligence told us that Fahim personally controlled up to 2,000 Afghan forces that he had moved into the environs around Kabul. We had maybe 100 to 200 in the area. ISAF had 4,000 to 5,000 troops, but they were not combat power. They were primarily civil support, intel types, and those involved in infrastructure support, such as quartermasters, transporters, and engineers. It would have been hugely difficult to counter him force on force. The U.S. policy in Afghanistan was in danger.

We took it up with Colonel Boardman. He had been tracking the situation for a while, but now it was focused. Some U.S. embassy officials had official contact with Fahim's people. Fahim was getting restless and telegraphing to the United States that it was his intention to become president of Afghanistan. He told us it would be a bloodless coup—Karzai could stay in the United States in exile and Fahim would take over here. Clearly, Fahim wanted a buy-in from the U.S. government.

Personally, I wasn't sure whether a change would make much difference, but our policy was to retain Karzai. I was asked to become involved in the creation of a Concept of Operations—essentially, a plan to "influence" Fahim and convince him we were serious. We had to scare this guy because scaring him was pretty much the only option we had.

We came up with a process to bluff him. I put out the word through the diplomatic, military, and intelligence channels that we knew he monitored that we were not backing down. The message was unequivocal: *We are not going to allow you to become president of Afghanistan. If you do this, you will die.* We had to make him blink. And if he didn't blink? We were going to lose.

We went through demonstrations of force to remind him of the power of the U.S. military by putting out word to increase the physical presence of troops in Kabul with more troop convoys coming into the city. Moreover, to deliver the message in a distinctly more intimate fashion, we sent a B-1 bomber at full afterburner buzzing over his house—and I mean over his house—just about 50 feet above.

Message delivered. It was two days later that we knew, through intelligence and diplomatic channels, that Fahim had backed down.

We were kicking ass all over the place. On the battlefield, the

Taliban were on the ropes. Wherever they were, we were. This was modern combat, where fewer than 800 men, with 400 or so newly minted ANA soldiers, using the best that modern technology had to offer, took on a force slightly larger than themselves—and dominated.

The one advantage that the Taliban did not have, which more than leveled the playing field for the purposes of Mountain Viper, was aviation. It turned mountain warfare into a game of deadly hopscotch that, with the right intelligence, allowed even a small force to move with vigor and determination that not even the Russians could match during their occupation.

We had solid intel on everything they did and we were able to blunt their all-out attack. They made the mistake of thinking they could take us on symmetrically—force on force—and bully their way back into power in Afghanistan. It failed abysmally. It was a huge miscalculation on their part.

Even so, like all good terrorist networks, they learned from it. It was a mistake they have not repeated since.

As Mountain Viper was winding down, Kate and I continued our cigar-smoking habit. One night, after we had our break for the evening, she hung around with me in the back of the tent I worked in at the SCIF. While chatting with me as I sat across from her, reviewing reports and e-mailing back to the States, she mentioned she had a sore leg.

During her intelligence training at Fort Huachuca in Arizona, she had sustained damage to her lower left Achilles, so severe that she couldn't run. She'd had surgery on it, but it still wasn't right. We spoke about the Huachuca Cannon run: a tough, two-and-a-half-mile dirt road that went straight up and down the mountains resembling those surrounding us at Bagram. I told her I'd torn a ligament in the same general area at Fort Huachuca while on the Cannon run.

"Well, it's acting up," she said. She was sitting on one of the desks, and she bent forward and dug at it. "I'm kind of having trouble walking."

In situations like this, it was always prudent to be polite and respectful, but I figured, there would be medicinal purpose in offering a foot massage. You know, one soldier helping another soldier.

"How would you like a foot massage?" I asked. "I'm sure that would help"—knowing that any such act would still require some privacy . . . and it would take an effort to remove the boots.

She straightened up, looked at me with those big, brown eyes, and a slow smile filled her face. She stood up, still smiling.

"No, I'd really like a full-body massage instead." Her smile was now a grin and, turning, she disappeared back into her work area on the other side of the SCIF.

Once my breath returned to my lungs, I thought, *Man, this is going to be interesting.*

• 8 •

TO THE FRONT

WHOA. I had made a personal commitment to focus only on the mission. I had to think about this.

I have always been careful and respectful of women in uniform to whom I was attracted, and I had a strong professional admiration for Kate—she was tougher than most of the 10th Mountain troops I had seen, but it was hard to ignore the fact that she was hot, too.

I did not know what, if anything, I would do about Kate's overture—and there were complications. I was still getting over the breakup with Rina. I had heard from mutual friends that she was dating, but it's not easy to stop caring about someone.

There also was the additional complication of something called General Order No. 1. It outlined a number of prohibited activities and standards of conduct for U.S. troops and civilians working for the military in Afghanistan, including the possession of alcohol, pornography, gambling, and sexual relations between personnel not married to each other.

Not that the brass had enforced it in any substantial way. It was treated more like a stern warning to frighten troops. It was well known that the troops had gotten smart about hiding their extracurricular activities. I had been told by several friends about finding troops "doing it" in cramped spaces like the small bomb shelters around our tent living area and Porta-Johns.

Yeah, Porta-Johns.

Shortly after our solidification of victory in Afghanistan in 2002 when large numbers of our troops started rolling in, General Order No. 1 was created by senior officers who didn't have a clue on how to lead troops. They had no sense of military tradition—especially army history—and of what worked and didn't work in the army during World War II and the Korean and Vietnam wars. They had this idea that we had to create "warrior monks" within the ranks of the military. Great. It wasn't good enough that these young kids had signed up to put their lives on the line for their country. Now they were expected to take a vow of celibacy.

If the kids serving in the military had wanted to be monks, I'm sure they would have found their way to the nearest monastery by now.

So I took every opportunity I could to ignore General Order No. 1. It was wrong at every level, and while I'd be careful with Kate (discretion being the better part of valor), if any opportunity presented itself, I would look forward to taking advantage of it.

Before any opportunity presented itself, Tim Loudermilk announced at the LTC morning standup that Special Forces had rolled up a guy ███████████████████████████ ██████ during a raid in ██████ the previous night. ██████ lay in a valley about 60 miles south of Kabul. It was the capital of the Patkia province and was once a stronghold of the Taliban—and considered to be on the front line of this unconventional war.

The detainee was being held at the Forward Operating Base just outside the city.

CJSOTF intel guys had visited the LTC and passed a series of messages they had received from their A Team ██████ The capture of an ostensible ████ had put a cramp in their style. They needed help from the LTC to determine, among other things, who he really was ██████.

Shortly after the stand-up, ██████, the senior FBI agent assigned to the LTC, came over. He had received the stack of messages and already read through them.

"Aren't you from ██████" he asked, his head cocked forward slightly as he faced me, his 6'4" frame too tall for the tent.

"Yep," I said. "Lived in ██████ for fourteen years."

"That's what I thought," he said. "Well, according to the ████ ████ we got from this guy, he's from ██████."

That's where I lived. Rina and I had bought the house there in 2001. "Really?" I said.

"Yeah," said John. "According to the information we have, he's from . . ." He named a community in ██████.

I stared at him. This was getting spooky. "I live within a mile of it."

John showed me a copy of the guy's ██████ Arash Ghaffari. Mustached, narrow face, dark eyes, looked to be in his mid- or late-thirties.

"Is this real?" I asked.

John nodded. "We got confirmation from ██████ that this is a valid driver's license."

"Has he told them what he is doing here?"

"Yeah," John said with a tinge of disbelief in his voice, "he said he was here as a tourist to visit his family."

Tourist? Here? We looked at each other, each thinking of the unsavory possibilities. Was he a terrorist over here for training? Part of a sleeper cell? What could he be planning? Several of the September 11 attackers had ██████. Who shows up in a freakin' combat zone to be a tourist?

Plus, he'd been rolled up with his cousin, Ali Ghaffari, whom the local Special Forces team had been monitoring for a while. A doctor who'd left Afghanistan during the Soviet takeover and settled in Iran, Ali Ghaffari had returned ██████ with his family during the

U.S. war with the Taliban. Intel collected by the A Team indicated that Ali Ghaffari had recently traveled to Iran and brought back the equivalent of ███████████ to cook up trouble for us infidels. Typically, the cash would be used to buy weapons and material for IEDs, obtain support equipment such as satellite phones, vehicles, etc. The let's-kill-the-Americans gear.

That money would go a long way toward hurting a lot of troops, and it had disappeared during the raid. Special Forces had rolled up Ali Ghaffari in his compound with five other men We didn't know who they were or what they were up to, and what the hell was ███ doing meddling in Afghanistan? The Iranians had secretly backed anti-Taliban forces during the time the Taliban had controlled Afghanistan. True, Hekmatyar had spent some of the Taliban years in exile in Iran. But the whole thing was just weird, and we had to get to the bottom of it—fast.

We believed there was the possibility of a larger plot. Maybe Ali Ghaffari had recruited his cousin for some long-term terrorist plan to be hatched back in the good ole ██████████████

Arash wasn't talking, John said. "He claims he doesn't know anything and just wants to go home. The Special Forces told him that ain't gonna happen, but he's been separated from the other prisoners and they're treating him as if he is a ███████. They're asking for guidance on what to do."

I went to talk to Rich, told him what was going on, and then headed out on some other work, my brain still ringing alarm bells over a guy from my neck of the woods showing up with someone who was clearly a terrorist enabler in Afghanistan. The whole thing stunk.

Tim and John found me later that morning. "We're sending John out to interrogate him and we want you to go with him."

"OK," I said, trying to imagine why they'd want me to go. "What exactly are you thinking?"

"You're from ████████, so you'll be able to determine if he's really from there," John said. "We especially want to see if he's planning something in that area."

"That's kind of a concern for me, too," I said.

"We'll fly out on the Ring helicopter," said Tim. "It's supposed to leave right before midnight."

The Ring helicopter was the U.S. military flying bus system in Afghanistan. The destinations were always the same, but the routes and times the helicopters flew along them varied for operational security reasons. There had been some losses, both combat and mechanical failure. It wasn't exactly a "safe" method of travel, but what was I expecting in Afghanistan? Greyhound?

Shortly before midnight, we headed for the flight line hangar with our kit. I had picked only essential items to bring with me. I didn't even take a sleeping bag. Instead, I took the ubiquitous poncho liner that every solider learned to use as a makeshift (and very portable) sleeping bag. I didn't know if I was going out for an overnight jaunt or a weeklong visit. That would be up to Mr. Arash Ghaffari.

While we waited for the mission briefing, I talked to a North Carolina National Guard aviator who looked and sounded like Dr. Phil in a flight suit. He would be flying cover for the mission in an Apache. All army helicopter flights required two to four attack helicopters as escorts because of frequent attacks on helicopters with small arms and some SA-7 surface-to-air missiles.

As we were talking in the mountain darkness, a sudden gust of wind came up, and I ended up with a mouthful of dust. By now, I'd gotten used to this during conversations. It was like particles of sandpaper suddenly settling between your teeth as you were talking. Even as my mind churned around the mystery of our alleged American citizen, we talked about more pleasant things. The National Guardsman was from Williamsburg, Virginia, and he and his family owned some hotels throughout the Eastern Seaboard. He was here to put his time in and was looking forward to going home he told me. Weren't we all?

In this night sortie, there were two CH-47s and two Apaches, and we went out to the flight line and sat down on the metal grates in the gusty wind next to the helos while the crews did their preflights and loaded pallets and cargo onto the aircraft. I later learned that the pallet next to me contained 2,000 pounds of C-4 high explosive.

We had to attend a preflight safety briefing within the hangar. While we were waiting, we took seats on the gray folding chairs lined up in front of the screen. One of the aviation admin troops, a young sergeant, obviously intrigued by the looks of our three-man team (two of us in civilian clothes with beards and guns and the third in desert camo), came up to me.

"You with public affairs?" he asked politely.

"No," I said.

"Civil affairs?"

"No," I said.

He tried again. "Special Forces?"

"No," I said. I paused for a moment and then said, "We're not really here."

I've always wanted to use that line.

He and I smiled—he finally got it.

"Destination?" he asked with a grin.

██████████

He walked away to put our names on the manifest and leave our unit affiliation blank.

Once the crew was done with the loading and preflight, we hopped on the cavernous choppers.

Truth be told, I'd always had a fear of flying in CH-47s. When I was a kid in high school in Portugal, I saw a photo of a crashed CH-47 and a headline that read 17 DIE IN CHINOOK ACCIDENT in the local *Stars and Stripes*. In the picture, you could see someone trying to get out, and that image always stuck with me. Then I sat down center cabin and thought about Alexander, and said a small prayer.

As the rotors on the 47 started, we all put on ear protection; Tim and I put on eye protection as well to try to keep the grit out. The crew chief moved around the cabin checking all manner of hydraulics and gauges. He also served as one of the two gunners who manned the large frame openings near the front of the aircraft. The top part of the loading ramp at the rear of the aircraft also remained open—I'd never seen them closed—so it was breezy even before we were in flight.

The other three aircraft, in turn, started their engines, and the flight began to taxi. There was an ethereal moment as the dust kicked up around our helicopter in the inky darkness of the taxiway and sparked as it hit the rotors. Fairy dust, John said. From the inside, it looked like a swirl of golden magical dust was picking up the aircraft and carrying us off into the blustery, dusty Afghan night.

There was no light in the cabin and the two door gunners wore night-vision goggles. You could see the two glowing points over their eyes and nothing else as they moved around like ghosts hovering in the great pool of black that filled the cabin.

We arrived at the ███████ Forward Operating Base on or about 0200. The landing approach was fast—I could just make out the frame of the horizon coming closer, noting our rapid descent as we hit the LZ.

As fast as we could, we cleared the chopper with our gear and moved to the vehicles close to the strip, which was nothing more than a stretch of asphalt road in an open desert field. I limped. In the inky darkness, I couldn't make out where the ground was as we evacuated the chopper. With my heavy body armor, pack, and weapon, I had landed hard on one knee and twisted it as I came off the back of the deck. It hurt like hell.

As the two Chinooks started to lift off into the night, we were pummeled by a searing blast of hot exhaust and dust.

The choppers were going on to the last stop on the Ring. The trip down to Kabul and back to ███████ would take them about an hour. That's all the time we had to conduct the initial interrogation of Arash. Then we had to make a decision: stay and do an in-depth grilling, which meant being stuck in ███████ and the end of civilization, until mission accomplished, or let the guy go and hop back on the 47 and return to Bagram. John and I agreed we'd make the call together after our initial contact. We had no real idea what we were going to find.

We headed in armored Humvees for the heavily guarded fort that I later would see resembled a small castle in the light of day. ███████ was a nasty neck of the woods. This had been, and remained, one of the areas most contested for control between us and the Taliban. Because of that, the fort was under sporadic mortar and rocket attacks from the enemy hidden in the hills.

The firebase was divided into two separate compounds that were within tens of meters of each other. One was manned by a Reconnaissance (Recon) element and the other a small security element of the 10th Mountain—a reinforced company from what I could tell. When the 10th Mountain soldiers comingled with the Recon guys, it was easy to tell them apart. The Recon all had some manner of facial hair and mostly opted out of wearing the normal desert camo uniform. Instead, they tended to dress in a motley combination of desert camo pants, T-shirts, keffiyeh scarves, and civilian baseball caps (from some distant U.S. university, bait shop, or favorite NASCAR driver).

The 10th Mountain had the short haircuts and the regulation uniforms. Their demeanor was stiffer and more formal—and tense. Their missions were very different. The Recon members were to engage the hearts and minds of the locals by day and do the rough work at night—recon missions, hitting suspect compounds, seizing weapons and explosives, trying to pluck out pockets of Taliban and al Qaeda. The 10th Mountain soldiers were "regular" army and fought using conventional small unit tactics. Their job was to provide security: counterbattery fire (to counter the Taliban shelling), combat power to ensure the base's security, and to go after any bad guys who showed up in the area.

In the darkness, I peered down at my Sunnto watch's altimeter. We were at nearly 7,000 feet above sea level. After the dust cleared, we were received by two ███████████ guys who looked like a combination of the bearded mobster in the movie *Goodfellas* and Dennis Hopper's crazed photojournalist character in *Apocalypse Now*. When we arrived at the Recon portion of the compound, I almost expected to find a fat bald guy slowly pouring water over his head in a cave. Marlon Brando at his best.

While the Recon guys had continued to interrogate Arash Ghaffari throughout the day, they still did not have a good handle on what he was doing and planning. We knew little more than the fact that he was the cousin of an HVT, and we knew that terrorists tended to do things as families. They trust each other, blood being much thicker than water.

"Has anything changed?" I asked the Recon intelligence guy.

He shook his head. "He won't talk to us."

We got a short briefing. Members of Ali Ghaffari's family had been in the compound, among them, ██████████████████████ ████████████████████████████████████ Six men had been captured and were being detained at ████████ It didn't appear that any of Arash's immediate family members, like a wife or kids, were there. Aside from the mystery of what the hell, if anything, Arash and family members had been planning for Afghanistan and the ████████████ was the puzzle of what had happened to the ████████ Disbursed among the enemy, it could buy a lot of dangerous stuff. Arash Ghaffari had denied knowing anything about the ████████ and said he had a plane ticket back ████████████ in four days—which by now had slipped to three. He wanted to go back to his family.

"You know, you've got about forty minutes until the helicopter gets back if you plan to leave tonight," the ████████████ Recon intelligence guy told us.

Tim, John, and I looked at each other. "We'll decide what to do after we see Ghaffari," I said.

Two members of the Recon led us to Arash Ghaffari. He was being held in a small office, the door to which was actually on the outside of the compound's main walls. The rest of the prisoners, including Ali Ghaffari, were being held as detainees outside of the compound—bound with black covers over their heads—under a long wall that had an overhead shelter. Harsh conditions compared to his cousin, Arash.

We entered the office where Arash Ghaffari was being detained, and one Special Forces guy flipped on the light switch while the other gave Ghaffari a shake. He had been sound asleep, and he sat bolt upright. His hands were bound in front of him with zip ties—similar to ties used to hold electrical cables together, only larger and more durable. He had one fastened around each wrist and then one looped through both of the wrist ties. He stared up at us from the mat on which he had been sleeping.

He was very thin, dressed in typical gossamer fabric Afghan shirt, casual pants, and sandals. My impression was that he was very frightened. I guess I would be, too. He knew that this guy in camo, plus two grim-faced ones in civilian clothes, hadn't just popped by to pay their respects. I can only imagine what he was thinking would happen next.

The truth was, violence wasn't on our agenda. John and I hadn't talked about our approach in great detail. We needed to get a feel for the guy first, but we knew that neither of us had any intent to use "enhanced" techniques. In any case, Arash didn't have to know this.

We all knew that harsher-than-normal interrogation techniques had been approved, and if you really wanted to do something, you could probably get approval to do it, but I didn't—and still don't—believe such methods work. John and I were trained interrogators, and that wasn't the way we operated. In fact, the FBI was on the lookout for cases of harsh interrogations in Afghanistan, and there were some prosecutions that came out of their limited effort to curtail abuse even in these early days of the war.

Later in my deployment to Afghanistan, I came face-to-face with the program of enhanced methods of interrogation—if you want to call that "interrogation."

We knew we were up against the clock. The helicopter was now due back for us in thirty-five minutes, if we could squeeze enough useful information out of the prisoner.

We introduced ourselves. I announced myself as Tony, an intelligence officer from the Department of Defense. John said he was from the FBI. Tim said nothing and stayed in the background, working his way through a bag of beef jerky.

We each leaned against a desk in the room and stared down at him for an uncomfortable minute. Then John asked the obvious question, "What are you doing here?"

"I'm here to visit my cousin," he said.

"We understand you are here to visit your cousin," John said, "but, obviously, your cousin has been arrested based on his activities. So what are you doing here?"

"I assumed it was safe here since the Americans were here," he answered. He spoke English well, with only a slight accent. That lent credence to his story that he was well educated.

"Sir, this is a war zone. People are dying every day," I said.

"I wanted to come visit my family. Yes, I know there is a war on, but it is not so bad in ███████"

We weren't getting very far. It was a freakin' *war zone* in ███████— this was the front line of the war. Who was he kidding?

"You were captured with your cousin. Your cousin is a known operative—he is going to Guantanamo—you are now on the same path," I said after he repeated several more times that he was just here for a visit.

"I cannot tell you things that I do not know."

OK, so he was sticking to his story. I decided to lay on the threats.

"If you do not tell us what you know, you will be going to Guantanamo."

He didn't much like that. "But I'm ████████████; I've done nothing wrong."

"You did do something wrong." I pointed out what should have become obvious to him by now. "You were with your cousin when he was captured. That makes you a combatant under the current rules of engagement."

Ghaffari persisted in saying that he was just here to visit his family. OK, fine. We would use that against him.

"If you value your family," I said, "you'll need to provide us information on your cousin."

We could just begin to make out the *whoop-whoop-whoop* of the approaching helicopter. We'd gotten nowhere. John and I glanced at each other. We read our mutual decision by the expressions on our faces.

We were staying.

John turned to Ghaffari. "We're done for now, but we're going to come back to talk to you again."

He nodded, still gazing at us with this innocent deer-in-the-headlights look.

Visiting his family, my ass, I thought. He knows what is going on with his cousin at minimum and possibly even more.

We left the room and conferred.

"We're not leaving," John told Tim.

Tim went into the ███ Team's headquarters room and asked them to radio the helicopter to direct it not to land and to proceed back to Bagram. As we walked past the entrance of the room, we could hear someone tell the helicopter, "The packages are staying. No need to land; you can return to base."

We agreed we had done enough for tonight. The Recon Team walked us to their "visitor" tents—a permanent set of GP Medium (general purpose) tents stuck between the wall of the fort and their makeshift bunkers, showed us where our cots were, and we pulled out our ponchos.

This was not going to be a cakewalk.

⋆ 9 ⋆

THE INTERROGATION

WE managed to sleep about three hours before the unforgiving Afghan sun awoke us as its heat bled through the roof of the tent. It was still near pitch-black in the tent, yet you could feel the heat just as if you were under a sun lamp.

The two Recon intel guys who were our hosts were already up and about—with as little sleep as us—working their sources to obtain information that might help us in our interrogation. One of the main focuses was the status and location of the missing ███ that was one of the primary objectives of their raid that had netted Ali.

The sky was clear and a brilliant blue as we sat down on a berm of sandbags, near the fleet of Humvees, to eat our breakfast of eggs, waffles, and bacon. Food was generally good—even at the front.

After the first bite of bacon and a quick sip of coffee, John and I were already sweating as we started to go over our strategy. We came up with a master list of questions. ████████████████████
████████████████████████████████████
████████████████████████████████████.

██

██

███████████████████████████.

First task: determine whether he was really from ██████████
██. That was my first focus. We went in and immediately got rolling.

"I live in ████████" I told Ghaffari. "I'll know if you're lying, so you might as well tell me where you are from if you are not from there."

He gave me a description of the neighborhood, and I quizzed him about a dozen local landmarks. The library down the street. The school he said his children attended. Two nearby grocery stores, including the one near the library and the other next to the gas station. He described the nearest gas station. He said he liked the one by the grocery store the best because the service was better. (He was right.)

Finally, after about forty-five minutes of intense but polite drilling, I gave John a small nod. He knew ████████ That much was true.

Now we were ready to refocus on why he was here.

"So what are you doing with your cousin in a war zone?" John asked.

He repeated his answer from last night. "Visiting my family. I thought it was safe."

"This is not a safe place," I said. "People are dying every day. How do you think it is safe?"

He persisted. "I wanted to come back and visit my family. It is not that bad in ██████—and I heard the ████████ army had won and everything was secure."

"We know your cousin had ████████ with him the night of the raid. Where did he get it?" I asked.

"I do not know," he said. "You must believe me."

"I'm sorry, I do not. We are told there is no way you could not have known about the purpose of the meeting or your cousin having ████████ Who were the men who were with him that night?"

He shook his head. "I am a good ███████████████ If I knew, I would tell you. I simply do not know."

We circled back around and talked about his background. He told us his family had moved ██████████████████████████████ to escape the Soviet occupation and had worked to survive there. He was younger ████████████ by ██████████

"What did your cousin do there?" I asked.

The answers got vague. Something about working in a government ministry.

"How did you end up in the ████████?" John asked.

He had found a way from ████████████, and he laid out a story that could be mostly verified. He had left ██ in the late '80s and moved to ██████, where he was a taxi driver. He had a ██████████ ██████ We would check to see if his kids were enrolled in the school he claimed they were. A fact that would be easily verifiable.

We wound up with some detailed questioning of his associates in ██████—the "circle of knowledgability." Who were his friends? Who and where were his other associates? Who had he talked to about coming here? Why was his wife not here?

He was reluctant to give up the names of his ██████ friends and associates.

"Look," I said. "If you have nothing to hide, then the more truthful you can be, the more information you can give us that we can verify, the better it is for you. But if you hold out on us . . ."

I leaned forward. Not close into his face, but it was meant to be a clearly menacing move. "I'm going to send you to Guantanamo."

He rocked back from his seat on the floor, an expression of shock rolling over his face. While I had mentioned this as a possibility last night, stating it again in the light of day in a more threatening way had a visceral effect on him.

I had pre-cleared to use the threat of sending Ghaffari to Guantanamo. If needed, I had been given the authority to detain him and send him to a wholly different life than the one he knew in ██████ ██ In Afghanistan, the military held the authority over detainees, so I had the authority to do so as a member of DoD in a war zone. John had no such power because he was domestic law enforcement.

"We're taking a break now," I told him. "You, sir, are not being truthful, and you will have to make a choice—soon—as to how much you love ████ or wish to cover up for your cousin."

Ghaffari pleaded. The mention of Guantanamo had gotten to him. ██████████," he said urgently. "I love my life in ██████. As God is my witness, I am telling you the truth."

I pressed harder. "I'm sorry. You are not telling the *whole* truth. Until we're convinced you are, there is a pretty good chance I will send you to Guantanamo. We can't take the chance of sending you back to the ████████ if we believe there is a link between you and a terrorist organization in Afghanistan. So you need to think about the fact that, right now, your next stop is not ████████. It's Guantanamo, and your life in the ████████ with your family, will be over."

I wanted him to chew on that over lunch. In fact, I wanted it to ruin his lunch.

He looked forlorn. The reality of his situation was sinking in. He couldn't just say a few things about loving ██████ and go home.

After three hours of questioning, we had a pretty good idea of who Arash Ghaffari claimed he was. John could send the info back to the FBI to verify his ████████ and ████████ over the periods of time he had described to us—and the smaller details regarding his children, their enrollment in school, and so on. Still, we hadn't come away with anything about his stay in Afghanistan that we didn't already know. He knew we were serious, and visiting his cousin had imperiled him. Now it was time to allow for the grim reality of a possible life in Guantanamo to sit like a granite boulder on his mind.

At lunch, sitting outside the compound in the dry heat, we conferred with the Recon guys, while Tim chomped on his ever-present supply of beef jerky, bags of which magically appeared constantly from his DCU cargo pockets. He had told me his wife had sent him a footlocker full of the stuff.

John, who was former Recon, found out while he was at the █ Team's HQ that several members of his former team were in the area, and he made arrangements for us to go meet them. He was

able to get on the computer system to Bagram to pass info. Once at
Bagram, his questions were relayed to the other agents and on to the
FBI Washington Field Office to verify the basic details of Arash's story.

John and I walked through the morning's interrogation. Even
though Arash Ghaffari clearly lived in ███████████, we did not know if
there was something more to him and his links to a known terror
enabler. That just made the picture scarier. Was he part of a sleeper
cell and were his associates part of that cell as well?

We agreed to focus on pushing him more on ███████ and his
associates and contacts. We did not want anyone stateside to over-
react or panic. We wanted to be cautious—and right.

After lunch, we walked back in and gave him a cold bottle of water
and sat wordless while he drank it and glanced nervously back and
forth at us. He received water regularly, but it was room temperature
at best. He clearly enjoyed the cooled bottle. We didn't say anything;
just let the awkward silence settle like a blanket over the room.

John looked at me, and I began.

"You told us you love your life in ███████," I said. John and I had
decided these would be our opening remarks. "We agree with you,
but if you want to protect your life and the lives of your wife and children there, you really need to be honest with us."

We decided to throw him off balance and switch between inter-
rogating him about ███████ and ██████ without telegraphing our
line of questioning.

It was apparent that he valued his family and wanted to return to
them. That was the carrot we could dangle in front of him—to allow
him to go back home.

"I understand how important your family is and how much you
want to be with them. But we've talked to the Recon troops who did
the raid, and I gotta tell you, you're not being up front with us," I
told him. "We know for a fact that while you may not have been
in the room with the other individuals, you know what happened
with the ███████ and until you tell us, we consider you part of the
conspiracy."

He was quiet for a full second, trying to measure how much we really knew. "I would never do that," he finally said. "I wasn't involved with what my cousin was doing. I have no interest in doing anything to hurt ████████████████████████

He was becoming emotional. His voice rose, and he rocked back and forth in his chair. "I want to go back to ██████████"

This was obviously a huge motivator for him. The more we mentioned taking that away from him, the more agitated he became. We wanted to use that. We didn't bring up Guantanamo again for a while. If he thought we were sending him there no matter what, then he would just shut down. We had to delicately employ the carrot (home) and the stick (Gitmo) with careful shifts in questioning.

Throughout the long day of interrogation, some important facts became clear. Ali Ghaffari, it was evident, was a real father figure to ████████████████████████████ had been killed in the initial days of the Soviet occupation when Arash was in his early teens, and Ali had taken over raising his ██████████████ This was one of the reasons Arash was so protective of his cousin. The psychological process of transference had occurred.

Arash Ghaffari also kept repeating how much he loved his life in ████████ and how important his family was to him.

Ya can't keep both, buddy, I thought to myself—and I still couldn't tell which he'd pick in the end.

"Arash, that's well and good, but you're not helping us here," I told him. Our biggest concern was what was going on in the ████████ ████—if anything.

We kept reiterating that he would have to tell us his recollection of the evening of the raid: what he was doing, who was in the compound, ties they had to him and to his cousin. The names of the people. Everything. We would keep going over and over the evening and what he knew about the ████ Then we would return to focus on ████████ and get him to talk about his associates there. The questioning on ████████ gave us more information to pass along to the

FBI but, just as important, it focused his mind on how important that place was to him.

By the end of the session, all three of us were exhausted, but we had established some important facts. He had a clear recollection of the raid and he knew names, although he wouldn't give them to us. While he wouldn't fully admit it, there were indications that he knew what had happened to the ███

Guantanamo was very real, and his family in ████████ was a huge emotional issue for him. That was motivating him to talk to us, but he was also trying to protect his cousin.

After midnight and after finishing off the last meeting with the Recon intel guys and John, I decided to check on things in ██████

I gave Rina a call on the Iridium satellite phone. One of the smarter things DoD had decided was to allow the ███████ to use the phones for morale calls. We'd often allowed the 10th Mountain troops to borrow our satellite phones so they could call home, too.

Since Rina had my power of attorney in the ████████, I wanted to check on my direct-deposit paychecks, how the house was, and that kind of stuff.

It was a melancholy phone call. We talked about what had happened with our breakup. Even though it was over, we both felt sad about it. I had to admit that I did miss her. I had the impression she felt the same way. We had agreed that, when we decided not to get married, it was time to move on. She was doing her own thing. I had heard from a mutual friend that she was going out with an Australian army officer who was visiting the States. This fact didn't exactly thrill me but, then again, it wasn't my business.

I couldn't tell her about the ███████ who had been captured and about the potential there was of a sleeper agent hanging around ███████ It would only have panicked her and, besides, we hadn't proven the case for or against him yet. We had a long way to go.

In the midst of the conversation, I heard a *whoosh* and a *thump*. Then another. Then another.

"Rina, hold on a second," I said. By the sound, the rounds were hitting well short.

"What the hell is that?" I said to one of the ███ guys hanging out near the gate entrance in his shorts and flip-flops. By now, the sky was illuminated by a 10th Mountain flare as they prepared for counter-mortar fire.

"Oh, the Taliban are mortaring us," he said. "I wouldn't worry much—they are terrible shots." He headed for the shower. No concern there.

Now I could hear the first volley of 10th Mountain mortars firing back at their best estimate of the Taliban mortar's origins.

"Shouldn't we all be in shelters or something?" I yelled to him.

"Nah," he said. "They usually don't get close."

Usually they don't get close? Oh, *that* was reassuring.

I told Rina that we were being mortared and I had to go, and asked her to make sure to look for a package from me for Alexander. The mortaring here had kind of panicked her. As we were signing off, she surprised me by saying, "I do miss you." It caught me off guard. I dodged the comment. But I missed her, too.

I was mentally and physically spent. After waiting to see if any of the Taliban mortars got any closer (they didn't), I went back to the tent and crawled under my poncho liner. Periodically, a mortar went off, then the 10th Mountain sent up a flare that lit up the sky with a bright white light that cast long shadows for a few minutes while they returned fire.

I figured, given the choice between sleeping in a cramped bunker or risking getting mortared on a marginally more comfortable cot, I would pick my cot. If they got me, they got me. I ended up sleeping through the night despite the constant—and loud—cat-and-mouse game outside.

The next morning, John had heard back from Washington. Ghaffari's account of his immigration to the ███ and his international travel listings were accurate. They also hadn't found any association between Arash or his circle of acquaintances and any known terrorist group in the FBI database. DIA had done checks on him, too, and so far the guy was checking out. So far, so good.

Still, he knew a lot more about his cousin and the operation in ▮▮▮▮ than he was telling us. We didn't know the extent of the Iranians' involvement in Afghanistan or whether they were involved in a sleeper cell in the ▮▮▮▮▮▮

We moved in for the second full day of interrogation.

I decided to open up by bringing up ▮▮▮▮▮ again. I told him that I had talked to my family back in ▮▮▮▮▮ the previous night and pointed out that he hadn't. He gave me a carefully vacant look. He was trying to be cool.

"It's a real shame that you, as a ▮▮▮▮▮, can't call your family right now," I said, "and you will not have the privilege of talking or spending time with your family until you open up. We feel we made some progress yesterday, and you gave us some good information, but there is a lot more you need to share with us."

There, I thought, *I've given him a little bit of carrot, but the message is that we've got a long way to go, my cousin.*

"Tell us about your life growing up in Iran," John said.

We followed with an intense line of questioning on Ali and Arash's upbringing in Tehran. How his cousin had made arrangements to send him to school there and how his cousin had watched out for him and raised the money to send him to the ▮▮▮▮▮ That sent off alarm bells, but Arash Ghaffari seemed very open about it. If we started talking about his cousin currently, Arash got more vague, so we stuck hard with their days in Iran, and some useful information started to emerge. Arash finally admitted that after the Shah of Iran had been deposed in January 1979, shortly before the Ghaffari family arrived in Iran, Ali had had "contact" with the ▮▮▮▮—the immensely powerful ▮▮▮▮▮▮▮▮▮ service. He had found work with them.

It was slowly becoming clear that Ali was, at some level, a player with the ████, probably as an intelligence officer. I knew from my work in other operations that the ████ was the self-appointed generator of chaos and evil for the Iranian people.

Ali Ghaffari was a bigger fish than we thought.

We cut the interrogation off at that point so we could discuss our strategy. This new point was an important one, and we needed to push hard on it. We rewarded him with a bottle of cold water.

We ended the session by telling him we appreciated that he was remembering more helpful information. We reminded him that the more information he remembered, the better the chances he had of going back to the ████████████ The idea was to reintroduce hope—for the moment.

After lunch, John and I strategized and tried to figure out what the hell was going on. Maybe there was an *Iranian* cell operating here, not an al Qaeda cell, not a Taliban cell, and not a ████ cell. If Ali was linked to the ████, then this was no shoestring operation.

At the break, we noticed a lot of activity around the base. Straightening up the mess hall. Stacking up supplies. Lining up vehicles. Some of the Special Forces guys were clean shaven and wearing crisp desert camo.

"What's going on?" I asked.

"General Schoomaker is visiting tomorrow, sir," one of them told me. "He's doing a visit to the front and we need to get things in order." Must be serious. They had started calling me "sir" again.

Gen. Peter Schoomaker was chief of staff of the army. He'd been appointed a few months previously to replace Gen. Eric Shinseki, who'd pissed off Rumsfeld by predicting (accurately, as it turned out) that the United States would need many more troops to keep the peace in Iraq than Rumsfeld wanted to send. I knew and respected General Schoomaker from my work with Able Danger, but I had no interest in running into him here with an ████████ prisoner under my wing. If General Schoomaker was coming, so was the press, which would snoop around. We had to finish up with Ghaffari and make him—and us—disappear by the next day . . . but disappear in the "right" way.

At the same time, though, we didn't want to take shortcuts. We had to proceed carefully and methodically through the minefield of Arash Ghaffari's fevered brain. We didn't want to become his enemy.

We wanted his own mind to become his enemy.

John sent back a cable ███████████████████████ saying we believed that Ali Ghaffari had some level of contact with the ████ and was probably an ███████████ and that we were going to explore the possibility that there might be an █████ terrorism cell in ███████ We had gotten additional intel from the Special Forces that they were convinced that the █████ was there during the raid and that it was supposed to be distributed that evening.

Our strategy with Arash Ghaffari was to build up his hope at the beginning of the afternoon and then crush it just before we broke for the night, no matter what he said.

"While we've verified that you're from ██████," John told him after lunch, "you have not told us what you've been doing for your cousin in the ████████

Ghaffari leaned forward again and spoke urgently. "I am shocked by what you say. I've done nothing for my cousin. He sent me there to live. ███████"

I jumped in. "It's very clear from our morning discussion that your cousin has connections with ████████. Our question is very simple: What, if anything, have you done to promote your cousin's activities in the █████████"

████████" Ghaffari repeated. "I would never do anything to hurt █████. It is my obligation to be a good ██████"

"You are 100 percent correct," I said. "You are obligated to tell us everything you know if you are a good ██████ You must tell us about your cousin's activities and what he asked you to do."

"By everything I hold holy, I'm telling you I have had no contact with my cousin other than correspondence."

"You're telling me you've never received any █████? You've not gotten any guidance on activities in the ████████"

"On my honor, I'm a good ████████ I want nothing to do with my cousin's activities."

"Then why are you here?"

Ghaffari looked frustrated. "Family. You must understand. Family obligation. When my cousin asked me to come back for a visit, I came."

Now, there was something new. His cousin had asked him to come back.

"I understand you are very close to your cousin and you honor him," I said, "but you are not honoring your country you now call your home and, therefore, you are not fulfilling your obligation to the ████████ by telling us something that is not true. I don't know how to make this clearer to you."

I brought back my ace. "You have to understand that the only place you're going to go is someplace warm in the Caribbean, and it ain't Puerto Rico, unless you come completely clean with us," I said. "So if you value your wife, your children, your life in ████████ you're going to have to tell us all that you know of what your cousin has been up to."

You could almost see the wind going out of his sails, and we could almost hear him thinking: *Oh God, we're back at that.*

John and I looked at each other and then looked at him. Clearly and concisely, we'd laid out his options—and choices—and a path to the future. He had to choose between his life back home and his cousin.

Some details started to come out. Arash told us more about his family leaving Afghanistan and going to ██████ and their life there. About his ██████ attending university in ██████ and being recruited into the ██████. About how his cousin had sent him to ██████

"So you're telling us that your cousin paid to send you to ████████ because he was ██████████████?" I asked.

"No, on my honor, I have had no contact with my cousin other than mail since I have been here ████████████████
████████

Then came the break we were looking for.

He leaned forward again. "My cousin and I—we traveled to Iran together while I was here," he said suddenly. John and I glanced at each other.

Arash leaned back and closed his eyes.

He was obviously struggling with his dilemma: His cousin ████████

"Why?" I asked.

The answers got vague again. They had traveled through Herat, the Afghan town closest to the ████████ on the bus. Then more vagueness.

We pushed him.

"You've given us a great deal of information, but you haven't given us everything," said John. "You have to give us the rest of the story. We have no authority to let you go unless we believe you've told us the whole truth—and you are obligated by your ████████ ████████ to do so."

"We're nowhere near that at this point," I added.

We took a five-minute break.

"What do you think?" John asked.

"He's given us more, but still not everything."

John wasn't getting anything back from Washington on this guy that indicated he was bad. His associates were checking out, but he wasn't coming clean on his activities, or the activities of his cousin, in Afghanistan. Checks are great—but not everything—and there was still more here.

We were frustrated. He was frustrated. It had been a long day. We went back in.

"Tonight, when the sun goes down, will be your last night in ███ and where you end up tomorrow is totally in your control," I told him, remaining propped up against the desk that I'd been leaning on for two days. "If you cooperate and tell us the complete truth about your cousin and what he has been doing, chances are excellent you will be released and able to make your flight back to the ████████. On the other hand, if you choose to continue to be less than truthful with us, then you will leave ██████ in handcuffs. You will move to Bagram, and from Bagram to Guantanamo. That trip will start tomorrow."

I never moved close enough to physically intimidate him. I didn't want him to be distracted by fear for his own safety. I wanted him to focus on my words so his mind could start gnawing away at them.

He was getting desperate, repeating almost to himself, "I love ████████ I love my life there. It is important for me to be with my family—my wife and my children. I am a loyal ████████"

"Let's go back to your trip with your cousin," I said quietly.

He knew that all the cards were on the table now. There was nothing standing between him and Guantanamo except us.

"Who gave your cousin the ██████?" I asked.

"The ████████████████ He has worked for them since ████████████████"

There. That was it.

The rest of the truth started to flow—never more than a trickle—but it was flowing.

He then went back to his life with his cousin ██████ before Ali had sent him ████████, and admitted that his cousin had become an ████████████ for the ██████ who worked against the ██████ He revised his story with the ██████ real work now the focus. It made sense.

Over an hour, it became clear that Arash had been called back by his cousin to be recruited into the fold. Payback time, in other words, for big cousin's "generosity" in sending ██████ to the ██████ ██████

Arash was going to become his cousin's operative.

"How did your cousin get the ████████████████" John asked.

"I carried it for him," he said. His eyes filled with tears. He was finally starting to break down at the knowledge of his betrayal of his cousin.

"How did you do it?"

"In my luggage. My cousin felt it would be best since I was an ████████ He believed that they would leave me alone coming into Afghanistan."

"How did you keep your passport from being stamped when you crossed into Iran?"

"My cousin arranged it."

"When did you give the ████████ back to your cousin?"

"Right after we crossed the border, and he brought it to the compound."

"You do know that the ████████ was involved in the meeting with the other men in the compound," I said.

"Yes," he said, "but I had nothing to do with my cousin business. I was asleep at the time of the meeting." That was true. The Special Forces had confirmed that.

By the end of that day, we had much more detail about what had gone down in the days prior to the meeting and his cousin's role in it, but we weren't letting him off the hook. We stuck to our plan to come down hard.

"You've done much better today," I told him. "We appreciate that you are a good ████████. I do feel that what you've said today helps us understand you and your cousin."

He let out a breath.

"But," I added, "I don't think it's enough to let you go home."

He put his head down.

"We're going to talk to you again in the morning. It's time for all of us to take a break. We'll have some food brought in to you."

"I must leave for Kabul tomorrow if I am going to make my plane home." He was pleading with us.

"Frankly, you aren't going to make any plane unless it's to Guantanamo," I said.

We left, and John got back on the computer while I smoked a cigar. The time was 2100. The 10th Mountain guys were still pushing back the insurgents with aggressive combat patrols in the foothills of the nearby mountains in preparation for General Schoomaker's visit. It seemed to work. There was only sporadic mortar and gunfire that night.

We were making progress, but running out of time. Clearly, if any info came back that Arash Ghaffari was associated with terrorists in the ███████████, he was done, but it didn't appear to be going in that direction.

Even so, we needed to know what, if anything, his cousin had been instructing him to do ███████████. We needed more information on what was going down in Afghanistan with the ███████ What was the ███████ really for? What other associates did his cousin have? Who were the men who had been rolled up with Ali Ghaffari?

The next morning, we found all of the Special Forces guys—even our two intel contacts—were now clean shaven and in clean desert camo. John razzed the guys about how good they looked. John and I pressed Tim about flights back. He figured that after General Schoomaker arrived, there would be helicopters we could hop on and get a ride to Bagram. Time was ticking down.

John and I discussed our final approach with Ghaffari. We decided to ask the same set of questions as yesterday and see if we could inch forward with that method.

When we got in there, however, the plan didn't work that way. Ghaffari looked awful. He was bleary-eyed and drawn. If he'd slept, it sure hadn't been for very long.

"We need to continue talking about your cousin and all of his activities to the point where we feel comfortable you have given us everything you can on him," I told him, presenting him with the stark choice we'd been laying out to him for the last two days. "You better make a choice between your life in ███████ and your cousin because, right now, unless you give us all the information you have on him and his activities, you will be loyal to your cousin, but you will end up at Guantanamo. If that is your choice, we can stop this discussion right now."

"No," he said. His voice cracked. "I will give you everything I have—anything you want to know about my cousin. As God is my witness."

"Tell us what your cousin was doing the night of the raid."

He admitted that his cousin had been instructed by ███████ ██████ to conduct terrorist attacks against ████████████ and create chaos for the U.S. Army and the ISAF in eastern Afghanistan. He told us that his cousin had been traveling between ██ ██████████, reporting on ███████████ to █████████████ back in █████. He gave us the names of the men who had gathered at the meeting.

By this admission, he was leaving himself open for death if his cousin ever found out. He had crossed the line. He had made his choice.

"What were the specific tasks your cousin gave them that night?" I asked.

"My cousin never shared with me the specific tasks or targets he was working on, but he had put together a number of groups to conduct terrorist attacks in eastern Afghanistan."

Interesting. The Recon could follow up to track these cells down.

"What did your cousin ask you to do?" asked John.

"Nothing," Ghaffari insisted. "He asked me to do nothing. I moved the ██████ for him into Afghanistan . . . that was it."

We believed him. At this point, he was pouring out his guts. I figured his cousin probably really did love him like a son, and was easing him into the family business.

"What happened to the ██████████" I asked.

He stopped for a moment. "You know my nephew was present at my cousins house?" he said.

"Yes, we do." We really did, we were briefed by the Recon guys on how the raid went down.

"One of your ██████ sergeants walked him out of the room," he said, as if that explained it.

"So?" John and I were baffled.

"My cousin—he gave the money to him, and ▮he put it in his medical bag ▮▮▮▮▮▮▮▮▮▮▮▮▮▮▮▮▮▮▮▮. Your ▮▮▮▮ sergeant walked him out of the raid to keep him from harm."

John and I rolled our eyes.

"Can you tell us where ▮he went?"

He said he didn't know but gave us the names of associates in ▮▮▮▮▮ where ▮he might have gone.

We moved back to his visit to ▮▮▮▮▮ with his cousin, and he gave us a detailed accounting of his cousin activities there and the people whom he believed were ▮▮▮▮▮▮▮▮▮ who met with his cousin. He methodically worked his way through the details.

I moved in to solidify our gains. We had to get him to understand that if he wanted his life ▮▮▮▮▮▮▮▮▮▮▮ back, he had to do something to prove it.

"Are you willing to work against your cousin?" I asked.

He looked up at me as if he had just been asked to kill his best friend.

"You've got to make a choice right now," I said.

"No, no, no, I understand," he said. He had no fight left in him. "My life ▮▮▮▮▮▮▮ is more important than my cousin, and I am willing to do whatever you need me to do."

He was looking down with what appeared to be shame, then he took a deep breath and looked up at us with new determination.

▮▮▮▮▮▮▮▮▮▮▮▮▮▮▮▮▮▮▮▮▮▮▮▮▮▮▮▮▮▮▮▮▮

He was now John's cat. It would be his job to take this guy on as an asset since he would be back ▮▮▮▮▮▮▮▮▮▮▮▮, and it would then be a ▮▮▮▮▮▮▮▮▮▮▮▮▮▮▮▮ John took over the questioning at that point, asking him a dozen questions, running through what we'd already asked him, and got clear and concise answers that were consistent with his previous ones. At the conclusion, John took a deep breath.

When John started the questioning, my thoughts were already gone. I had already started to think about our return to Bagram and getting back on the task of targeting the ▮▮▮▮ in ▮▮▮▮▮ This was good stuff but as far as I was concerned it was now history. We needed to keep moving forward, and I did not see a big threat to ██████████ here, so it was time to keep pressing on the bad guys.

We learned what we needed to know. It appeared that Arash Ghaffari was not part of a sleeper cell in the ██████████, but he had a front-row seat on some nasty stuff in Afghanistan. He'd given us the intel we needed to determine that the Iranians were, indeed, getting involved in the war here and were relying on an intelligence agent—Ali Ghaffari—to do their dirty work. They had given him ██████ to form terrorist cells and begin conducting operations against the ██████ in Afghanistan. By getting to Ali Ghaffari early on, we were able to stop him in his tracks and to stop the Iranians—cut out the cancer before it had a chance to grow.

John and I were getting ready to leave when Arash stopped us. "Wait," he said. "I feel very strongly that there is something I have to admit to you so that you understand that I am a good ██████."

John and I looked at each other as we stopped in our tracks. We had thought he had told us everything.

"I must admit to you something that is very, very important . . . to clear my honor."

John and I just stared at him. What had we missed?

"I must admit that my wife and I had traveled to Iran before," he said.

"Yeah, you told us that," said John, puzzled.

"I did a terrible thing." He was speaking rapidly, and John and I tensed. Shit. Maybe this was about nukes.

"In my religion, there are specific things one can do to help ensure his children are right in the eyes of God."

Oh, boy, I thought, this was about to go into any number of directions—all of them very bad.

"Well, I'm not sure how to say this." He looked up at John and me, seeking an affirming look—or something.

"Consummation of our child is very important in our faith," he said, staring at us fixedly.

"OK . . ." John said. Where in the hell was this going?

"I must admit to you that in one of our trips to Iran, we visited a special mosque."

"And . . . ?" I said. What did this have to do with nukes or terrorists? We knew, of course, that terrorists used mosques as staging grounds. "We're listening."

"I must admit to you . . . I am so ashamed of this . . . my wife and I had sex in this mosque to conceive our son."

Whoa . . . sex in a mosque—now that is ballsy!

"Was that it?" I said to him, still waiting for info of military value. Maybe I'd misunderstood.

"We conceived our child in a mosque in Iran." Ghaffari looked back at us, surprised. "This isn't important to you?"

The tension in the room evaporated. I was fighting hard not to break out laughing, and I glanced at John. He was, too.

"We're *Americans*. We don't care about things like that," I told him.

Ghaffari looked disappointed. It was clear it meant a great deal to get that off his shoulders. He'd expected a bigger reaction from us.

"Don't worry about it," John said, "no big deal. You are good to go."

As we left we recognized it for what it was: What it showed us was how much we'd broken this guy. No one admits having sex in a mosque to the U.S. government. To *Penthouse Forum*, maybe, but not to Uncle Sam.

With that, we were out of there.

John and I went to the Tactical Operations Center and gave them a detailed verbal dump of everything we'd learned. By now, the Recon intel guys had an inkling that the nephew had been involved in evacuating the ███ and there was a full-blown search under way for him ████████████████

They were confident they would chase down the nephew for the ███ and go after any other remnants of Iranian activity in the area.

We told the Recon guys to let the guy loose. They gave him back his belongings and took him into ███, where he could get transportation to Kabul to catch his plane. It would be up to the

We grabbed our kit, and the Special Forces drove us out in armored Humvees to the landing area.

Within minutes, we heard the *whoop-whoop-whoop* of a flight of Chinooks and watched them lumber in with an ever-present two-bird Apache escort.

We had finished just in time.

A huge backwash of dust hit our faces as the two Chinooks landed while the Apache orbited above looking for bad guys. General Schoomaker and his staff came off the 47 closest to us. He looked over at us, but knew better than to come over and talk to us. He knew undercover intelligence folks when he saw them.

The two Chinooks lumbered slowly into the air, whipping us with dust and debris as they clawed the clear blue sky for altitude.

Before the Chinooks were gone from the horizon, we could hear the *whop-whop-whop* of a single Air Force UH-60 Black Hawk with an Apache escort arriving over the same stretch of weathered asphalt road.

As it touched down, Tim shouted at us.

"This is the one we're supposed to get on," said Tim.

With my kit and a still aching knee from my bad exit from the Chinook three nights back, I moved toward the door of the now stationary Black Hawk.

As the door opened, out came Christiane Amanpour of CNN in a bright yellow nylon jacket, cameraman in tow.

She stopped and stared at us, clearly surprised but intrigued. She seemed on the verge of speaking to us, but I motioned to John and Tim, and we quickly moved past her without a word and onto the chopper.

I gave her a thin smile and helped the crew chief slide the door closed behind me.

Within two minutes we were back in the sky and rolling. A short

Japanese journalist, whose Kevlar vest appeared ten sizes too big for him, sat to my immediate right and directly across from John. Tim and I sat against the starboard door and its window.

We flew near the nap of the earth back to Bagram, never rising higher than 2,000 feet above sea level but mostly staying below 1,000 feet. The terrain varied from scarred desert—areas pockmarked with craters from past artillery barrages—to jagged rifts of rocky mountain terrain in which the striations showed layer after layer of the Earth's history now open to the sky. At times, the jagged mountains towered over the chopper. It was a roller-coaster ride.

Having been on similar types of flights years ago, I'd had the wisdom not to eat lunch before the flight. Tim had apparently not been so savvy. He had been grazing all morning on his supply of beef jerky and, on the flight, kept offering the bag to John and myself.

I never had taken any jerky from Tim to this point, and neither had John, but I think John was to the point that he was going to take a piece just to be polite. At that moment, the Black Hawk went into a swooping dive. I felt my stomach go up into my throat. Just as John started to reach for a piece of jerky, Tim pulled the bag away and forcefully replaced all the jerky he had eaten earlier in the day into the bag.

He finished puking, calmly closed the bag, and put it back in his cargo pocket. . . . Cryin' shame. He'd ruined a perfectly good bag of beef jerky.

The mountain ranges were connected by long stretches of open desert—stark, empty, completely lifeless rolling dry mud baked to a light tan. By my count, we passed five separate mountain ranges. About 5 miles out, when we reached the John Wayne Pass at the last mountain range before Bagram, our Apache escort faded back and entered a separate approach pattern to Bagram.

After having run through my mental "things to do" list, my thoughts turned to Kate. I had some planning to do for her, too.

· 10 ·

IMPROVISED RAID

SO much for plans. A short time after my return from ██████, I was holding a gun in the lobby of Afghanistan's Post Telephone and Telegraph Company (PTT), while a little old lady chattered away in Pashtu on one side of me and an ominous crowd of men gathered on the other. If we didn't get out of here within a couple of minutes, it was going to get very, very ugly.

I took another glance at the growing group of men and tried to look as if I were actually listening to the old lady, while I carefully moved the selector switch on my M-4 from SAFE all the way to AUTO. Why the hell were John and Lisa taking so long?

This episode had started with a fairly innocuous request from ██████ Sgt. Lisa Werman, who came up to me after one of the morning stand-ups shortly after I got back from ██████ ██ ██ ████████████████████████████████ Can you come over to my office and take a look at it?"

"Sure," I said. "Let me finish a couple of things and I'll be over."

I'd acquired a reputation as kind of a tech head. I'm not sure it was deserved, but I was willing to give it a try. The phone had been captured off a bad guy killed in Khowst. ████████████████████ ███████ The phone might hold key information on his network of associates. There was a big problem, though: Lisa and her folks couldn't break in to it.

I headed over to the ████████ office in the BCP (Bagram Collection Point), or prison—a handmade sign by one of the troops over the entrance proclaimed it to be HOTEL CALIFORNIA. Frankly, I had been avoiding the place. There were problems over how prisoners were being interrogated. Suspicious deaths had been reported, and there were ongoing investigations. I wanted nothing to do with it. Despite my reputation as a troublemaker, I really don't go looking for trouble, and as long as I was operations chief for our HUMINT projects in Afghanistan, my people were not going to do anything that would remotely show up on the radar as improper or illegal without good reason. No matter what, I did not allow abuse.

The BCP was an old hangar converted for the task—large, dark, and foreboding. Painted the typical Bagram tan outside, its windows were painted black. I turned in my weapon, was issued a badge, and went inside for the first time. Inside, the PUCs (persons under control) wore what looked like bright orange scrubs. A few shuffled by me, being taken, blindfolded and shackled, to interrogation rooms located off a walkway that ran along the wall above the first floor. There was constant noise—banging against cell bars by prisoners, yelling by guards, which had the effect, by design or happenstance, of never allowing the detainees to feel at ease.

The ████████ office was on the second floor in a secure area off the walkway. It wasn't much bigger than the area where I worked in the 180 HUMINT tent and was crowded with enough technological equipment to put a man on Mars. Computers, a few radios, wires, antennas, a digital camera with a giant telephoto lens, ████████████ ██

██
████████████████████████████ were crammed onto the desk. It looked more like a high-tech workshop than an office.

"What's up?" I asked Lisa, a petite brunette with a spunky attitude—kinda like Katie Couric in combat. Lisa had been unable to unlock the captured phone. It was a blue Nokia, fairly typical for the era, but Lisa said there seemed to be some kind of ████████ ████ code that wouldn't let us unlock the phone ████████

She handed it to me. "You see?" she said. "We get a signal, but I can't even make a call."

I turned it over in my hand. "What options do we have?" I asked her.

"Well, we could send it back to Washington ████████, but the value of the info would be degraded by the time they got to it," she said.

"Do you want to stop by the new GSM (Group Spécial Mobile—the most popular standard for cell phones) store right next to that Internet café in Kabul?" I asked. "We can see if they can get into it."

"Sure," she said. "Great idea. That's a brand-new telecommunications provider. They're selling phones to the Afghans like hotcakes."

"Which is interesting," I said, "since most Afghans don't make more than $300 a year."

"They're pretty much dirt cheap," said Lisa, "and the plans are better than those in the United States. When is the next convoy going to Kabul?"

"Tomorrow," I said.

"Let's do it," she said.

The next day, we performed our typical 80 to 100-mile-per-hour run from Bagram into Kabul without incident, and the FBI vehicle didn't even blow a tire as it was apt to do every hundred miles or so. We brought with us five 10th Mountain troops, mostly tactical intel types who never get out of the wire, so they could shop at the weekly ISAF bazaar.

We took the phone to one of the commercial telephone ventures popping up in Afghanistan that we figured might be compatible to their network. The idea being to see if they could open it for us. We had John with us and another guy from the FBI, along with a translator. With the FBI providing security outside, Lisa, Dave, and I took the phone into the vendor to have him take a look at it. The rest of the troops set up a secure perimeter around the parked vehicles outside.

The vendor was polite, but openly skeptical about his ability to do anything with a phone from another network. After hooking it up to a computer, he fiddled around for a few minutes but soon gave up, shaking his head. "No, I cannot open it," he said in passable English.

"What's going on?" said John as we emerged from the store.

"He couldn't get it open," said Lisa.

"Is there anywhere else in Afghanistan where we could get help to break into the phone?" I asked Lisa.

"I think it's part of an older GSM system run by the Afghanistan Telephone and Telegraph Company," she said.

"The telecommunications center?" I asked.

She nodded. "That's where I think we would find the help to break into this phone. Plus," she said, "we might be able to download 100 percent of the entire country's phone infrastructure—all of the technical data and all of the phone numbers in the system." That would include the database containing the names and addresses of the phone users ███ ███ ████████████

Basically, it would be the Rosetta Stone. It would give us the information we needed to better eavesdrop on the terrorists—████████ ███

████████ A lot of people knew this information was there but it was difficult, politically and logistically, to get at, and the Afghans never would have volunteered it.

"Wow," I said. "But that's Indian territory." I gave them the street location. "It's the heart of where the bad guys are hanging out these days." The Taliban were infiltrating the phone companies and putting their trusted personnel into jobs within the companies to protect their interests.

John shrugged. "I've been down there before. Doesn't seem that bad to me."

"Yeah, but you were not trying to steal something that is potentially important to the Taliban."

Dave looked at John and me and said, "There is a bookstore that I've wanted to check out again." Dave collected rare books and on missions he liked to visit the small bookshops scattered around the city and had used them as cover stops in the past. Despite the risks, he'd stopped by the bookshop next to the building.

"Oh, now *there's* justification for us to go there," I responded.

"Just what are we after?" asked John.

"We're apparently after a ton of shit," I said. "We want the data to break into this phone and, while we're at it, we'd like to download all the data for every phone on the system. But we don't know where this data is kept in this place." I glanced over at Lisa, who kinda shrugged.

"So . . . ?" said John.

"John, we don't even have a floor plan for the building, and we can't just walk in and take the place over."

"So . . . ?" repeated John.

I was getting a little exasperated. "We do not have enough folks to set up a perimeter, and we haven't done a rehearsal."

John was still undeterred. "Tony, we don't need a rehearsal. We can just go in."

Dave chimed in. "Yeah, and we could use my stopping at the book cart as cover." Great. Now my navy friend had become an expert on clandestine operations.

"John, are you sure about this?" I asked. "I've already been warned about abusing you guys on these missions." I had been reminded recently that the FBI's job in country was debriefing and site exploitation to look for the possibility of attacks on U.S. soil. It wasn't planning raids on Afghan organizations or conducting combat operations.

Through his beard, John broke into a wide grin. "I don't know of any abuse going on here."

I grinned, too. "All right. Dave, what are your thoughts?"

"Hey, shipmate, you're the OIC of this mission," Dave said. "It would help ███████, but we don't have a clear picture of what's inside of that building if we go in."

"How close is the bookstore to the telecommunications building?" I asked, in light of this apparent interagency willingness to take this mission on.

"It is a little book stand, actually, about 80 meters from the rear entrance of the building."

"Do you know the basic layout of the building and can you diagram it for us?"

Dave thought for a moment and then drew a series of squares and lines on the dirty side window of my truck. "I know where the front is, and I think I know where the back is—here and here."

"Now," I asked Dave, "do we know for a fact that the technical room that we need to get access to is in this building?"

"Yeah," said Dave. "We know from our intel that it's in there."

"It looks like a big building . . . do you really think the device that will unlock Lisa's phone is in there?"

"Yep," said Dave.

I called over Lisa, who had walked back and was leaning against Dave's vehicle as she continued to examine the phone.

"Do you have your laptop with you?" I asked.

"It's in the truck," she said, gesturing toward the vehicle.

"If we get you access, do you have the right tools to be able to hook up your laptop and download what you need off the network?"

She looked at me like I was slightly unhinged.

"Yeah, I do," she said. The tone in her voice was questioning.

"How long would it take you?"

She thought for a minute, still eyeing me like I was crazy. "Ten minutes."

"You're sure?" I asked. "Ten minutes."

She corrected herself. "No, fifteen minutes."

I turned to Dave. "Can you browse for books for fifteen minutes?"

"Easily," came the answer.

"OK, John, you're the raid expert here. What do we need to do to get in there and pull this off?"

Realization of what we were thinking about trying to pull off began to dawn on Lisa and she joined our planning circle. I saw her eyebrows go up and her eyes widen.

"This is the deal," John said to us. "We'll need to clear and hold a secure corridor in." John drew a line along the path that Dave had put on the window. He continued, "And since we have limited radios, we'll need to stay within visual distance of each other—kinda like bread crumbs to follow—each in sight of the other all the way into the interior."

"Can you rapidly secure a path to get us safely into that building?" I asked John with some disbelief.

John turned to Dave. "What's your estimate of the distance from the street to the room you need to access in the center?" he asked.

Dave thought for a moment and took a guess. "A hundred meters. Maybe a hundred and fifty."

We only had six people for this mission: John, the other FBI guy, the translator, Dave, Lisa, and myself. We had far too few people to set up a secure perimeter, so the secure corridor idea had merit.

"There's no way we can secure the route," I said. "We're going to have a hard time stringing ourselves out and having line of sight on each other." I thought out loud. "We would be fifteen to twenty meters apart." I looked around at our small band on the Afghan street. "Can we do that?"

"Yes," said John immediately. "Or, I believe so."

I turned to Lisa. "Are you OK with this?"

Lisa wasn't going to miss this bus. "If you can guarantee I'll have enough time, I'll be fine."

Then I looked over at our translator. "Can you explain to them technically what we need and persuade them to allow Lisa access to the room?"

He nodded. "Yes, although I don't think any explanation will be needed if he comes with us." He pointed to John, who towered over all of us. John grinned.

"OK, then this is the deal," I said. "Let's dump the rest of the 10th Mountain folks off at ████████ and do a quick rehearsal of how we're going to do this. We'll diagram it out again and do a run-through." As the commander of the convoy, it was my job to move everyone to and from Kabul safely. I didn't want any nonessential personnel to go with us on the mission and risk the chance they'd play John Wayne if they got nervous.

Everybody nodded in agreement.

We moved the last two miles to the ████ to drop off the rest of the crew that we'd brought to town and hung on to the three vehicles. In the lobby of the ████ we sat on two chairs and a couch and did a quick run-through. Dave described the exterior of the building and where he thought the target material might be in its recesses. We decided that one of the FBI guys would remain with the vehicles, Dave would stay outside as a lookout (he would try to stay inconspicuous by pretending to shop for books), while John, Lisa, the translator, and I would go in.

Then we moved out to execution. We would only get one shot at this.

The PTT office, which also doubled as the Kabul post office, was the tallest building in town. A sullen slab of a building, it sat on a street with a few scruffy trees and clusters of makeshift shops around its front and side.

NATO and ISAF troops had been shot at in the area, and bombs had been tossed at them. Nevertheless, we figured that by keeping a low profile with just the six of us, in civilian clothes, we could come in under the radar and be in and out before anybody knew what happened.

That was the theory. Now we had to test it.

We moved into position, parking the vehicles along the street near the rear of the building in a line and in a way that wouldn't make it obvious to any observer that we were headed for the telecommunications center.

One FBI guy stayed behind with the vehicles, while the rest of us moved casually, but deliberately, for the back door of the building. Dave took up position by the bookshop next to the telecommunications building. He appeared to have a good view of the street in case anybody appeared who could cause us trouble. We hoped.

The remaining four of us—John, myself, Lisa, and the translator—then slipped in the back door. From that point on, I had only limited sight of Dave, and it would take a couple of seconds for him and the FBI guy who was guarding the vehicles to get to us if there was trouble inside.

The pucker factor was way up as we moved in.

In a line we walked into a crowded L-shaped lobby, with a caged counter that ran around the lobby from the back door to the front. Groups of two or three people were coming in every minute or so. I stationed myself toward the rear end of the lobby, where I could see both the front and the back doors.

John motioned that he, the translator, and Lisa were moving behind the long counter. They stopped one guy, and I could see Lisa talking and then the translator gesturing and speaking. The guy didn't look happy. At first he shook his head, and then Lisa and the translator spoke to him some more. Finally, he gave a reluctant nod and opened a door to what appeared to be the back room. My eyes, still adjusting from the bright light outside, could not make out what was in there.

All three disappeared. I turned my attention to the lobby. Every now and then, John would poke his head out and nod. I'd walk back to see Dave still standing at the book stall.

I had the impression from John's nods that the guy had given Lisa the device she needed to unlock the phone. Then, I learned later, they had developed a ruse to get the guy to leave the room. That's when

Lisa grabbed her computer and linked it up to the control system for the network.

Fifteen minutes. She said she needed fifteen minutes. The clock was ticking.

I looked around the lobby. This could end up being the longest fifteen minutes of my life. I kept glancing out the window for a glimpse of Dave and also kept an eye out for John.

People started to take notice of me. It wasn't hard. An armed Westerner standing in the lobby of their phone company/post office. While they wouldn't be able to tell if I was an American, I certainly wasn't UN, since they didn't carry guns and wear body armor. More and more people glanced my way. Then they stared. Then they stopped and stared.

An old Afghan woman came over to speak to me. She was wearing a black dress and had a white head scarf and held a large, blue carryall. I tried to move away from her, but she wasn't deterred and followed me around, chattering away. Even when I attempted to tell her I didn't speak Pashtu, she didn't stop talking. More and more intense-looking men were coming in off the street. I saw one look my way and whisper in another's ear. He glanced grimly at me and then headed out the door.

Trouble.

Then John popped his head out and I tilted my head inquiringly at him. Finished? He shook his head and held up his hand to me, palm toward me, fingers spread. Five more minutes. I groaned. Goddamnit. This was going like molasses in winter.

A group of men standing just outside the lobby was beginning to grow. First there were two or three. Then six. Then a dozen. Two had AK-47s that were clearly visible, but not yet pointing my way.

Word had gotten out that something was going on.

Finally John appeared and nodded. Lisa, computer tucked against her, was right behind him.

"How did it go?" I asked.

"I got *everything*," she said. "It was amazing. Just amazing."

"Glad you are happy," I called after her as she moved out the back door and into the alley.

I moved toward the back door and saw the man who had been with John and Lisa come out of the room and move along the counter, speaking tersely to a man who appeared to be a colleague. His tone was not a happy one. He saw me and froze—apparently he did not know if I understood what he had just said—and he now looked at me with fear in his eyes.

I eyeballed the growing crowd of grim-faced men and then looked back at him.

The men were moving into the lobby like bees in a hive that had been disturbed. I swung my weapon, still on AUTO, around as I walked backward, back into the light of day.

Finally, I hit the door and backed through it onto the street. Dave had spotted John and Lisa and had signaled to the FBI guy to start the engine on his car.

Dave casually took the computer from Lisa, who brought her M-4 up, pointing it at the building to cover me as I moved. I continued backing down the alley at a deliberate pace and onto the street, watching for any threat to come flying out the back door of the PTT.

John hopped in the FBI truck, while watching to see if anyone came around from the front. Lisa climbed in with Dave, while the translator got in with me. I was last. I started my truck, picked up the Motorola radio, and said, "Go!"

We took off.

Wow. Not bad for not having detailed diagrams of the building and little knowledge of what was kept at the PTT.

It took a good quarter hour for the adrenaline rush to wear off and for my perception of reality to return to normal—about the time it took for us to drive back to the Ariana and rendezvous with the 10th Mountain troops who were waiting for us to bring them to the bazaar.

After we parked the trucks and dropped off the troops, we went for pizza at the Italian army-run club room near the ISAF HQ.

We were amazed that we'd pulled off the raid—a real "interagency effort," if you wanted to call it that—involving Washington, the FBI, and the DIA. Not that we could talk about it much back at Bagram without our collective HQs coming down on our heads for having decided on our own to go on a dangerous mission without clearance.

We all took our pizza outside into the small garden area without talking. Each of us was still coming down.

"Dave, tell me you at least found a book while you were waiting," I said as I finished my pizza and took a long swig of Coke.

"Nope," he said after taking a bite of his pizza. "Lots of old texts, some real quality stuff, but he would not come down on price. Maybe he'll sell it to me next time."

"Yeah, maybe . . ."

We reassembled the convoy, now with the 10th Mountain troops present, at about 1600 hours in the VIP parking area of the ISAF HQ. One of the British NCOs came over to question what we were doing in "his" parking area.

"Fighting a war," I replied.

"Sir, you should do that somewhere else."

He was right. Perhaps the Bahamas would be a better choice of location for the next war.

After the usual wild ride, we landed back at Bagram. It was quite a trip—in and out without a scratch—into what was Indian Territory, in broad daylight. We wouldn't be able to take any real credit for it because of internal politics, but no one on the team really cared. Lisa would pass the information along to Washington although how it would be used we might never know. But we had accomplished the mission: Extracted critical information that would not normally have been shared, or made available, by the Afghan government.

Now it was time to chill and smoke a stogie or two with Sergeant Kate.

· 11 ·

IED

WHOOOOOOM...

The giant blast washed over us, coming at us through the tires, the firewalls, and the windshields of the convoy I was commanding. We were in the crowded center of Bagram village, within sight of the base.

Shit. An IED.

I could see a mushroom cloud billow up just off to the right of my windshield near the gates of the base.

I grabbed the radio. "Keep going!" I shouted into it. We had to get out of this mess and into Bagram Air Base.

Then again, bedlam had broken out around us. The usual heavy traffic ground to a halt. It was as if the cars suddenly got stuck in cement. Panic-stricken drivers hopped out of vehicles and began running back and forth. As the smoke billowed up, pedestrians dropped their goods and joined them. Bicycles were thrown down in our path. People screamed and pushed, and knocked against our vehicles. No one seemed to know where to go, what to do.

There was no way we could get through this gridlock. I ordered everyone out of their vehicles to set up fields of fire.

We were trapped 300 meters from the gate with no way to move forward or backward—in a perfect kill zone.

Up until that point, it had been a—relatively—quiet day. It was a Friday, and we'd convoyed into Kabul, dropped off the intelligence folks for their operation, and then gone over to Kabul International Airport to drop off John and pick up two new FBI agents who were starting their tour of duty. John's ninety-day tour was done, and it was time for others to take over.

Kabul Airport was originally built by the Soviets in the 1960s when Afghanistan was starting to modernize and actually was attracting thousands of tourists each year. It was heavily bombed by U.S. forces about a month after the 9/11 attacks. The eastern portion of it was now controlled by ISAF, while a smaller section was used for commercial traffic—whatever there was of it in a combat zone. The FBI flew in and out of the third section of the airport, which was controlled by the CIA.

John hopped out of the truck carrying his bags, and we shook hands, not saying much. We'd been through a lot together.

"Well, brother, it's time to go," he said.

"It's been a lot of fun," I said, thinking back on our marathon ████ interrogation of Arash Ghaffari and John's role as enforcer in our raid on the telecommunications center. "If you come back, I hope we can work together again."

John grinned through his beard. "I hope so, too."

I introduced myself to the new FBI guys, Brad Daniels and Kent McMillan. Brad was goateed but with the same broad grin as John, and Kent was thin and wiry, with close-cropped brown hair.

"Welcome," I said. "Who's driving?"

Brad and Kent looked at each other, and Brad gave a small shrug. "Hey," he said. "I'll drive."

"Let's get going," I said.

I had some tasks I wanted to accomplish before we headed back to

Bagram, and it was already midafternoon. We had to get back to Bagram before dark. Besides, the mess hall served Alaskan king crab on Friday nights, and you had to get there early before it got too rubbery.

"Stick with Tony," John told them. "He's going to take good care of you."

With that, he moseyed over to his plane, a two-prop Bombardier that he would fly in to Tashkent in Kurdistan. From Kurdistan, he would fly commercial home.

"I've heard good reports about you," Brad told me, "that you've done a great job helping us out here. I'm looking forward to working with you."

"Same," I said. "You've got some big shoes to fill—literally."

My sense was that Brad was as gung ho as John, although he didn't have the deep experience John had since John was former Special Forces. It would be interesting to see how they performed when they were tested, and, guaranteed, this country would test them. I just didn't know that it would be so soon.

In the convoy, I took the last vehicle. The intelligence personnel took the first vehicle, and I put the two new FBI guys and John Coleman, an FBI agent who had come in with us from Kabul, in the second vehicle since Brad and Kent had the least experience. I figured that if something went wrong, I'd be the guy in back doing command and control.

We headed over to ISAF headquarters to meet up with the intelligence folks. We generally staged our convoys in their VIP parking lot, which annoyed the hell out of them, but what were they doing to do—shoot us?

We stopped briefly at the bazaar on the ISAF grounds in between the Afghan and ISAF checkpoints, where you could buy everything from eighteenth-century muskets to the latest pirated DVDs. Walking around the colorful, noisy event, with its carnival atmosphere, it was easy to forget there was a war on. Nevertheless, I pulled the new FBI agents back to reality with a safety-and-operational-review tactics brief, going over how to drive inside the city and then the driving techniques when we hit the open road. Hit it full blast, I told them. I gave them radios and my handle, which was "Fox." They chose handles for themselves. We also went over emergency reaction drills if a vehicle was hit by an IED.

"We're going to stop first at the Italian PX," I told them. "I need to pick up some cigars." The Italian compound was just north of Kabul, and I had promised cigars to a number of folks, including Kate. Our late-night cigar breaks were continuing, and I certainly didn't want to run out of them. I was still mulling her massage offer, but the opportunity hadn't come up to take her up on it. She was back stateside on home leave, and I wondered what would happen when she got back.

Brad turned out to be a cigar smoker. "This is great," he said, "buying Cubans legally."

From the Italian compound, it was only a five-minute drive over to the Russian tank graveyard, so I took them there. It was kind of a rite of passage for new members of the LTC—a reminder that in our testosterone-fueled combat atmosphere, it was important to stay humble.

It was a stunning sight, especially the first time. The graveyard sat up on a high plain that overlooked Kabul against a backdrop of brown and gray rock mountains. Faded green Soviet vehicles—T-64 and T-72 tanks, BMP armored personnel carriers, BRDM armored cars, and more—were stretched out on a tan, flat plain as far as the eye could see. Row after row of them. The numbers were in the thousands . . . it boggled the mind. Some were obviously shredded from being destroyed in combat, others you had to walk right up to to find the combat damage, but all were dead hulks in fading green paint, rust, and covered, increasingly, with graffiti.

The first time I had visited the graveyard, it looked like a vision from hell. It was a 120-degree day, and the green hulks seemed almost translucent from the heat waves coming off the vehicles. In the backdrop, three dust devils, spread almost equally apart in a steel blue sky, slowly turned above Kabul.

It was no less spooky today.

Many of the tanks had golf-ball-sized holes with the telltale melting marks around them of a direct hit of a shape charge—likely an RPG—that burned through the 10-inch steel and turned the interior of the tank into hot gas and shrapnel. It would have been an ugly way to die.

The Soviets were just one of many empires over the last several hundreds of years that had attempted to occupy Afghanistan and had left in defeat. All that was left were these weapons rotting in the desert. The huge amount of waste stretched out before us was dizzying, and it served as a strong warning to would-be invaders of what could lie ahead.

It was hard to imagine all the wealth the Soviets wasted here, I thought as we roamed around the wreckage, the FBI guys taking pictures. (We also had weapons at the ready; I'd been shot at on a recent trip there.)

The haunting landscape was a stark monument to Soviet misjudgment—a nine-year conflict that killed 14,000 Soviet soldiers and God knows how many Afghans. The Soviets were finally driven out by the Mujahedeen, backed by the United States, Pakistan, Saudi Arabia, and other Muslim nations.

It was a vivid example of the kind of trap that Afghanistan could become—and had become—to great nations that sought to conquer it. To have invested so much energy, resources, and blood for a large, landlocked piece of real estate that, in the end, meant nothing.

The lessons for Americans were all around us. By October, I had been there for almost four months, and had come to realize that Americans needed to maintain a small, agile footprint; to remain above the tribal entanglements and work to show the Afghans the path to a peaceful, prosperous society. We could help them along that path, if they so chose. Or, we could contain them should they choose not to go that route. It was up to them.

We'd already made so many mistakes here. Working with the Muj to expel the Soviets but then looking the other way as, next door,

Pakistan developed its nuclear capability and nurtured groups like the Taliban and other terrorist groups right under our noses. Underfunding pro-Western groups like the Northern Alliance as well as Ahmad Shah Massoud, the "lion of Panjshir," and hyperfunding radical Islamists like Hekmatyar, who would take it upon themselves to shell Kabul after the Russians had left, simply to prove the point that their belief in Mohammed was better than any other Islamic sect. Kinda like if the Baptists one day decided they didn't like the Mormon approach to Jesus Christ and decided to shell Salt Lake City—not acceptable in our Western culture but fully acceptable in Afghanistan's tenth-century take on the world.

This would have to change if there was to be any real progress. We could help shape that change—creating economic incentives and cultural benefits—but it was hugely important that we not become a central component in the change. Or in ten years, we might see a large plain filled with Abrams tanks, Bradley fighting vehicles, and Hummers.

After one last look, we hopped back in our vehicles, took a dusty back road to the New Russian Road, and headed back to Bagram.

I had just let down my guard after the usual tense race into town when the IED went off, and I could see the mushroom cloud. It was a grayish tan billowing cloud rising over the horizon, set against the mountains and a crystal-clear blue sky, over the adobe-style mud huts that made up the village of Bagram. I could see it to my right, out of my window.

Mushroom clouds are never good, I found myself thinking. I could feel the concussion like a force—a wave of some sort.

There was nothing between us and the threat ahead except a lot of hysterical Afghans. We were totally exposed, stuck behind a pileup of Taliban taxis and a truck and hemmed in on either side by the mud huts and shops of Bagram. There were no alleys nearby, but even if there were, there was no way I was going to take the convoy off the main road and trap us in an alleyway—the perfect kill zone.

I thought fast. It was important that we keep the vehicles running and not move too far from them since it's faster to escape by vehicle than on foot. Out of our trucks, we set up a perimeter with overlapping fields of fire to cover 360 degrees. Upfront, the ██████ guys took 90 degrees on either side of the vehicles, as we had rehearsed. The FBI guys took 120 degrees—from the other car back to my vehicle. I got out of the left side of the Toyota and took the remaining area.

We struggled to say focused, surrounded by confusion and hysteria. To maintain concentration, I literally had to take a step outside myself. *This is Tony playing me in a movie*, I told myself. It was a way of detaching to get over the shock of what had just happened. Don't worry. It's just a movie.

Over the noise, I shouted for the DIA guy who had been in my backseat to call the base and tell them an IED had gone off outside the gate and that we were stuck. I heard snatches of what he was saying into the sat phone, giving them our convoy number and asking for help. I glanced over. I didn't like the look on his face. Whatever they told him, it wasn't good news. I started watching the roofline and looking in every window up ahead.

Then I saw them.

Dark, shadowy figures on the roofs and in windows on the left, holding Kalashnikovs. Maybe a dozen. I couldn't tell for sure.

I pointed to the FBI guys to look up. I could see them tilt their heads up and then look back at me, fear dawning.

The gunmen could advance toward us, we couldn't move away from them, and they were too far away for us to take a shot at them. Besides, there was the danger of hitting a civilian.

It was the longest five minutes of my life.

They seemed to lie in wait, biding their time, waiting for us to move closer so they could get a better shot. We were trapped farther down the road in that sea of humanity, and I knew they would realize this shortly and begin moving in our direction. *Where the hell was help?*

In front of me, I saw one of the ██████ guys suddenly stiffen.

Barely visible, two Humvees—machine guns manned and ready and a Mark 19 grenade launcher mounted on top—loomed in the distance, coming out of the Afghan-controlled gates of Bagram. Out of the windows, I could see an MP yelling at the Afghans, getting them out of the way as the vehicles made their way slowly toward us. Drivers looked up, saw what was coming, and jumped into cars and trucks to creep out of their path. Pedestrians retreated to the side. Bicyclists picked up their bikes. Inch by inch, the traffic cleared just enough for the Humvees to make their way through. It was an agonizingly slow trip toward us, as the MPs shouted and waved at the crowd.

I made a circular motion with my finger to my convoy. Mount up! Let's go! They got the message and hopped back in the trucks, M-4s pointing out the windows. We moved forward, weaving over to the right where the traffic was thinner. They finally reached us. One pulled up parallel to me.

"Sir, you guys all right?" a sergeant shouted.

"Fine," I said. "We appreciate you coming out to help us."

"No problem," came the reply. "Anybody behind you?"

"No," I said.

"Good," he said. "We're going to follow you back in."

I looked up. The figures had faded away. What saved us, I realized later, was that the blast had gone off too early and the traffic had compressed so quickly, we hadn't had a chance to move into their kill zone. They screwed up. Otherwise, we would have been dead.

It was time for king crab, and I didn't care how rubbery it would be. Never a dull moment. Never a dull freakin' moment.

• 12 •

AL QAEDA HOTEL

"I'VE got something for you, shipmate."

With a slight grin, Dave was standing, sentinel-like, just outside our HUMINT tent getting printouts off the network printer, as I was passing by.

"I hope it's some of that Starbucks coffee you just got," I joked. Starbucks was the coin of the realm in Bagram. In all of Afghanistan, for that matter. Elixir of the gods compared with the tree bark the military poured. I always donated the Starbucks I got in care packages to Dave's mess—and we all shared in the booty.

"Even better," said Dave, a glint in his eye. "My foreign analyst has found some significant intel you'd be very interested in. She's found a spot where there is real potential. I'd like her to brief you on it."

"Sounds promising," I said. "When?"

"How about right now?" He paused. "There's a spot she's calling the 'Al Qaeda Hotel.'"

Whoa, I thought. *This must be good.*

"Let me grab my mug, and I'll meet you at your tent."

I met Captain Knowles and Dave at his office tent. She had gathered her briefing materials, and the three of us went into the big briefing room of the main tent.

Dave and I sat down, while Captain Knowles put some maps on the table and then positioned herself by our big map of Afghanistan on the wall, which also showed its eastern border area with Pakistan—often called Pakistan's "lawless territories"—and for good reason. The FATA, or Federally Administered Tribal Area, was where bin Laden had escaped to in 2001. It was an area that Pakistani journalist Ahmed Rashid, an expert on the Taliban and al Qaeda, would later call a "multi-layered terrorist cake."

"Based on ████ analysis, we've identified three primary centers of gravity for known and suspected al Qaeda and Taliban operatives in Pakistan," Captain Knowles told us in her flat foreign accent. Attractive, with bright, intelligent eyes, she was a waif-thin brunette who bicycled everywhere in Bagram. More important from our perspective, she was extraordinarily gifted in her intelligence work. ████
██
████████████████████████████████ and I had the distinct impression that most of the ████ at Bagram had figured out by now who I was. The ████ military was a small world.

Captain Knowles pointed at the wall map and moved her hand down. "The three known centers of gravity are Quetta to the south . . ." She moved her hand up slightly. "Wana, here in the center of the Pakistani territories . . ." She pointed farther up. "And Peshawar up here."

I had a feeling this was leading up to something very interesting.

"We have the best intelligence," she said as she turned and gestured toward the map on the table, "on Wana."

I squinted to focus on the very small spot on the map.

"Wana?" I had heard of it, but it never really stood out in the jumble of facts, locations, and events that I had been trying to familiarize myself with since coming to Afghanistan.

Wana, I found in researching it later, was a Pakistani city about twenty miles from the Afghan border and the main town in South Waziristan, the largest of the seven tribal areas in the FATA. South Waziristan was the perfect lair for terrorists—towering mountains, deep forests, steep ravines—and Wana was its administrative capital: a market town with a resident population of about 50,000, and thousands more coming in to do business each day.

"Captain, Dave mentioned something about an 'Al Qaeda Hotel,'" I said to Captain Knowles.

"Absolutely," she said. "Let me show you on the Wana map."

We headed back to the table where she showed us a higher-resolution map of the central city of Wana, including a U-shaped building that she said was used by transients and visitors. ███ They're linked to activities that occurred during Mountain Viper," she told us.

Dave expanded on Captain Knowles's comments. "There are significant indications that they are using Wana to regroup and come back."

"You mean the insurgency," I said as the light went on.

"That is a very unpopular word," Dave said, looking up at Captain Knowles, who was still standing over the map of Wana. *Oh, yeah, right,* I remembered. *We were supposed to be in rebuilding mode. There wasn't supposed to be an insurgency in Afghanistan. Silly me.*

"Yes, we mean an insurgency," said Captain Knowles. "In the case of Wana, there are indications that this is a major command-and-control node that is not simply a terrorist-training facility, but a full-blown military headquarters. It is clear that this location is involved in the Taliban's effort to retake southern Afghanistan."

"All well and good," I said with a tick of impatience, "but what specifically do you believe we can get in this hotel?"

"We believe that a dozen dedicated rooms are being used by the Taliban," she said serenely.

"And we are talking about al Qaeda senior leadership," Dave added.

That was a shock.

"Really?" I said. "What do you mean?"

"Well, nothing we can pin down, but the ████████████ pattern is similar to those we know to occur around known al Qaeda leadership," said Dave.

"You mean there could be Tier 1 HVTs there?"

Dave and Captain Knowles looked at each other. "Precisely," said Captain Knowles.

I looked at Dave. "Why don't we just bomb it when we think one of the al Qaeda guys is visiting?"

He shook his head. "It's a location with a lot of civilians. Attacking it would result in a lot of civilian casualties, plus a degradation of intelligence ██████████████████████████████ ██████████ this target."

I put my hands in my lap, stared down at them, and started to think. "What do you need from us?" I asked him. I looked down at the table and recognized that it was built in the same U-shape as the Al Qaeda Hotel.

"I thought we should partner on this," said Dave. "Can you get some folks in to put eyeballs on the facility? I figured you might have some good ideas based on your previous life on how to enhance our information from the location." I instantly thought of my friend, Lt. Col. Jim Brady, ████████████████, where he was the DIA rep. The initial part of any operation wouldn't be hard because we could do those cross-border intelligence-collection operations, but to do anything "active"—such as raids, renditions, or any other offensive operations—would be a whole different ballgame.

"The first thing we need to do is verify what's going on at Wana," said Dave.

"I'm with you," I said. "How soon do you need this?"

"I'd like to get this started before I leave country in three weeks," Dave said.

"I think we can do that," I said. "But if we're going to do anything to support ██████ operations, we'll need to get Washington started on it immediately."

"Agreed," said Dave. "I can have you talk to Washington directly to lay out what you think we'll need."

He stood up. "Colonel Negro has some thoughts on this, too."

"Have you talked to him specifically about this?" I asked.

"No, not about Wana, but he's talked about doing the night-letter thing." That was where we planned to influence operations to intimidate the Taliban where they lived in Pakistan. Night letters—a centuries-old tradition—had been co-opted by the Taliban into something more sinister. Colonel Negro figured we could return the favor by putting night letters in their safe havens in Pakistan. I had volunteered to be on the first mission in. Night letters are a throwback to earlier centuries. The Taliban posted threatening letters on the village bulletin boards and on doors to intimidate local populations. We wanted to do the very same thing to them: post letters on the doors of Taliban leaders residing in Pakistan threatening them with harm, death, and all manner of bad things if they crossed the border and did anything in Afghanistan.

"I'm aware of the night-letter idea, and I think it's a good one," I said.

"This would be a good location to consider it for."

We finished our coffee. I wondered what kind of amenities the Al Qaeda Hotel offered. Frequent Jihad Stay Points for every visit, maybe.

Captain Knowles gathered up her papers. "I'm going to go back and finish my tasks and leave you to think," she said. She knew we would be talking about matters she couldn't be a part of. While she had a top-secret SCI clearance, we still did not share some intel ██████████████████████ details with her.

"You know that Patrice Sullivan is our desk officer," Dave said after she left. "Patrice used to work for you, didn't she?"

"Yeah, she did, and I spent a lot of time trying to keep her on task," I said. "When she was with Stratus Ivy, she was a constant, though enthusiastic, pain in my ass. She once slugged an FBI special agent in the face during an exercise where she was playing 'terrorist.'"

Dave grinned. "I don't think we would be asking her to do any-thing operationally. We really need her to come up with a good suite of technology for us."

I realized that Dave was thinking two jumps ahead in the chess game, already planning to do an operation.

"I suspect Patrice is still tied into Doug V.," he said. Doug was one of the most brilliant minds in the intelligence community.

"I think you're right about that," I said. "If we limit her to the technology, we should probably be OK. This will mean buying local stuff to use."

"You need money for that?"

"No, we've got enough cash," I said. "I just need to see if I can get Jim to send his crew into there."

"How soon?" Dave asked. He really wanted to get this under way before he left.

"I can see Jim the day after tomorrow at the Ariana, and we can talk about it," I said.

"Can I go with you?" Dave asked.

"Absolutely," I said. I was starting to turn over what I'd heard in my head.

"Then it's a date," Dave said. "You want me to do the convoy clearance or do you want to do it?"

"Why don't you do it and put me down as commander," I said. I wanted to focus. "I'd like to think about this. I think I have a concept."

With that, I returned to the HUMINT tent. I had a lot of work to do.

As I settled in front of my computer in my office, my brain began to wrestle with the concept of exploiting the Al Qaeda Hotel as an intelligence target but, more important, how to reduce its effective-ness as a command and control headquarters—and perhaps even cap-ture a major HVT there.

I wondered how we could best leverage and take advantage of this information. We had broken the back of the Taliban offensive; their attempt to come across the border and engage us militarily had failed.

Nevertheless, the Taliban and al Qaeda were shrewd and ruthless adversaries. They would come back at us, though probably not in a similar fashion.

OK, so we knew that, but rather than waiting to see what they dreamed up in the Al Qaeda Hotel, we needed to launch an intelligent, effective, offensive operation. As George Patton, my hero, said, "In war, the only sure defense is offense, and the efficiency of the offense depends on the warlike souls of those conducting it." That was gospel for me.

The intel that Captain Knowles had brought us gave us a clear advantage. We now knew of a safe haven in Pakistan that was a beehive of activity. The key was how to plan with precision to identify specific HVTs who frequented the hotel and to destroy their ability to resupply, rearm, and recruit. We needed to go there in order to stop them from coming here.

That's when I thought back to the movie *Apocalypse Now* and going up the river.

• 13 •

THE "HEART OF DARKNESS"

I'M a big fan of movies. One of my top ten favorites is *Apocalypse Now*, based on the novel by Joseph Conrad, *Heart of Darkness*. The movie, set in Vietnam, tells the story of Army Capt. Benjamin Willard, played by Martin Sheen, who is sent into the jungle to assassinate Special Forces Col. Walter Kurtz, played by Marlon Brando. Kurtz has gone AWOL and is believed to be insane.

I first saw it in Lisbon and, while I didn't get it as a kid—other than the fact that it was a realistic and visually stunning war movie—it stuck with me.

I got it now.

In the movie, the mood darkens as Willard's boat navigates up the fictional Nung River, and Willard's obsession with Kurtz deepens. The movie chronicles Willard's travel through a surreal world of war and revelation, much like I was finding myself in the middle of Afghanistan. There were a growing number of parallels between the Vietnam War and our efforts in Afghanistan. Scary parallels.

I thought about the stunning stuff the foreign analyst had shown us.

The Al Qaeda Hotel. I thought about Willard's journey up the river and into the "heart of darkness." Maybe we were going to have to do something to get at these guys where they lived; the remote area where Kurtz called his home was as remote as Wana was to us.

Operation Dark Heart. That's what this would be.

Over the next twenty-four hours, I mapped it out: a long-term operation to destabilize the Taliban and al Qaeda and reduce their ability to reconstitute and train. ███████████████████████

███

███ I can't go into too much detail, except to say that we would know everything that was going on there.

I'd learned a lot about the Taliban since being in country. They were vulnerable—and not just militarily. They were focused on reestablishing their extreme form of sharia, or Islamic law, across Afghanistan, but their partners in crime, al Qaeda, had a broader, more global agenda—fighting the United States and its allies and overthrowing Western-friendly regimes in the Middle East.

We could use that against them.

I was typing furiously at this point. We needed to accomplish three goals.

First, enhance the intelligence from the Al Qaeda Hotel in Wana by conducting tactical operations. ███████████████████

███

███████

Second, understand everything going on there in such a detailed way that we could plan bold psychological operations. Exploit the differing ambitions of the Taliban and al Qaeda and their allied terrorist organizations. Sow confusion and hostility among their leaderships by posting anonymous night letters in Pakistani villages known to be Taliban and al Qaeda strongholds. To intimidate and influence them, we needed to move like shadows to disrupt them and make them fear for their own mortal existence. We had to stop seeing their actions through the prism of *our* culture and, instead, view it through *their* eyes, and we had to take it to their level. Turn them against each other. Use their mysticism, their fear of bad omens, their obsession with anything related to Allah, and their profound fear that Allah would be displeased with them—and try to find a way to feed into that. Kill one and then melt away. Kill another, then disappear. The idea was to make them so worried about their own survival in Pakistan that they wouldn't have the time or ability to focus on Afghanistan.

Third, once we had struck fear into their hearts and had gained sufficient intel from the Al Qaeda Hotel, destroy it, and move onto the next known Taliban safe haven. There were two more—one to the north and one to the south. Continue that strategy until there was no longer any viability for al Qaeda or the Taliban to reconstitute or re-arm. We would have achieved "functional defeat."

To do that, however, we had to be willing to do cross-border operations into Pakistan using black special-mission capabilities. The Pakistan government couldn't know about this. Because once the Paks knew, the Taliban would find out. Plus, the Paks were very sensitive about U.S. incursions into their country, and technically we were allowed over the Pak border only if we were in "hot pursuit" of a target.

So we needed to be creative with the authority we did have, and do what was tactically and strategically necessary to keep up our momentum from the victory we had achieved in Mountain Viper.

We had beaten the Taliban in the south before they could retake Kandahar, and we had beaten them badly, but we also knew as long as they had a safe haven they could retreat to in Pakistan, they would regenerate, get stronger, and come back. We had to strike at their heart of darkness. Get them where they live. Take away their security, their ability to plan and conduct operations.

Twenty-four hours later I had a plan. I leaned back in my chair and read it over again.

This just might work. No, it *would* work.

If politics didn't get in the way.

Dave and I headed out on a convoy for Kabul. Once there, the ███████ folks went to do their thing, while Dave and I met Jim Brady ███████████ to discuss the operation and get his buy-in before we went to General Vines and pitched it to him.

I'd known Jim for years. He was the single most effective operator Defense HUMINT had. Jim was a close friend that I had known since my days at INSCOM in the late 1980s. He had been a coconspirator on many of my past black operations—official and unofficial ones. He was very good at getting information out of people and somehow did things that didn't piss off leadership. He got away with shit that I would never get away with.

Also, he was a good friend. The last time I'd seen Jim was on my supposed wedding day three months ago when Rina and I had broken up. He was going to be my best man and had walked into an emotional scene at our house. His magic had worked on me then.

A small room had been set up for the meeting at the ██████. In the hotel's heyday, it was probably the reception area for the second floor of the hotel. High-backed chairs like those in an eighteenth-century English manor were scattered around—a touch of the British colonies that still remained in this wrecked capital. I had spoken to Jim on the phone, pushing a button to get it on the secret level, giving him an idea of what we wanted to talk to him about. He sounded excited about zeroing in on a known center of gravity since they hadn't made much progress on their own, ████████████ but he hadn't heard the details yet.

He was waiting for us. "Hey, brother, good to see you," he said as we came in, and we gave each other a hug. "I like the goatee."

"Your face is like a baby's ass," I told him. "Where is *your* freakin' beard?" With hair slicked back and smooth features, he looked like Alec Baldwin from *The Departed*, where Baldwin played a Boston police captain.

"It always comes out like baby fuzz," he said with a grin.

"Maybe when your testicles drop, the problem will solve itself," I joked.

"Hey, the last time I saw you, your testicles were pretty far up there." He laughed.

"You got me there," I said. "Speaking of testicles, here is Dave Christenson. He is an intelligence officer ███████████████ here in country." Dave shot me an annoyed look as he shook Jim's hand.

"Tony speaks highly of you," Dave told Jim.

"Yeah, well, I know where his desk is in Clarendon. He knows I'll Super Glue everything down if he doesn't say nice things," Jim said.

We each grabbed a chair and gathered in a semicircle.

"We've got a concept I want to talk to you about," I told Jim.

"And I want to talk to you about some things we want to do at Bagram that'll need your approval," he said.

"OK, you first," I said.

"We want to get into the BCP," he said. "We think one of the detainees had access to one of the HVTs we're after ███████████

Since I was head of HUMINT ops in Afghanistan, he had to go through me to get into the BCP.

"I don't hang out there much, but I can get you access," I said. "Whatever you need, we'll get you. What do you have in mind?"

Jim briefed me on a creative concept for gaining intelligence on bad guys. ███ ███ Almost like counterintelligence operations.

I was impressed. It was sound, and it was legal.

"It's great," I said. "I'll get Lisa, our operator there, to get you in."

Favor done. Now it was my turn.

"What do you have for me?" he wanted to know.

I leaned back in my chair, hands on the back of my head, and looked him square in the eyes.

"Operation Dark Heart."

He gave a high-pitched laugh. "Really? Did Jeff Murphy go rogue and create his own army of tribesman? He was going native the last time I saw him."

"Something like that," I said, leaving the joke about Murphy—one of my favorite colonels—alone for now. "You familiar with Wana?"

"My guys have been through it. Not a pleasant place."

"We need to go back there." I briefed him on the intel, then on the concept of operations.

Jim leaned forward, hands on knees, and listened intently. When I finished, he thought for a moment. *Here goes,* I thought. *Our first hurdle.*

"Excellent," he said finally. "We're on board. This'll give us access to the HVTs that we want to get. Even if our specific guys aren't in Wana, it's a promising start to gain insight into their comings and goings."

This was a win-win for both of us. It was a win ▮▮▮▮▮▮▮ because it gave them a path to exchanging information on the HVTs as well as a viable shot at killing or capturing them, and it gave ▮▮▮ ▮▮▮▮▮ a real opportunity to reduce the effectiveness of the safe havens to regenerate forces and plan operations. It got to the very heart of both issues.

Jim promised to dispatch one of his teams within twenty-four hours to do an initial recon of Wana, and he recommended we get together at the Safe House in Kabul for a briefing on what they found and to discuss the way ahead.

"Jim, I'll leave this intel for you to study," Dave said as he handed over a package of paper—copies of the key information.

"Good luck with that." I looked at Dave. "He'll have to learn to read first."

"Hey, there are pictures in there, too," Jim said, leafing through the packet. "I'll figure it out." He suggested that we both brief Randy "Big Red" Hoover on the concept, and I agreed. Hoover was chief of the DIA ▮▮▮▮▮ detachment in Kabul and ran the Safe House there. It also gave us an opportunity to watch cable TV and sleep—at least for one night—in real beds.

Jim dispatched his guy to rent a room in Wana with a visual line of site of the Al Qaeda Hotel. Within ten days, we had a detailed report on the first recon.

This was gonna be a complicated, multifaceted operation. We would be using imagery from the National Imagery and Mapping Agency. ██

██

██

████████

The recon, to determine operational feasibility, would go on for thirty days. So far, it looked good, but we still had to get operational approval ultimately from General Vines, the commander of Joint Task Force 180.

I was drawing on my experience in running a black DoD special-mission unit that involved offensive operations aimed at strategic targets, such as certain countries, as well as transnational targets like al Qaeda. Some of these operations were so sensitive and successful, and the intelligence take so unique, that we could not put it into any database or transmit it electronically. I had briefed CIA Director George Tenet about them. The first time, he was in shock. He looked over at my bosses—Lt. Gen. Pat Hughes, director of DIA, and DIA director for operations Maj. Gen. Bob Harding—and said, "Holy shit. You guys are doing *this*?"

They grinned their asses off. It isn't every day you catch the DCI off guard—in a good way.

Then again, that was all half a world away and many years past.

After our meeting, Randy and a two-vehicle convoy showed up in front ████████. He would take us to the Safe House. Dave and I put on our "Hajji hats"—flat-topped Afghan hats worn by the local men—so we could look, in profile, like any other van loaded with locals.

DIA operators conducted ███████ operations the old-fashioned way. They fanned out over Afghanistan building up Afghan spy networks that provided us with crucial intel on the movements of the Taliban and al Qaeda. They were presided over by Lt. Col. Randy "Big Red" Hoover.

██
██
██
██
██
██
██
██
████████████████████████████

Bill Wilson said he'd gotten word that DIA wanted me kept away from the house. There was always this fear by DIA leadership that I would somehow "take charge" and go off in my own direction if given half a chance. Or something like that. Rich and Randy totally disagreed, and I had an open invitation to visit whenever.

██
██
██
██
██
████████████████

There was a debate over whether the Safe House ███████████ would do the ████████ operation—and how long we could keep this from the CIA, because they couldn't be trusted not to pass the intel along to their sources in Pakistan since the CIA considered the country their personal territory. We were going to do this as a Title 10 operation, which legally did not require CIA coordination, but, as a courtesy, we'd have to notify them at some point. Randy happened to be meeting with station chief Jacob Walker every day.

"I'm going to have trouble keeping this from him," Randy said.

"How much do you think we can get away with without telling him?" I asked him.

"The moment we start coordinating with ███, he's going to find out and ask some hard questions."

"OK, I can keep it under wraps until we get close to execution," I reassured him. "Dave can keep this off CIA's radar."

Because of our success in Mountain Viper, Randy told me, Jacob Walker had done a request to Langley to put all of Defense HUMINT under his control.

"You've got to be kidding me," I said. I could only interpret the move as professional jealousy.

"Nope," he said. "Jacob has sent a request to Langley, arguing that it would present a better integration of in-country collection efforts."

"They haven't been very successful, and I think I know why," Randy said.

"I think it's because they're arrogant and tone deaf," I said, "but do you have specifics?"

██
██
██████████████████

"Tradecraft 101," I said. "What are you telling me?"

"Yeah, that's the way I do business with my team," Jim added.

██
██
██████████████████

Jim and I looked at each other.

"*What?*" I said.

"I kid you not," said Randy. "When Jacob sends his guys out, they go in three trucks—two trucks with security and one truck with case officers. They're more worried about protecting the case officers than they are in getting intel."

"That explains a lot," I said. "Essentially, they want us because we're doing the work and they want the credit."

"That's my view of it," said Randy.

"Have you talked to Padro Vario (DIA director of operations in the United States) about CIA wanting to take over DIA HUMINT operations?"

"Yeah, Padro knows it's coming, but at least he is prepared."

"Well," I said, reaching for a bottle of water, "the way they want to play this, based on the CIA's chumminess with the ISI, we don't want them anywhere around us."

With that, I walked Randy through the basic concept of the operations. ██
██████████████████████ He got it at once. He broke into a big grin and flashed me a thumbs up.

"This is great," he said. "I'm on board. Let me know what we can do." Then he looked at me warningly. "The problem is going to be Peter."

"Well, we can postpone his knowledge of the ████ mission," I said. "He does know that Wana is a location of interest because of the HVTs there, but since this is a ████████ target, we'll just inform him rather than asking permission."

Randy and Jim nodded.

"So we're agreed that Jim has the lead in this mission area," I said.

"Agreed," they said.

"What can we do about the overall border area? We don't know how loyal the Afghan border police are," I said.

"We're working on that," said Randy ██████████████████
██████████████████████████████████████ and that should give us significant insight."

Now that we had Randy's buy-in, we headed back to Bagram to begin preparing for the staff concept briefing for General Vines. He didn't have to approve the operation—yet. He just needed to know about it so we could get started. Approval, assuming we got it, would come later, but I had to brief Colonel Negro first.

Dave and I decided to brief him after the LTC stand-up. After it, the FBI rep, John Hays and Tim Loudermilk, Colonel Negro operations officer, remained, and the CIA rep departed. Dave watched him leave the SCIF to make sure he was gone. Colonel Negro gave us a suspicious look.

"What's up, airborne?" he asked.

"Sir, we have a concept that we gave your staff hard copy on regarding cross-border operations into Pakistan. We need your guidance and approval."

"What ya got?" he said.

Dave and I gave him a forty-five-minute presentation of the concept of the operation, looking over our shoulders periodically to make sure the CIA rep didn't reappear. We detailed the task organization, the timelines, the technology, and the ultimate end-state of Operation Dark Heart.

After, Colonel Negro gave us a big smile, and Dave and I looked at each other in relief. He got it. Colonel Negro sat back. "Have you talked to Colonel Boardman about this?"

"We haven't said a word," I said.

Colonel Negro thought for a second. "Well, General Vines needs to see this, and the sooner the better."

"We agree on that," I said, "but if we take it to Colonel Boardman, he's going to say no. And we don't need the senior intelligence officer becoming a problem in this operation." Boardman liked to hoard information. He considered all intelligence assets in country as belonging to him, and we believed our job was to run operations—to achieve results—not just to collect intelligence.

Colonel Negro glanced over at Tim. "What's General Vines's calendar like for the next two days?"

"I've already checked, and he's got a window of an hour and a half tomorrow. About ten. Right after the J2 briefing."

"Did you check where Colonel Boardman's going to be?" Colonel Negro asked.

"He's scheduled to be in Kabul."

Colonel Negro turned to us. "Can you do the briefing tomorrow?"

"Yeah. Easy," I said. "Dave's folks will brief first on the intel. I'd like to do the concept and content briefing. Sir, can you jump in and request that he give guidance on what to do? I'd appreciate that."

"You got it," Colonel Negro said. He turned to Tim. "Make sure you put this on General Vines's schedule as an LTC briefing, and don't put in any names of the briefers."

We were nervous about the next day's briefing, even though we were only briefing General Vines on the concept of operations, illustrating to him how it fit into his larger mission objective for Afghanistan and obtaining his planning guidance for implementation. It wasn't meant—yet—to get his approval. Eventually, though, he would have to give us a thumbs-up—or a thumbs-down.

In the briefing were Dave Christenson, Tim Loudermilk, John Hays, as well as Captain Knowles, the FBI, and reps to the LTC from ███████ CJSOTF Information Operations. We used the video-conferencing room. It was smaller, but used for the most sensitive briefing because it was the most secure—as secure as you can make a tent.

Major General Vines was no wilting lily. White-haired, slightly balding, but rugged, with keen eyes that seemed to look right through you, he had served in Panama, Operation Desert Storm, and three years in Somalia—not a cupcake posting. Standing near him, you got this feeling of refined aggressiveness. Many military officers aren't comfortable with spooks. They know—and care—little about what we do. They seem to regard it as ungentlemanly or something, and they sure don't like the fact that we're often not in uniform. Yet I had the sense that this didn't bother Vines one damned bit. He had a war to fight—despite what the Pentagon was saying.

He always let you know where he stood and whether he believed you were doing a good job. He had developed a strong reputation as a war-fighting general, one who was more and more at odds with Pentagon leadership, which wanted to move away from the Afghan war to reconstruction operations. Albeit we were presenting him with a concept predicated on the idea that the war was not over and people were still dying—an inconvenient fact for a Washington obsessed with the Iraq war.

We stood up as General Vines came in and he asked us to take our seats. He looked around the room and greeted Colonel Negro in a slight Southern accent; he had been raised in Alabama.

"Juan, what have you got for me?" he asked briskly.

In his typical quiet manner, Colonel Negro laid it out. "We've got a concept of operations that we want to give to you today that will allow us to better conduct leadership-targeting operations while simultaneously supporting the objective of Task Force 180."

"Sounds good. Let's go," said General Vines.

With that, Colonel Negro looked at Dave.

"Sir, the intelligence that's driving this operation was discovered by Captain Mary Knowles, and she will first brief on the intelligence in which she has identified three key centers of operation of al Qaeda and Taliban leadership in Pakistan. She will be followed Major Shaffer with the concept of operations."

For about ten minutes, Captain Knowles laid out for General Vines what she had told us about Wana, pointing it out on a map on the flat panel screen on the wall. He looked up at her. "So this fits with what you have been telling me regarding the creation of multiple safe havens in Pakistan?"

Captain Knowles glanced at Dave, then back at the general, looking for approval to say more. "Yes, general," she said. "While you do not see them here on this map," she said, pointing to locations north and south of Wana, "there are two other major safe havens we now know of—one near Quetta and the other near Peshawar."

General Vines nodded. "Thank you, captain. Great briefing. It enhances my understanding of the target."

We all sat for about thirty seconds as she gathered up her notes and quietly departed. I felt kind of bad for her. She would never know the outcome of her work.

Colonel Negro gave me a brief smile as I began my presentation.

As I stood up, I realized that I was the only person in the room not wearing a uniform, and it worried me for a moment—I hoped that my goatee, Nike golf shirt, and tan tactical pants would not affect the general's view of my briefing.

"General," I began, "as you know, we were successful in integrating multiple intelligence capabilities. ████████████ In addition, this concept has been coordinated with ████████ and its personnel ███████████████████████

General Vines nodded. "You did great work."

"Thank you, sir," I said. Good. He was on board so far. "We'd like to continue that concept in what's called Operation Dark Heart."

Then came the detailed briefing, to which General Vines listened without comment. It took about an hour, each representative giving a short briefing on his specific organization's role in supporting the operation. I gave the task organization—who would be doing what—and pointed out that the CIA was not involved.

Throughout the briefing, I kept glancing at him, trying to gauge his reaction, but he was expressionless. Damn. What if he didn't approve of the concept? Without that, we were dead in the damned water.

After, he stared at us for a moment before speaking. Then he rocked us back in our chairs.

"Gentlemen," he said, "if you want my approval, you've got it."

We stared at him, shocked.

"This is outstanding," he said. "It's the most integrated I've seen you all since I've been in country."

This was way more than we had expected. Not only did he buy into the concept of operations, he'd given us the go-ahead to execute it.

In the midst of my relief, though, there was one aspect I wanted to make sure I was absolutely clear on—the CIA.

"You do understand that we're proposing that this be done without CIA participation," I told the general.

Colonel Negro spoke up. "Sir, with all due respect, we believe we have the legal authority based on current guidelines to conduct operations within cities along the Afghanistan-Pakistan border without CIA coordination."

Here, we were dealing with the division of authority between the CIA and DoD. Since Afghanistan was a war zone, it was covered by Title 10 of the U.S. Code, which governs the armed forces. The area of vagueness came in the fact that we would be conducting operations on the Pakistani side of the border, where the CIA felt it had authority under Title 50 of the U.S. Code, which covers foreign intelligence operations. Having conducted most of my operations over the past ten years in DIA under a combination of both Title 10 and Title 50 authority, I had been involved with the policy debates about what the distinction really meant. We were successful in using Title 10 when necessary. In some cases, we informed the director of Central Intelligence but didn't request concurrence, so I felt comfortable working in this area for General Vines.

"I understand," General Vines said. He moved quickly past that issue. "Let me know when you are ready for implementation. I want updates every thirty days. Got it?"

We all nodded, still slightly in shock.

He gave us a hint of a smile. *I'm pleased*, he seemed to be saying, *but this isn't going to be easy.*

"Anything else for me?" he asked.

We all looked at Colonel Negro, who shook his head no.

General Vines stood up. "Thank you for the briefing. Good job. Drive on."

We all stood up until he left and then collapsed in our seats.

I looked over at Colonel Negro. "Did I hear what I thought I heard?" I said.

Colonel Negro just smiled. "Boardman is going to be very unhappy about this."

"Yes, and so is a certain chief of station when he figures out what is going on," I said.

I looked over at the ████████ rep, a navy lieutenant, and asked him to pass the general's comment along to Jim and to ask him to execute the first part of the mission.

Operation Dark Heart was a go. Soon after that, Kate finally collected on her massage request.

I didn't quite know what to expect. I'd never given a massage in a combat zone before, but I dug out some hand cream scented with lotus flowers that I'd picked up at the ███████████████████ ██████████████████ and figured it would do in place of massage oil.

By some miracle, and some careful planning, the whole DIA crew that I shared a tent with was out to the four winds from Bagram for the day: Ken the debriefer was tied up doing a debriefing for ISAF, Greg had gone forward to the front and was working with Ray Moretti in Kandahar, and Special Ed, Jack, and Chris W. went to visit the Safe House to pick up Chris W.'s new bed.

The Safe House was being upgraded with new beds, and Randy said they'd have a couple extras and wanted to know if we wanted them. I turned him down. I wasn't going to take something unless the whole team could have it.

Chris W. didn't see it that way and decided to bring one back for himself. After all, he was an air force officer, we joked, and not really part of the military. Chris W. enjoyed the Safe House and spent as much time as he could there. You gotta admit, cable TV, real running water, real food made by a chef, and no rockets being fired at random over your head was kinda attractive. So he had taken Special Ed and Jack to the house that day to bring back the twin-sized bed and somehow crowd it into our tent.

The previous night, at about 0200, while sitting side by side and smoking a cigar and chatting, Kate's leg kept gently bumping mine— one of those small flirtations. It was a welcome touch.

I finally could not hold back anymore and leaned over in her direction until my mouth was about two inches from her ear. In not much more than a whisper, I told her that she could collect on her massage after her overnight shift.

"How did you arrange this?" she asked quietly, when I told her about my absent tentmates. She put her hand on my right upper leg and leaned in to whisper into my ear.

With her head still leaning into my body, I whispered back, "I'm the ops officer. I move things around. I was able to move everything at once to create some space."

I could feel the heat of her body as she stayed just inches from mine, the weight of her hand still on my thigh.

I added, "Are you still up for a full body massage, or would you like me to just do your feet?"

I could feel her almost shiver as she took a breath.

"Everything," she answered. I tried not to be obvious as I swallowed hard.

She finished her cigar and pushed off my leg as she got up and put her hand on my shoulder.

"You'd better be good," she murmured.

"I'll try."

So the next morning, I waited in the empty tent for her to come off her shift. Even though it was October and the nights were cool, the morning sun had already warmed up the tent to the comfortable midseventies.

The door opened and in walked Kate. I stood up and, in a split second, that high school awkwardness reduced my age from forty-one to seventeen.

"Hey, how are you?" I asked.

She smiled as she touched her hair with both hands. "Great, and about to get better. Just came from the shower."

She walked over and stood about six inches from me. I didn't move.

She smelled heavenly—like roasted almonds with vanilla—and her black hair was still damp from the shower. She looked me right in the eye.

"How are you?" she said with a wide grin.

"Uh, fine . . ." I mumbled. What a time to lose my ability to come up with glib comebacks.

I put in an audio disk of '80s music. The Psychedelic Furs' "Love My Way" started to play. OK, here we go . . .

The massage soon transitioned into cuddling—and to other things. After it all, I held her, both of us sweating from the exertion and passion, and both of us starting to drift toward sleep.

"Do you ever think of death?" Her question came out of the blue and as not much more than a whisper.

I had thought about death—about how I'd considered suicide when I hit bottom before I joined Alcoholics Anonymous—but had tried to put death out of my mind since my deployment.

"Yes, sometimes."

"What do you think heaven will be like?"

"I don't know." And I didn't. I thought for the moment. "Perhaps it's what we believe it to be. Maybe God allows us to pick our heaven."

"I had never thought of that," Kate said. "That would be nice."

"What do *you* think heaven is?" I asked. I started to stroke her black hair.

"Feeling safe . . ." she said as she faded off into sleep in my arms.

Not able to sleep, but enjoying the energy circulating between us, I lay there and felt her breathing as I held her.

Safe. What a concept.

✦ 14 ✦

ABLE DANGER

THE event that would change my military career started innocuously enough with an announcement by General Bagby at the morning meeting. Members of the 9/11 Commission investigating the September 11 attacks were at Bagram, he said, and if anyone had any information for them, we could meet with them.

Two words immediately leaped to my mind: Able Danger.

I hadn't thought much about it since coming to Afghanistan. To tell you the truth, I hadn't thought about it much for a while. I'd forced myself to stop thinking about it. The frustration was too great.

I approached Colonel Negro after the meeting. "Sir, I have some information that the 9/11 Commission might be interested in. It's about an operation I was working on called Able Danger. I've mentioned aspects of it to you because we used some technical operations there that I'm proposing for Dark Heart. What do you think?"

"Write up a talking points memo, send it to me, and I'll send it along to General Bagby," Negro said. "I'll see what he says to do."

I went back to my office and, in front of the computer, the memories of that operation came flooding back. Christ. We *had* those guys, and we blew it. We all freakin' blew it.

I started typing, bulleting points to talk from if I was asked to brief, to show the 9/11 Commission what we knew more than a year before the attacks: the basic details of ███████████████████ ████████████████████████ the concept of operations and notable details; of Able Danger, and the notable and numerous problems. The commission had to know the whole story—or as much as I could give them in one session.

In 2000, while targeting al Qaeda, our Able Danger task force had discovered two of the three cells that later conducted the 9/11 attacks. Including Mohamed Atta, the lead hijacker.

I figured someone had already clued in the 9/11 Commission since I was not the only one who knew. By my count, ten folks in all of DoD had that information. We—actually, the army—had found evidence of al Qaeda cells operating in the U.S. in 1999 through its data mining program. Within DoD, there was knowledge of al Qaeda operating for the better part of two years before September 11, 2001. We had known, for example, about the threat that al Qaeda posed to U.S. interests based on the 1998 U.S. embassy bombings in Dar es Salaam and Nairobi. I assumed the commissioners were aware of some of that, but I wanted to walk them through the entire operation just in case. It was important for them to learn the whole story—or as much as I could give them in one session.

Able Danger. Where would I start?

Suddenly, I was out of this combat zone in a godforsaken country halfway around the world, and it was 1999 in Tampa, Florida, again.

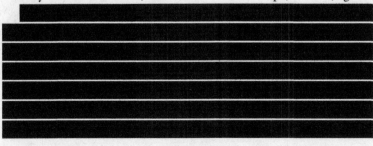

███████████████████ we took cutting-edge, "out-of-the-box" technological concepts and developed them into real intelligence operations. Much of it was so black that we couldn't talk about the existence of the operations on any computer network, even at the top-secret level, so I had to keep a lot of records in hard copy only and work on stand-alone computers. I often briefed higher-ups in person rather than sending an online memo.

I got involved in Able Danger in September 1999, when I was at SOCOM headquarters in Tampa for my annual reserve training. Because of my work on Stratus Ivy, I was brought in to brief Gen. Peter Schoomaker, then SOCOM commander.

Schoomaker, a stout officer with graying short hair, decisive eyes, and a low, deliberate voice, stopped me in the middle of my Power-Point briefing. He asked me a key question about one of the black operations that involved the penetration of a major transnational state. I gave him a key phrase that was code for the exact nature of the capability. Schoomaker got it. "I need you for a special project," he said.

He turned to one of the colonels in the room. "I want you to read Major Shaffer into Able Danger ASAP." He left no room for negotiation. It was a done deal.

The next day, navy Capt. Scott Phillpott, who managed the project, took me to the Special Technical Operations office, presented me with a three-inch-thick briefing book, and said with a big smile, "Here ya go. You're going to like this."

I remember opening the briefing book, starting to read, and then stopping.

Oh my God. This is the A ticket. The ultimate mission.

We were taking the gloves off and going after al Qaeda.

At that point, in 1999, it was clear that al Qaeda was a formidable and deadly opponent. In 1993, a car bomb was detonated below the North Tower of the World Trade Center. The 1,500-pound device was supposed to bring down the towers, but it didn't. Still, it killed six people and injured more than 1,000. According to the narratives of the event that I respect, this was al Qaeda's first decisive, though not entirely successful, strike on U.S. soil.

Then there were the 1998 attacks on the U.S. embassies in Nairobi and Dar es Salaam orchestrated by al Qaeda. Truck bombs killed hundreds of people and injured thousands.

Schoomaker's concept was to bring together the best and the brightest military operators, technicians, planners, and intelligence officers from the army, the DIA, and SOCOM. They would combine cutting-edge technology with traditional human intelligence operations and link both directly into military planning.

It was like bringing the best minds from Apple, Hewlett-Packard, and Microsoft together to focus on a single challenge. The mission here was to discover the global "body" of al Qaeda and, with this information, prepare offensive operations options. Those options could include everything from raids to highly complex psychological operations to manipulate, degrade, and destroy al Qaeda.

In other words, gather the intelligence to kill the largest and most dangerous terrorist operation in the world.

Gen. Hugh Shelton, then chairman of the Joint Chiefs of Staff, had directed that SOCOM have the lead command on Able Danger. This was the first time that SOCOM was the lead command. Usually the regional commands—CENTCOM, EUCOM, SOUTHCOM, or PACOM—would be the lead command with SOCOM supporting their operations, but in this case, the rationale was that al Qaeda was a global transnational threat that didn't have one particular regional focus. It was a huge departure from tradition, however. SOCOM would be telling the regional commands what it needed, not the other way around.

With the approval of the DIA director of operations, Maj. Gen. Bob Harding, I put several folks to work on a herculean effort to try to assist SOCOM in several key areas of its mission.

The first was to map something that had never been mapped before, using a clean-sheet approach in which no existing methodology existed.

My staff coordinated—almost as a concierge for SOCOM—the operational requirements and documents. Our task included getting copies of the large, classified "corporate" databases of DIA and ███—terabytes of data. The patterns found in open-source data would confirm, or be refuted, by comparing them to information and patterns contained in classified databases.

We would follow the data wherever it took us and build a global map of al Qaeda. Since we were not terrorism experts, we had no preconceived notions or bad habits. We were "pure" in our drive.

Still, it wasn't just about the data.

We would find ways to support the military operationally when it started to act against al Qaeda. ████████████████████

████████████████████████████████████
████████████████████████████████████
████████████████████████████████████
████████████████████████
████████████████████████████████████

████████████████████████████ was a key, vetted asset, with solid access to the Taliban and al Qaeda, whom we'd had on the books for years, and he was our ticket into the heart of al Qaeda. Using the knowledge we would amass through Able Danger, ██████

████████████████████████████████████
████████████████████████████████████
████████████████████████████████████
████████████████████████████████████
████████████████

For the first four months of the project, our SOCOM Able Danger team floundered because it lacked operational methodology and usable intel. The "clean sheet" approach was more like a sterile one.

I had used the U.S. Army's Land Information Warfare Activity (LIWA) unit to support two other black operations that Stratus Ivy was running: LIWA had provided key data that had helped us plan operations, and I was impressed with its results. So I recommended to

SOCOM that it look at LIWA and its massive database and data-crunching ability. One of the lead organizations on Able Danger was LIWA, which had begun to adapt to the information age and was considered the army's lead data-mining center. Its idea was to use high-powered software to bore into just about everything: any data that was available—and I mean anything. Open-source Internet data, e-mails believed to be terrorist-related, nonsecret government data, commercial records, information on foreign companies, logs of visitors to mosques obtained from an outside researcher, and much, much more.

Even before moving in to assist Able Danger, LIWA had begun looking at global terrorist infrastructures. Over six months in 1999, it had acquired a vast four-terabyte database and had assembled all these scattered pieces of information about al Qaeda into a comprehensive global picture.

Its researchers did huge sweeps of the Internet and used highly advanced algorithms to compare and amalgamate data. It was a powerful way to link individuals and organizations and make sense of disparate streams of data. It was like Google on steroids.

Within two months, LIWA had produced some impressive results in establishing a global map of al Qaeda using only open-source data. Its model was based on targeting methodology developed by J. D. Smith, an analyst for Orion Scientific Systems (a LIWA contractor), who deconstructed every individual involved in the 1993 World Trade Center bombing into basis data points—the year they were born, their associates, tribal affiliation, mosque memberships, and so on—and built an algorithm. It was then used to examine immense amounts of publicly available data and identify other potential terrorists by comparing them to the original '93 World Trade Center terrorists. As we identified individuals who matched those characteristics, we looked at their associations with other like individuals and started to create a map of a worldwide organization and its direct links with al Qaeda leadership.

In early January, I brought charts produced by LIWA from Fort Belvoir to Able Danger's operations in Tampa. I remember opening them up and laying them down on the table in the conference room located next to Schoomaker's command suite.

"This is what they got for us," I told Scott Phillpott, the operations officer of Able Danger. "They say they can do more of this."

We both looked at the charts, blown away.

They were two-dimensional representations of the large open-source database containing between three and four terabytes of information on known and suspected al Qaeda operatives, enablers, and affiliates. The charts had hundreds of photos (from passports, visas, and other sources) and names (sometimes multiple for one individual). Some photos were grouped on the chart by terrorist affiliation, others by suspected geographic location.

One group was the "Brooklyn cell," as we came to call it: associates of Omar Abdul Rahman, the "blind Sheik," who was serving a life sentence for the 1993 bombing of the World Trade Center.

An al Qaeda cell in the United States.

Scott stared at the chart, transfixed. "This is it," he said. "This is exactly what we need."

We both leaned over it, examining photos of some of the most dangerous people in the world as they stared up at us.

Scott pointed to one in the Brooklyn cell. Thin-lipped, close-cropped hair, a sculpted face. Eyelids pulled partly down over a set of dead eyes. The photo was grainy, but it still captured a sinister feeling.

"That's one scary-looking dude," Scott said.

I remember several names under the photo. One of them was "Atta."

The significance wouldn't become clear to me until much later. At that point, it was just a menacing face set within the Brooklyn cell.

I was just satisfied that Scott was impressed with LIWA's work.

██
██
██
██
██
██ we

were aiming for the electronic records used to track individuals being trained in terrorist tactics.

In my Bagram office, I sat back in my chair, staring at the bulleted points I had made on my computer screen, the memories of that time coming back in waves. The bureaucratic resistance we had faced was positively epic—even for the military.

Senior DIA officers—men and women who never left the air-conditioned environs of the DIA Analysis Center in Clarendon—wanted Able Danger to become exclusively an analytical operation, and there were several attempts to take Able Danger away from us and give it to the director of Intelligence and its Office of Transnational Counterterrorism. They would focus only on the analysis of the data and would rarely produce actionable information.

Other problems persisted. Several agencies treat their intelligence information as if it were proprietary in nature. This was typical of DoD. Intelligence agencies do not like to share their data with the operations side of the organization despite the fact that it is all U.S. government. Senior bureaucrats like to believe the data is exclusive to their command—owned outright. Sharing it might enable some sister organization to be successful. Imagine that. An intelligence service being successful in its mission because it had data from another agency. Cooperation and sharing—even if it resulted in successful identification of threats before they do harm to the United States? Nonsense. That wouldn't be cricket.

In early 2000, after an Able Danger briefing to DIA deputy director Jerry Clark, he told the DIA officers who were at the briefing to drag their feet and slow down the process of providing people and data to our effort. He didn't see the need to "share" DIA's best resources. ███ also refused to provide SOCOM access to its database. My deputy worked her magic and was finally able to convince ███ to give us a copy, which we then sent on to SOCOM.

It got worse. After refusing to provide us with all of DIA's information, DIA finally gave us the data—raw data, everything it had collected—20 terabytes of data on a bowling-ball-sized hard drive known as the Military Intelligence Database (MIDB). However, it came in an unusable format. It appeared that DIA techs had purposely tried to "scramble" it to make it unusable. Fortunately, an experienced programmer on the Able Danger team was able to create an algorithm that corrected the problem.

Behind some of the resistance, in my view, was sheer denial within DoD that al Qaeda was even a threat to the United States. A senior DoD black-operations program manager once told me that I was wasting my time, that al Qaeda wasn't really a danger because the United States was such a lucrative fund-raising center for it through Muslim charities. Its leaders would never be so stupid as to attack us and risk cutting off that funding.

Right.

Later in 2000, a huge roadblock was thrown up—by our own government. Scott called me.

"You will not believe what is going on here."

"What?" I had assumed that things were going well.

"The SOCOM lawyers are telling us there is a whole group of folks we can't look at because they are here legally in the United States or they are affiliated with folks who are here legally. They are 'U.S. persons,' they say."

"That's loony," I said. "Clearly, they're on our radar because they're linked with terrorist organizations. That makes them a valid target."

"I agree with you," said Scott, "but the lawyers won't budge on it."

I broke out President Reagan's Executive Order 12333. It restricted the use and retention of information on U.S. persons for intelligence-collection purposes, but it clearly had an exception for information on individuals suspected of criminal activity, affiliated with, or suspected of being a part of a terrorist organization.

I tried talking to the DIA lawyers, but they didn't want to get involved. This was a SOCOM project and they wouldn't touch the controversy.

On my next trip to Tampa, I saw the chart I had brought them; there were yellow Post-it notes over most of the photographs on the

Brooklyn cell. The SOCOM lawyers had determined they were off-limits to the Able Danger effort. Not to be looked at or evaluated as potential targets.

Shortly after that, the Army got cold feet because of the "U.S. persons" issue, determined that it wasn't in compliance with DoD intelligence oversight policies, and shut down all army support, pulling LIWA out of the project.

Not to be deterred, Schoomaker directed the establishment of a replica of the LIWA technology and the project was revived and expanded.

In the meantime, SOCOM still wasn't allowing any action to be taken on the suspected terrorists with the Post-it Notes on their photographs. I decided that if we couldn't use the data on those individuals, then maybe the FBI could since these guys were operating in the United States. I set up a meeting between SOCOM and the Washington field office of the FBI, where I had some contacts, but, at the last minute, SOCOM canceled it. I tried again—and again. Each time, I would get a call from my baffled FBI friends wanting to know where the hell SOCOM was.

I called Scott. "What's going on?" I asked. "Why aren't you guys showing up for these meetings?"

It turned out, he told me, that SOCOM had been advised by their lawyers not to go. He told me that SOCOM lawyers had forced them not to show up for the FBI meetings because they feared controversy if Able Danger were portrayed as a military operation that had violated the privacy of civilians who were legally in the United States on green cards or valid entry visas.

Never mind that they were freakin' terrorists.

The first week of October 2000, while sorting through data and looking for al Qaeda centers of gravity, a surprising location showed up on the radar: Yemen.

During an update to General Schoomaker, just prior to his retirement, one of the analysts assigned to the project told the general that al Qaeda's activities were the second highest in Yemen. This was

significant. Schoomaker noted it and suggested that the intel be for-
warded to Central Command to make them knowledgeable of the
threat.

The threat information on Yemen was passed to the CENTCOM
representative assigned to Able Danger, but the information was never
passed on, and Lt. Commander Kirk Lippold sailed his ship into the
Port of Aden with no knowledge of what had been discovered about al
Qaeda half a world away in a SCIF in Garland, Texas. On October 12,
2000, he and his crew fought valiantly to save their ship after al-Qaeda
militants in Yemen bombed his destroyer, the USS *Cole*, in a suicide
attack that killed seventeen U.S. servicemen.

After General Schoomaker retired in October 2000, his successor,
air force General Charles Holland, didn't seem to understand the
Able Danger concept. From Schoomaker's retirement on, Able Danger struggled to survive. Holland ordered Able Danger to terminate
its activities sometime in late January 2001, and directed that it become a SOCOM J2/intelligence analysis project. It was rolled into the
Special Operations Joint Intelligence Center and was consumed in the
dark waters of the river of bureaucracy.

Ironically, it was clear that higher-ups wanted projects like this.
When I was with Vice Adm. Tom Wilson, then director of DIA, briefing General Hugh Shelton, chairman of the Joint Chiefs of Staff, in
early 2001 on a parallel clandestine operation, I explained to him that
the Internet tools, techniques, and procedures we were using derived
from Able Danger. Shelton nodded and said he remembered Able Danger and approved our new project immediately.

"The people of this country think we are doing things like this,"
he told us. "We *should* be doing things like this."

Shortly after the meeting with General Shelton, my work with Able
Danger ended. Maj. Gen. Rod Isler came in the winter of 2000 to replace Maj. Gen. Bob Harding who, as deputy director for operations
overseeing Defense HUMINT, was one of Able Danger's few supporters at DIA.

Isler, who didn't want anything to go wrong on his watch, though, was no fan of Able Danger or other projects that I was working on. Every operation Stratus Ivy was running was high risk/high gain—and all too high risk for him. Isler ordered me to "cease all support" to Able Danger.

The old arguments about DIA being more for analysis than operations came up again.

"It's not your job to provide direct support to SOCOM or chase terrorists," Isler told me. By this point, we were practically shouting at each other. "You shouldn't be involved in operations." I was as close to hitting an officer as I had ever been.

"Sir, if we don't do this, who will?" I argued. "The objective of Able Danger is to penetrate al Qaeda leaders to the point where we know what they're doing so well we can prevent attacks. That was the ultimate objective."

"Well, it's not your job," he said.

I was stunned. "Sir, if it's not our job, whose job is it?"

"I don't know," he repeated, "but it's not yours."

I stormed out of his fourteenth floor office in disgust. It was the beginning of the end of Stratus Ivy, and I knew it. Shortly after that, one of his deputies started making preparations to move me to Latin America, where I had no background or interest—anyway, salsa makes me break out in hives.

Then the September 11 attacks happened. It was devastating: To know we were right, and the critics were wrong. . . .

Shortly after that, Eileen Preisser, who had run a good portion of the Information Dominance Center at LIWA, called me to have coffee and told me she had something to show me. Eileen was the brilliant scientist who put together the core technologies at LIWA and had managed the effort that had identified Atta. Over coffee at a bagel shop in Springfield, she showed me one of the charts produced by LIWA back in January 2000 that Scott and I had looked at. She pointed out the Brooklyn cell.

"Look," she said.

I was confused at first. What was I supposed to be looking for?

"Look," she repeated, gesturing to the photographs in the cell.

I was getting annoyed. "What's your point?" I said.

She was even more emphatic. *"Look at the chart,"* she said.

OK. OK, I thought. *I'll look at the chart again.*

It took a while, but I found him. Mohamed Atta. The same sculpted face and strange eyes that had been plastered across every television in America. It was the man I had seen more than a year before when Scott and I had stared down at him in the SOCOM conference room.

Mohamed Atta. Mastermind of the 9/11 attacks. Hijacker in control of American Airlines Flight 11 that was the first plane to strike the World Trade Center.

I had a sinking feeling at the pit of my stomach. We had been on the right track. Hell, we were even on the right *train*. Despite that, because of the bureaucracy, we had been stopped. Otherwise, we might have played a role in stopping the 9/11 attacks.

I asked Eileen what she planned to do with the information.

"I don't know," she said grimly, "but I plan to do something."

I knew she would. She was a woman of action.

On a warm September day, about two weeks after 9/11, I was on my normal afternoon run from the Pentagon to the Lincoln Memorial, when I got a call on my cell from Eileen.

"You'll never guess where I am," she told me. She was sitting in the outer office of Scooter Libby, then assistant to Vice President Cheney, with Rep. Curt Weldon, Rep. Chris Shays, and Rep. Dan Burton. They were going in to brief Steven Hadley, assistant national security adviser to the White House.

I was surprised, but relieved. The Atta information, and our work on Able Danger, was being provided to the right government leadership. I really expected that the Able Danger team might even be reconstituted.

I moved on then. I was confident that the information was in the right hands.

To this day, I don't know who finally pulled the plug on Able

Danger—or why—but I do know that a lot of people were more concerned about their careers and getting that next promotion than they
were about protecting their country. The army and SOCOM were
ahead of their time in doing something about global terror. It was not
a "failure of imagination" that resulted in the 9/11 attacks. It was pure
bureaucratic bumbling and intellectual corruption.

In the end, being right and ahead of our time had gone nowhere.
The people who had failed their country had been promoted and had
moved up the military hierarchy rather than being fired and moved
out.

I stared at my computer. It was time to tell the 9/11 Commission
what I knew. It was the right thing to do. I had gotten an e-mail that
I was on the agenda for the next morning.

Members of the commission and their staff had gathered in the
large command dining hall behind the two-story stucco command
building in the CJTF 180 building and had set themselves up around
folding tables. There were six people when I came in, including General Bagby, all clustered at one end of the table. Some of them didn't
look too interested. Clearly, they were wondering why they'd ended up
in a war zone.

Until this point, I hadn't paid much attention to the commission,
formally known as the National Commission on Terrorist Attacks
Upon the United States. It had set up shop the previous year, in November 2002. Its mandate: "to prepare a full and complete account of
the circumstances surrounding the September 11, 2001, attacks," and
to provide recommendations to safeguard against future attacks. I
had figured that after Eileen had passed the information on Able
Danger to the National Security Council, everything was taken care
of. I was wrong. I didn't know that at the time.

I was part of the first group of witnesses who would talk about pre–
9/11 intel and intelligence failures. Commission executive director
Philip Zelikow—a rather gaunt figure with a long face, glasses, and a
subdued demeanor—greeted us and settled into his seat. I felt kind of

awkward in my golf shirt and baggy pants. This wasn't something I looked forward to, but I just wanted to make sure they knew about Able Danger. It was important.

My turn took about an hour. I followed the bulleted points I'd made on my memo to myself. I outlined everything from ██████████ to General Schoomaker's ordering me into Able Danger to the data mining to the actionable options to be taken against al Qaeda, which we'd outlined in January 2001. That got people's attention.

All listened intently as I walked through my narrative, hitting bullet after bullet, but the kicker came when I mentioned that Able Danger was successful in "discovering two of the three cells that were successful in conducting the 9/11 attacks—to include Atta." There was a shuffling of people in their chairs, and the commission staff appeared to be all of a sudden uncomfortable.

I listed the bureaucratic roadblocks that had been thrown up in front of Able Danger, how LIWA had been pulled from the project, and how I'd tried to alert the FBI to this finding before the 9/11 attacks and how the SOCOM lawyers had shut me down. In the end, I explained how, despite multiple and strenuous attempts to revive it, Able Danger was finally shut down, and its work had been sucked into the gullet of the military bureaucracy.

There was a stunned silence when I was finished. General Bagby finally spoke. "Very compelling report, Major Shaffer," he said.

"Thank you, sir," I replied.

The commission then moved on to the next witness, and I stayed to listen. After the commission stopped for a break, I was getting ready to leave when Zelikow came up to me.

"What you said today is very important," he told me, handing over his business card. "We need to continue this dialogue when you return to the United States. Please contact me when you return so we can continue this discussion."

My next thought was instantaneous. This was going to be trouble. DIA did not like us talking to anyone outside the organization, but this was damned important.

"I'd love to do that, but I'm not back stateside until late December or January," I told him.

"That's fine," he said.

███

██████████████████████████████████

I left the room to go back to work, shoving the whole episode into the back of my mind. I had to go back to the war.

· 15 ·

TIPPING POINT

WINTER had come to Bagram, I had set the briefing to the 9/11 Commission aside, and Operation Dark Heart was now in motion. ████

Just as we started to cook, we were hit by some stunning news one morning late in October. General Vines had been absent from the general's briefing, which was unusual for him. General Bagby announced after the briefing that the general had left the country. A medical issue, General Bagby said. The general had been evacuated out. He was gone.

Wow, what kind of medical condition would cause someone to instantly vanish? Vines didn't strike us as the kind of general who would just up and leave without some kind of thank-you to the troops and staff—especially since the recent battles had gone well.

But just like that, he had vanished.

We found out later it was a medical ailment that was resolved, and he eventually returned to duty. It's funny how often small, seemingly minor twists of fate that appear to have little importance at the moment prove to have huge consequences later. It wasn't until later that I realized this was one for me.

Usually generals leaving a post will overlap their successor by a few days and have a change-of-command ceremony—a tangible transfer of authority and command from one leader to another. If they have to leave quickly, they will at least do a walk-through of the troops, but as far as we knew, even a walk-through hadn't occurred.

We respected and appreciated General Vines. He knew how to fight a war, and he let us do our jobs. He understood how to establish and assign objectives that were clear and achievable.

Plus he didn't buy this Pentagon charade that the war was over and that we were in peacekeeping mode. He realized that battle wasn't over—not by a long shot.

Maybe that was the problem. It was clear that the White House party line was that the war was finished—move along, folks, nothing to see here—and we were supposed to just rebuild the country. OK, so we hadn't gotten bin Laden yet. That was no big deal. He was just around the corner, on his last legs.

Sure.

General Vines knew the score, understood the intel and, in Patton-like style, wanted to take the war to the enemy—to show him no quarter. The Taliban was still there and was a threat to the long-term stability and economic programs that were just then taking root in Afghanistan. General Vines knew that he had to break the back of the counteroffensive before the Taliban could come back and take the country again.

Privately, we assumed, he'd had to push back against Rumsfeld's aggressive effort to turn activities in Afghanistan into a reconstruction-focused, postcombat, "permissive" environment, and to declare that the large-scale combat was over. After all, the focus of the main effort was Iraq. We wouldn't want any bad news to tarnish the brilliant victory achieved in 2001 and 2002 in Afghanistan.

General Vines had been the first top U.S. military commander to publicly confirm the Taliban resurgence out of Pakistan into Afghanistan at the beginning of Mountain Viper. Also Mountain Viper had proven that the war was not over, and that a committed enemy was willing to mount major operations. It would take a leader of General Vines's focus and wisdom to keep up the effort, to aggressively seek to engage the enemy, and to keep him off balance while the civil-military programs could take hold.

We assumed his relief would be cut from the same cloth.

With Vines's departure, that moved up the arrival of Lt. Gen. David Barno who, unlike Vines, would be commander of the combined forces in Afghanistan—the first overall commander of NATO and U.S. forces. (NATO had assumed command of ISAF in mid-August 2003.)

Combined Forces Command (CFC) became headquarters to the two military elements in country—NATO/ISAF and CTJF-180—

which General Barno would command. Brigadier Gen. Lloyd James Austin III arrived within weeks to assume the takeover of CJTF 180.

Eventually, General Barno would need to endorse Operation Dark Heart, but we weren't too worried. Vines had been sold on it, and General Bagby was behind it as well, so we expected General Barno to display the same degree of enthusiasm.

Only a few days after General Barno arrived, one of General Bagby's staff officers summoned us. Grab your armor and weapons and go, he told us. General Bagby wanted us to helo to Kabul with him right then to meet with General Barno. I was asked to brief on the successful use of HUMINT in the recent combat operations. After running to the hooch to grab my body armor, we sprinted from the 180 compound to a waiting Black Hawk, rotors spinning, with General Bagby on board.

I had deposited the slides and notes for my presentation on Dark Heart in an envelope and stuffed them in a pocket of my cargo pants. We were also going to pitch the Dark Heart operational concept on behalf of the Leadership Targeting Cell. Col. John Ritchie, the new 180 senior intelligence officer, would introduce us at the briefing. Bill Wilson had left, and Maj. Chris Medford had assumed the duties of chief of the HUMINT support cell at 180.

General Bagby, Colonel Ritchie, and Colonel Howard were all big supporters of Dark Heart—and all knew what was at stake.

It was a tense ride to Kabul for me. I would rather have taken my chances with IEDs and rocket-propelled grenades in a convoy. I preferred being on the ground than in the air, where surface-to-air missiles could get you in a blinding second. I figured that on the ground, if you survived the initial phase of an ambush, you could still fight. In the air, there was nothing to do but fall helplessly to the ground, strapped into a shredded multimillion-dollar airframe. Nonetheless, in this case, there was no way to say no.

It was only a fifteen-minute flight at 2,000 feet. We flew around the mountain range that we normally drove through and landed in the NATO section of Kabul International Airport. A VIP convoy of up-armored SUVs was waiting to rush us to the American embassy, where General Barno had his temporary headquarters in the Defense attache's office.

I was used to traveling undercover in soft-skinned, civilian vehicles, but we still drove at top speed through the city, this time with sirens blazing. I'll tell ya, I didn't feel any safer in a car with 2,000 pounds of steel plating, even if it meant it was supposed to be impervious to small-arms fire and more survivable if it hit an IED. I felt damned conspicuous, as if we were wearing a big sign reading WE ARE AMERICANS. ATTACK US.

We quickly arrived at the U.S. embassy, which would have barely passed for a midgrade office complex in the United States. It had closed in 1989 during the Taliban's stay, but had reopened in December 2001 after the Taliban had been supposedly cleared out of Kabul.

My thinking was straightforward: The previous general had approved it, and the facts were conclusive and compelling. Today's briefing would give General Barno the basic idea of the mission and maybe he would offer us some expanded guidance.

I knew only a little about General Barno; there hadn't been time to study up on him. He had served in combat as a Ranger company commander in Grenada during Operation Urgent Fury in 1989. He'd commanded a parachute infantry battalion in the 82nd Airborne Division. Most recently, he'd been in Hungary as the commanding General of Task Force Warrior, which was supposed to train Iraqi forces in support of Operation Iraqi Freedom, but he apparently had no experience with dark operations.

He also had no background in Afghanistan. Not that I was any expert—but within a few months of arriving in country, I had known enough to understand that the problem wasn't just in Afghanistan. It was also in Pakistan, and that any long-term solution had to be based on resolving the insurgency in the Pakistani tribal areas and stabilizing Afghanistan. That's what our intelligence was telling us. That was what my gut was telling me.

General Barno was sitting in a chair behind his desk as I entered his office, following General Bagby, Colonel Ritchie, and Colonel Howard. His office was Spartan, with the light of the late afternoon sun spilling into the window, causing the dust in the air to almost glisten.

General Barno was a tall man, probably six foot two—and thin, with sharp features and a flat effect. General Bagby introduced us, and General Barno, wearing a crisp, pressed Desert Camouflage Uniform, moved out from behind the desk to shake our hands. It was a wet-fish handshake. His movements were almost robotic. I thought I sensed a slight grimace of disapproval when he shook hands with Major Howard and me, but I could have been imagining it. We were the only officers in the room not in military uniform, and I always felt a bit self-conscious with my goatee, too.

We all found seats, and General Barno returned to sit behind the desk. "Gentlemen, it is good to meet you all. What will be the focus of this briefing?" he asked.

As we began, General Bagby spoke in glowing terms of the work performed by the Defense HUMINT team in country. I was surprised and impressed at the clarity and detail of the information he presented, all without notes. He had been paying attention. He walked through the Mountain Viper success and the other successes by the Safe House in Kabul and Ray Moretti in Kandahar.

Colonel Ritchie followed, pointing out that while he had only been in country for about a month, he was impressed with the HUMINT effort and that, in addition to the combat operations, Defense HUMINT was playing a key role in the Leadership Targeting Cell effort based at Bagram. Colonel Ritchie explained to General Barno the specific mission of the LTC.

General Barno sat back in his chair, not commenting or asking any questions, but soon after I began my briefing, I sensed trouble. General Barno folded his arms and squinted at us, expressionless. I gave a half-hour review of the intelligence and walked him through Dark Heart, listing significant assets, their access, and placement.

I got the feeling from General Barno's expression—or lack of it—that the information was not resonating. Like when you are talking to your mother-in-law about a great episode of *Saturday Night Live* . . . just not getting through.

I explained about identifying three primary centers of gravity within Pakistan that were serving as the recruiting, training, planning, and command/control locations for the Taliban and al Qaeda recovery. I told him about the ████████████████████ layer of the intelligence driving the operation. The desired operational end state, I briefed him, would mean the reduction of Wana and the destruction of the Al Qaeda Hotel and we would accomplish the mission objectives through its three phases—then go to the next and do the same thing. Wash, rinse, repeat. Through a combination of precision strikes and assassinations, destroy the whole of the Al Qaeda Hotel and create the appearance of tribal rivalries as the source of the violence.

I then sat back, hoping that by some miracle General Barno was a great poker player, and he was holding back his enthusiasm.

There was silence.

"And so, the overall idea is to keep the Taliban off balance—and do so with surgical precision using ███ CJTF 180 ████████ assets. . . ." I added in the awkward quiet.

General Barno finally spoke up.

"I appreciate what you're saying, but I don't agree," he said abruptly. "I don't believe we should be going into Pakistan. What if we get caught?"

I tried to reassure him. "Sir, the chances of that happening are very slight." My temper flared a bit. "We've been doing this for more than a day or two, and we're good at it."

General Barno smiled thinly. "I can't accept that. It's my job to use all the resources available to me. Therefore, I think it's important that the Pakistanis pull their own weight."

John Ritchie and I glanced at each other. *This guy just wasn't getting it.*

I tried to talk him down. "Sir, with all due respect, the Pakistanis aren't pulling their own weight and they're not going to pull their own weight. They're part of the problem."

"How do you know that?" he shot back.

"Because we've caught a female ISI operative participating with the Taliban in a Taliban raid."

"How do you know that?" he persisted.

"Sir?" His question came as a shock. His lack of understanding knocked the wind out of me.

"How do you know she was ISI? What raid are you talking about?"

I told him about the female ISI operative we'd rolled up during the Taliban offensive against one of our outposts in Khowst and that her link to the ISI had been proven through ███████ analysis █ █████████████████ She was now being processed to move to Guantanamo.

He shrugged it off. "Well, I believe that to be an exception. She was probably a rogue."

Ritchie and I glanced at each other again. *Where the hell was he getting this shit from?*

I tried again. "Sir, it's clear from all intel that the Pakistani intelligence service is actively supporting the Taliban."

Ritchie took a turn on the merry-go-round.

"Sir," he said, "what Major Shaffer is telling you is absolutely true. There is clear and compelling evidence—solid intelligence—that the Pakistani Intelligence Service is at best compromised and, at worst, a coconspirator with the Taliban. Operation Dark Heart would probably give us a better picture of what is actually going on between the ISI and the Taliban."

Unbelievably, General Barno shrugged it off. "I don't care. We've got to give the Pakistanis a chance to pull their own weight." His chest seemed to puff up as he sat forward to emphasize his point. "I see myself as a General MacArthur–type of commander. It is my job to use all the capabilities I have as the combined forces chief."

What the hell? MacArthur? What a flippin' ego, I thought.

Then he dropped his bombshell. "Give the Pakistanis the intelligence you've gathered so far. They've got to take action against the Taliban themselves."

I almost fell out of my chair. "Excuse me, sir?"

He enunciated his words more slowly, as if I were a kindergartner using scissors for the first time. "I need you to pass your information to them."

I leaned forward. This guy couldn't be serious. "Sir, this information was obtained through a number of clandestine methods and sources. To provide the Pakistanis with it is to reveal to them sources and capabilities. We can't do that."

"Major Shaffer you need to find a way to do it," he said impatiently. "I don't support the risk you are proposing here to conduct operations in Pakistan."

I wasn't ready to give up yet. "Sir, if we don't do this, there will be a full-blown insurgency within a year. We know from intel that these guys want to come back in and capture whole pieces of Afghanistan. They attempted to do that in their fall offensive, and we were able to prevent them. But they are going to keep coming."

Now General Barno was getting pissed. "Major Shaffer, *I don't care.* I will not support any cross-border operations into Pakistan. You need to understand that. Find a way to pass the intel to the Pakistanis."

There was an uncomfortable silence. We all sat and stared at each other. I was quietly seething and trying to figure a way out of this. *OK, fine, the guy's new. We'll find a way to convince him. I'm not giving up on this.*

Ritchie finally looked around the silent room. "We need to get back to Bagram," he said. I got up gratefully.

"Absolutely." I turned to General Barno, struggling to keep from speaking from between clenched teeth. "Sir, is there anything else?"

"No, gentlemen," he said. "You have my guidance."

This guy was a royal ass.

As we walked out of the room, Colonel Ritchie put his hand on my shoulder. "Tony, stay focused," he said quietly after we'd gotten out of the room. "We can revisit this later and I'll support you. Let it go for now. I give you my word, this isn't over yet. Let me work to try to get his mind changed. We don't want to let it go."

General Barno hadn't been listening to the facts. He had notions that were misguided at best and dangerous at worst.

As we climbed into the up-armored Suburbans to head for Kabul International, Colonel Ritchie told General Bagby that he believed the intel collection should be maintained as long as possible, and that there was no way to easily or quickly pass the intel to the Pakistanis. General Bagby nodded in agreement and suggested we all meet at Bagram within a couple of days to discuss all this.

My mind, however, was still back in the briefing—running the tapes—trying to figure out how I could have adjusted my briefing to be more compelling or clearer in order to convince General Barno of the urgency of Dark Heart.

General Bagby looked at me. "I'm very sorry that General Barno didn't better accept what you had to say."

"Sir, this is really important," I said as he listened in silent sympathy. "We have to find a way to do this."

It was one of the worst times of my life. Déjà vu all over again. Was everything I had done wasted? Had we wasted our freakin' time? In some ways, I felt like I did after the September 11 attacks. Through Able Danger, my team and I had done everything in our power to prevent a disaster, but others had made bad decisions that resulted in our failure to help prevent those attacks. Now, this time again, my team had done everything we could to be successful in identifying the source and location of the hard-core bad guys. Now we were being told to give away the intel we had on them to more bad guys.

Colonel Ritchie gave me a pep talk. Don't give up, he said. We'll get this back on track. Right now, we needed to focus on the new operation he had just been briefed on—to go into the winter mountain safe havens of the enemy. A new task force, Task Force 1099, was coming in to run it. But Colonel Ritchie guaranteed me that we would get back to Dark Heart. We were not going to walk away from it.

I stared out the window, looking at the throngs of people, carts, and bikes, and the shanty buildings as we flew by, wondering what this all would mean for them. Kabul had seen its first real period of stability and relative lack of violence in years, but how long would it last? How long before a determined adversary, with many thousands of followers—radicals who would die for their cause—overwhelmed the 10,000 troops we had in Afghanistan, a country of 25 million people? Tough odds.

There was no way we were turning over our intel to the Pakistanis. No freakin' way.

Then again, I also knew I didn't have much control over the situation.

THE "DEATH STAR"

"HEY, airborne," Colonel Negro said from across the tent as he walked my way. "Someone here I want you to meet." I was writing a dispatch home on one of the LTC's unclassified Internet computers.

It was evening at Bagram. In my report home, I was trying to put the best face on what happened after the General Barno disaster, and the words were just not coming quickly. The Negro interruption was welcome.

He came over with a tall colonel I'd never seen before. Looking up at him, I thought he kinda looked like a military version of Ed McMahon—silvery hair, bulbous nose—but with shrewd eyes and none of the jokiness.

It was Col. Brian Keller, the senior intelligence officer for a top-secret operation ramping up, Task Force 1099, under the command of Maj. Gen. Stanley McChrystal. As Colonel Negro and Colonel Keller explained it, ████████████████████████████████ its replacement, TF 1099 would continue the same black operations mission, but because of a new Washington emphasis on getting the big HVTs (Osama bin

Laden and Saddam Hussein) the task force would operate simultaneously in Afghanistan and Iraq. The goal was: capture or kill both bin Laden and Hussein by the end of spring '04.

In Afghanistan, TF 1099 was beginning to set up for Operation Winter Strike—to go after al Qaeda and HIG leadership, known to have their winter headquarters high in the Hindu Kush Mountains in Afghanistan and, in the process, to hunt down bin Laden. The thinking was to be bold and dynamic, and to go where no other army had been.

They were talking my language.

Colonel Keller and Colonel Negro took seats across from me. They were bringing in all the clandestine big boys, they explained. It included four major, top-secret elements: ████████████████ ██ ████████████ an elite SEAL Team; the CIA Special Activities Division; and the "Night Stalkers," the 160th Special Operations Aviation Regiment, which provides aviation support ████████████ ████

The spearhead of the effort would be the 75th Rangers. Colonel Keller, a Ranger, made that abundantly clear.

Colonel Keller told me he had ideas on how he wanted to use HUMINT to support their forward battle area operations. He wanted to create a "scout" unit—obtaining a number of local indigs to serve as ground guides and scouts. It's something that the U.S. Army has used throughout its history, going back to the U.S. Cavalry in the nineteenth century. It really hadn't been used so far in Afghanistan. We had relied on paid informants who stayed undercover, but now that we were headed into more remote locations, they would need native scouts to lead them through there and work with the indigenous population.

After he completed his overview, I jumped on the opportunity and gave Colonel Keller a two-hour briefing on everything we were doing, including Dark Heart and our focus on Wana. Maybe with a bold new approach, they would take on Dark Heart. I included info on the ISI agent we had captured working with the Taliban as proof that Pakistan had its fingers deep into the conflict.

His focus, however, was elsewhere.

"Tony, you all have been doing great work here," he said. "Juan has filled me in on most of it. However, our focus is going to be the Hindu Kush Mountains for now. Wana may be their command and control center, and it's important for the overall war effort, but our focus is on their winter safe havens in the mountains."

I tried again. "Sir, there are some safe havens in Afghanistan, and they probably feel pretty secure in them based on history. However, now, especially after breaking the back of their fall offensive, the intel indicates that most of the leadership is probably now in Pakistan."

Colonel Keller looked at me and smiled and took a deep breath.

"Yes, we are seeing the same thing, but, for now, it's not an option. Frankly, and this cannot leave the room, McChrystal is trying to get permission to conduct operations on both sides of the border. However, for now, CENTCOM and the Pentagon have told us we have to stay on this side."

Traditionally, from November to the end of February, adversaries of all flavors in Afghanistan called an informal cease-fire. Everybody would retreat to winter headquarters, lick their wounds, and do nothing of an offensive nature during the winter months. This custom went back hundreds, maybe thousands, of years.

When you think about it, it was a pretty asinine custom since your enemy got time to recoup and gather strength, and then could come out swinging come springtime.

In 2002, when our main effort was to use the Afghan Militia Forces (AMF) to battle al Qaeda, there was no need to go into the mountains. At the end of the year, there was a clear victory: We and our Afghan allies had made the Taliban and al Qaeda combat ineffective in Afghanistan. We then pounded them again in Mountain Viper, and their attempt to come across the border and engage us had failed militarily. Now they had re-formed, and it was clear we had to do something.

TF 1099 initial strategy was to try to catch the enemy off

guard by pursuing them into their winter safe havens in the mountains. Maybe they could get bin Laden, al-Zawahiri, and others. At the very least, they had a chance at picking off some of the chief lieutenants and allies. There were indications, for example, that Hekmatyar and his folks were now the outer ring of bin Laden's protection—and therefore, a very worthwhile target. If you could find Hekmatyar, then bin Laden probably wasn't far behind.

Still, it wasn't going to be easy. In Iraq, where 1099 was hunting Saddam Hussein, it was more of a traditional military operation since the country was occupied by more than 130,000 U.S. troops and the guy wasn't very well liked among his people. The hunt for bin Laden and his types would be more of an intelligence mission because they were believed to be hiding out in the mountains—on one side of the border or the other—with help from Muslim radicals and tightly knit tribal communities that had traditionally rebelled against any foreign interference. Even with TF 1099 combat power rolling into town, there would be no more than 12,000 U.S. forces in Afghanistan—a miniscule amount compared to Iraq.

So Keller needed our capacity for HUMINT operations in the mountains. ███████████████████████████████████ He required feet on the ground to track down these guys.

We had people who could help, including a local governor on our payroll whose people could watch the border to see if they escaped over to Pakistan. Keller was excited about this and asked me to organize a meeting between himself, his team, and our Safe House case officers on how we could support Winter Strike.

So I swallowed my disappointment over Dark Heart. Operational concepts tend to cycle in and out of popularity depending on timing and leadership, and I believed that the timing would be right at some point to revisit Dark Heart again after Task Force 1099 had finished with Mountain Strike.

Or so I told myself.

I did a mental salute and chose to drive on. "Whatever you need from us, I'll do everything within my power to support the operation," I told Colonel Keller.

Task Force 1099 began arriving in Afghanistan with a vengeance. It had the best technology, the best weapons, the best people—and plenty of money to burn. I had worked with 1099's parent element for years. ███████████████████████████████████████ As the cutting edge of SOCOM and, in reality, the whole Department of Defense. They were ████████ always ready to jump in and perform the nation's most sensitive, high-risk missions—and had generally done them well.

This capability grew out of the screwups of the 1980 Iranian hostage crisis and the failures at "Desert One"—the staging area that was supposed to be used for an assault into Tehran to liberate the American hostages held there. The debacle at Desert One was attributed to our lack of a standing, well-funded, well-trained, mission-ready, cutting-edge Special Forces unit ready to jump into any crisis anywhere on the planet. ████████████████████ were the answer to that need.

As 1099 started to roll into Bagram, the very fabric of the base changed. It brought almost a surreal energy. At one point, fully loaded C-17 transport aircraft were landing at Bagram every thirty to forty-five minutes, spending about an hour off-loading and screaming rapidly back into the sky again. I could see pallet after pallet of material coming off the C-17s, neatly lined up and filled with enough high-tech gear to run a country.

The number of personnel swelled. While its predecessor unit, ████████ ████████ had been a tight unit of some 200, Task Force 1099 was going to have several hundred more than 2,000.

They set up their initial headquarters in the old ████████████ command center, but only temporarily. As their folks arrived, they tripled the size of the old ████ compound and built row after row of "B-Huts"—plywood buildings that could serve as anything from offices to sleeping quarters. Massive tents went up. As they unpacked and set up, tent after tent was filling with equipment and technology.

Task Force 1099 had brought its A game.

The largest new structure on the compound was its Tactical Operations Center (TOC), warmly referred to by all as the "Death Star." It was a large green domed tent, which looked black in certain light. It was connected to another tent (known as the Joint Planning Area) that was the size of a football field.

You could have staged several Barnum & Bailey circus performances in there—if you brought in enough elephants on those C-17s.

On one end of the Joint Planning Area was the large communications room that housed most of the hardware to drive its cutting-edge ADP (automatic data processing) systems. On the other end—bleachers for briefings and planning sessions. Like fingers from a hand, off-shoot tents ran all along the Joint Planning Area tent. Generally the size of basketball courts, they were designated for single-unit activities—one for an operation center, another for the 75th Ranger's Operations center, another for its current operations, and so on.

These areas weren't hurting for technology, either. Within each one were long desks full of laptops, charts, and flat-screen TVs lining the walls. Back then, those flat screens cost 10 grand a pop. It was impressive although, frankly, I couldn't connect how having the biggest and most flat-panel displays in the whole of Southwest Asia would help to win the war.

Most of the Ranger folks were in uniform but, as a signal of the covert nature of their operation, there were small changes to name tags and no patches of any sort to identify them. Some didn't wear uniforms except when they were in the final planning stages or conducting a raid. Most of the time they dressed like they were preparing for a commercial for Mountain Hardware—guys in great shape wearing the latest in civilian outdoor gear.

All in all, there was a swagger in the steps of most everyone in █, all guys who had volunteered to work at a whole different level and thrived in the most challenging of environments. I had trained with them during peacetime in their secret training areas. ███████ ████████ They train like they fight.

Once you are in ███, at any level, you are expected to perform at the top of your game. There is a whole different level of professionalism and personal accountability. While all soldiers, marines, sailors, and airmen are expected to perform their duty as directed, ████ ██████████, you do so with very little supervision and are expected to show and take initiative. The initiative and personal accountability parts are difficult standards to achieve and maintain, therefore the number of people who are accepted and retained █ ████ is limited. Regular troops are generally focused on "process and regulations"—and that is their job. These folks, at all levels, are taught and encouraged to focus on mission accomplishment over following a set process.

When in doubt, accomplish the damn mission and screw blindly following the process.

The 1099 grand entrance didn't sit well with some organizations that had been working in country for a while. The ████████████ ████████████ Green Berets (army's Special Forces)—were bitching about it because they'd spent months working in remote areas with indigenous populations trying to accomplish the same basic mission. Their perception was that their work was being pushed aside, and their perception was largely correct.

Even so, that's the military. One minute you're in and the next minute you aren't.

I and the other Defense HUMINT folks ended up trying to serve as peacemakers between ██████████████████ It wasn't fun.

I was designated to head the HUMINT Support Detachment (HSD) 1099, which would also mean functioning as a liaison to CJTF 180.

Not that I got rid of my other responsibilities, of course. I was still running convoys for ████████████ and doing what-all for CJTF 180. It just meant grabbing less sleep and depleting the ███ Starbucks stash even more than usual.

I informed Bruce Gains, DIA's operations officer for Afghanistan with oversight and management of the clandestine missions, and others at Clarendon of our intent to support 1099 its mission. There was static. I would have expected nothing less.

Two primary teams would support Winter Strike. I wrote two separate Concepts of Operation (CONOP) for our support to 1099. CONOPs, which are the architecture and framework for any given military operation on the battlefield—the equivalent of a business plan in the corporate world or a script if you're an actor.

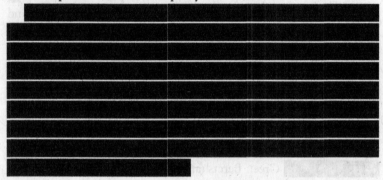

The second CONOP was for Randy and the house. They were both going to focus their existing operations on Winter Strike. Their case officer team would work directly for the Rangers. I would direct them on behalf of Colonel Keller.

While all the supersecret special ops stuff looks cool in the movies, Hollywood never addresses the tons of paperwork and coordination that have to be done. In the real military world, you don't tell everyone to be at the helicopters at dawn, and expect things to just "happen." The reality is more sobering and slow.

As I slogged my way through the CONOPs, I accepted the idea of going into the winter havens. It showed commitment on our part that we would do what was necessary to win. I still felt strongly that to be fully successful, we had to go into Pakistan, but if we couldn't do that, the more we could do to stir things up, the better.

· 17 ·

BRONZE STAR

I was still too busy running operations and supporting the house to steam too long about the General Barno briefing, and with CJTF 1099 rolling into town, my workload was increasing exponentially. However, whenever I had a moment of free time, the tapes would start running of the event, and I'd start to simmer again, wondering if I could have done something or said something differently.

As Task Force 1099 swooped into town, a group of us decided after a long week and a late-afternoon after-action meeting to go to the north dining facility (DFAC) to see if their steamed crab legs were any better than the center DFAC's crab legs. The north DFAC was about a mile walk off the CJTF 180 Compound and, while getting sandblasted by the wind as you walked wasn't fun, it was good for stretching your legs. You'd see soldiers of every nationality—Poles, Koreans, Japanese, Canadians, etc., and all ranks, from private to full colonel—walking along the sides of the road. Everyone getting equally shellacked by the wind and burned under the desert sun.

Colonel Negro suddenly decided to join us. That was unusual.

Most colonels don't comingle with the "simple warriors." They tend to stay together like a pack of elephants. Safety in numbers, I guess, but this time, a bunch of us—Colonel Negro, Maj. Tim Loudermilk, Maj. Chris Medford, FBI agent Ben McFarlane, and I—walked to the north DFAC in the twilight. Once there, Colonel Negro and I went through the mess line last and took seats by the wall facing one another. The fare wasn't bad. Besides king crab legs, there was a good amount of vegetables and fresh fruit. I grabbed an apple and stuffed it into my cargo pants pocket for the midnight shift.

After a loose session of war stories and jokes over dinner, the colonel and I ended up alone at the table when the others went up to get dessert.

He leaned back in his chair, folded his arms across his chest, and looked at me for a minute. "Airborne," he finally said. "I've been impressed with your actions over the past four months. You've redeemed yourself."

"Sir, thank you . . . I think."

"You've done an outstanding job," he told me. "I've never seen a spook do as much as you."

I was surprised. "I'm just trying to do my job, sir," I said, answering honestly. "I'm here to get things done."

There was something about Colonel Negro that inspired you to speak frankly. He had a good bullshit meter. "And," I added, "I'm having the time of my life."

Colonel Negro smiled. "You've really forced me to reassess my view of case officers. In fact, I'm so impressed with you, I'm putting you in for an award. Tim is working on that now."

I was caught off guard. "Thank you, sir." I thought back on my checkered past with DIA. "DIA would never do something like that."

Colonel Negro nodded and smiled again. "I understand," he said, "but it's that very attribute—always pushing to achieve the mission—that I want to see you recognized for."

"Sir," I said, "you don't need to do this. I do appreciate it, don't get me wrong, but your recognition is fine. I just enjoy working for you and supporting the LTC. . . ."

We both looked up. The rest of the troops were returning with ice-cream bars for the colonel and me. As the conversation turned to complaining about the crappy Porta-Johns, I thought about how this was one of those best-of-times, worst-of-times periods.

The bad: Dark Heart, a major initiative of Task Force 180 that we believed would have hit at the core of the Taliban and al Qaeda, had been killed off—at least for the time being. I still hoped, with John Ritchie helping me, that it was just suspended and would be reconsidered later, but right now, it was dead in the water.

The good: working for Colonel Negro and the LTC. And here, Colonel Negro, a commander whom I respected more than just about any other officer I had served under, was looking to reward me for work that I honestly felt was just a part of my job.

I also thought about Kate, another first-class part of my stay in Afghanistan, but one that came with, well, issues and probably an expiration date.

Despite our crazy work schedules, we were managing to spend time together. We stole moments for intimacy. The heavy-duty stuff, yeah—but even the simple stuff, like junior high all over again. Watching movies or sitting in the truck near the flight line, holding hands and listening to the local radio station, with jets taking off and landing. Nothing adds to romance like the smell of burnt JP-4 jet fuel coming off the runway, I guess.

In that harsh environment, it's amazing how the touch of another human takes on greater importance. Also acts of kindness. Once I left the tent at 2:00 A.M. with a killer sinus headache, and she came by to check on me when she came off her shift at 7:00 A.M. I returned the favor by always making sure that she had enough cigars, even when she couldn't make a convoy to get them herself.

By far, she was the best shotgun who rode with me on my convoys. She was fearless, as far as I could tell. Probably because of her rugged

Alaskan upbringing. No matter where she was—on a convoy, on foot in and around Kabul—she was always on top of the situation. I got a kick out of the fierce way she would direct the troops to secure perimeters around a convoy when we had a tire blow (which was fairly often). She didn't take any shit from anyone.

I was drawn to her energy and her enthusiasm. She had become popular with the ██████ team and although I didn't push her in their direction, it was a natural fit. Her ability to keep her cool and think quickly under stress was something that would serve her well if she decided to try and join the ██████ program. I thought she'd make a great HUMINT case officer and offered to write her a letter of recommendation and get her plugged into a recruiter if she wanted.

She wasn't sure. She told me that she had her "own plans" for her life. She never spoke to me about them in specific detail—just general stuff. She was on the road to being promoted to staff sergeant at the very young age of twenty-three and she was thinking about going to Fort Huachuca to become an instructor after she completed her combat tour. The kids coming through the school would have greatly benefited from her knowledge, no doubt about that, but I figured she would get bored quickly and long to be back in the shit within thirty days.

Her only real shortcoming was her youth. She was so damned confident that her life was going to turn out the way she had planned it. I'd been there: promoted young, thinking I knew more than I actually did. So then you have to learn some tough lessons. In fact, if there was anything painful about our relationship, it was to know what she didn't yet realize—that control is an illusion.

That realization comes with age, and we never talked directly about the nearly twenty-year age difference between us. There were glimpses, like when we commented to each other about how fate had put us out of sync by two decades. There was real love between us. She admitted it to me, and I to her. It reminded me of a line from Shakespeare's *Merchant of Venice* that I'd memorized in high school. "For love is blind, and lovers cannot see the pretty follies that themselves commit." I quoted it to her once. She thought it was cute. I knew it was true.

So, with all its pretty follies, the clock was ticking on our romance, even as the autumn turned into winter and our time together kept us warm. We both had other people and other issues in our lives that we'd have to eventually deal with.

I would also learn just how illusory my control over my life really was.

It was the reality of going back to our real lives that was coming into focus. Even more so when it came time for the presentation of the Bronze Star.

It came at Colonel Negro going-away party. His tour of duty was up, but he turned his good-bye party into an awards ceremony. Like most things he touched, he was making sure it wasn't about him but about the team he had put together. He wanted to reward us.

The ceremony was at the small covered outdoor-barbecue area sandwiched between the plywood B hut (we called them Haji Huts since local Afghans built them) that the LTC staff used for its recreation building and the State Department's white trailer that was to serve as President Karzai's secret residence if there was a revolt or coup.

The event was pretty informal. We all stood around eating Sun Chips, Pringles, and well-cooked hamburgers, washing them down with high-quality, German, alcohol-free beer.

"Gentlemen," Tim called out. "It's time for the awards."

While Colonel Negro had told me he had nominated me for the Bronze Star, I didn't know it had been approved. I figured it would eventually be awarded when I got back to Clarendon.

Then he called me forward.

After I came up, I turned to face the group to the right of the colonel. He smiled and nodded at Tim, who read off the citation. Phrases stuck in my mind: "commitment to mission accomplishment in the most extreme circumstance . . . performance in a combat zone." As I stood there, all the things that I'd seen and been part of in the last four months came rushing back: the 105-degree arrival, the combat convoys, the ███████ interrogation, the away missions, the raid on the telecommunications center, the IED and near ambush, Mountain Viper and Dark Heart . . . all rolling around in my head as the words were read. The emotions were raw and settled at the same time. I was grateful to be alive and to be doing what I'd always wanted to do. Everything was happening for a reason. It was a strange dichotomy of being in a crazy situation but also doing what I had been trained to do in the most challenging of operational environments.

As Tim completed reading, I stood at attention as Colonel Negro pinned the medal on the left side of my chest. Medals are always pinned on the left over the heart. The Bronze Star—awarded to service members in combat—was a one-and-a-half-inch star suspended from a red, white, and blue ribbon. On the reverse, it read HEROIC OR MERITORIOUS ACHIEVEMENT along with a place to have my name engraved, although no one I knew got their medals engraved.

██
██
████████████████████████ The text describing my actions that led to the Bronze Star would also have to be sanitized to take out the top-secret info.

Colonel Negro said a few words, telling the group what he'd told me at dinner—that I had restored his faith in spooks and how I had effectively integrated the clandestine HUMINT capabilities into the operations of the command. Then I said a few words, noting that I believed that this war, not the Iraq war, was the real war because this was where 9/11 had started and we had to make sure that another 9/11 didn't come from this region of the world.

"Thanks to all of you for helping me accomplish the missions. My main job is to make you all successful," I told them. I turned to Negro. "And, sir, I appreciate every opportunity you have provided me to fight the war and to serve you and the cell—it's truly been an honor."

There was scattered applause from the group, and I nodded thanks to them.

"Tony, thank you," Negro said and then turned to the group. "OK, let's go finish those hamburgers." With that, the award ceremony was over.

I looked around at the group I'd been working with. This medal ceremony was just a brief pause for me—for us.

I had the feeling that the eye of a hurricane had just passed over.

· 18 ·

MADRASSAH

IT quickly became clear that 1099 was under enormous pressure to produce quick results. Within the first forty-eight hours of its official arrival, even before it had a chance to move into the "Death Star," it was already being pressed to make progress, even though its forces weren't ready. They hadn't even assembled their helicopters. They were still all lined up on the tarmac in large pieces, and the task force was still operating out of ▮▮▮▮▮▮▮▮ old Russian-built structure. Though they were supposed to instantaneously come up with bin Laden.

It was not pleasant to watch.

I had wrapped working in our 180 space and had just sent the final CONOPs off to Clarendon at about 2300, shortly after 1099 hit town. I decided to go over and check in with Colonel Keller to see how their efforts were progressing. It was the last week of October; there was a crispness in the air that comes with autumn, and the moon was just over half full as I walked the quarter mile from the 180 compound to the growing 1099 compound. I showed my badge to one of the Rangers who was pulling guard duty at the outer perimeter. He looked at it with a penlight and waved me through.

I had never seen the █████████ building so full. It was packed with people in constant motion, all scurrying around like ants, with purpose and diligence. I moved through the crowd as if I were invisible to them all, making my way to the Ops Center and a huge 10-foot-by-8-foot display screen that showed the current intel. That night, there was feed from a Predator drone orbiting around a fixed spot of interest.

I stopped for a minute to try to figure out what the hell the Predator was looking at.

Colonel Keller came over. "We've got some information from the CIA that Hekmatyar and his deputies are meeting in this madrassah right now," he said, looking up at the screen, and then turning his gaze back to me. "Can you get someone up there right now to check it out?" He gave me the location.

Jesus. There? Not in a hurry.

"It'll take two to three days to get one of our clandestine teams up there," I said.

Colonel Keller looked unhappy. Clearly, the geography of Afghanistan hadn't sunk in with him yet. "We'd like to get your guys to confirm the meeting. We're uncomfortable with a single source. There is no way to get there tonight?"

"I don't trust single sources, either." I paused for a moment to phrase my words carefully. "Colonel, my best guess is three days," I said, "and I don't recommend you guys do anything against that target at this point because we just don't know. I think we should stand down."

He relented. "I agree. We can't do an air assault. Our assault helos are still being off-loaded from the C-17s. The only option is to bomb it, and I'm not going to recommend that we do that."

"Great," I said. "Let me go over and call the house from my desk at 180. I'll give this to Randy and have him confirm the time it will take to get the guys in there."

Colonel Keller looked relieved. "Let me know tonight what the bottom-line estimate is to get your folks to put eyes on target at this location. And I still need the list of your assets in country."

"Sir, will do. I'll be back at oh two hundred with an update." That was settled. I left to go back to the 180 tent, get the estimate for Keller, and grab a cigar with Kate.

I got Randy on the phone, and we spoke at the secret level about the location. He said he could get one of the Afghan teams there in probably two days. I requested that he start planning to dispatch them, and that I'd be seeing Colonel Keller to get final confirmation to send them.

Other than the constant growl of A-10s and C-130s taking off every twenty minutes, the Bagram night was fairly peaceful. I used a small LED flashlight to avoid obstacles in the pitch-blackness after the moon had set and arrived back at 1099 HQ at about 0200.

They still had the damned drone focused on the madrassah.

I found Keller. "What's going on?" I asked.

"We've been directed to bomb it," he said grimly. "George Tenet got involved. He feels that their information is solid. He called General Abizaid and told him it was solid intel and that he needed to take action on it." (General Abizaid was commander of CENTCOM.)

Colonel Keller looked really pissed. "So we've been directed to do something. I said we could have some people there within two or three days to verify the presence of an HVT. I was told no, that we needed to get going without it."

I looked up at the madrassah. Its time left to exist was now measured in seconds, and I was horrified. Shit. They *were* in a rush—and recklessly so. Why? What if we were wrong?

I stood next to Colonel Keller as the screen suddenly went white with the impact of the precision bombs that had come off a B-1 bomber some 38,000 feet up and many miles away. No sound. The white flash was then followed for about five minutes by white and gray smoke—an optical trick from the infrared sensor seeing the flash. Its aftereffects were limited to a monochromatic palette.

I was stunned. This was some friggin' grand entrance into country.

"Sir, we need to know what was there—if we got the target or not," I said.

Colonel Keller agreed.

"The 10th Mountain can chopper in a sensitive-site exploitation team in there within a day. I'd like to send in the FBI to see what they can get—if that was an actual terrorist command and control node." Again, Keller agreed. Over the next day, I worked to coordinate the team going in, and made sure an FBI agent was included for the site forensics analysis. FBI agent Brad Daniels went in with them.

The team got there about a day later via helicopters since stealth was no longer a requirement. I had asked Brad to call me immediately when they arrived and had loaned him one of our Iridium satellite phones.

Brad reached me after lunch at CJTF 180.

"Brad, what do you have?"

There was a brief silence. That wasn't good.

"Tony, there are no bad guys here. No males at all. Looks like all the victims were women and kids. There is nothing for me to do here . . . nothing."

So much for the CIA's single source.

I instantly thought this was a tribal issue—that someone had gotten smart and played us against them to do their dirty work. Some of these rivalries went back hundreds of years.

We'd been suckered.

Part of my job was to make sure we had the right people at the right place at the right time to conduct operations. I had to try to prevent instances where we didn't have the right folks to gain ground truth—that is, tell us what was really happening. We needed to be more precise in our use of lethal force.

Shortly after, I was called in to a meeting in Brig. Gen. Stanley McChrystal's office with Colonel Keller.

General McChrystal had plenty of experience in Special Operations, most of it classified. I knew he had served as a Ranger in the 1980s and as commander of the 75th Ranger Regiment in the late

1990s. He was an impressive officer. He was lean from an obsessive running habit; a driven workaholic, he operated on just a single meal per day and few hours of sleep per night. His reputation was that of an aggressive, but imaginative, commander.

General McChrystal stood up. "Tony, good to meet you," he said, before immediately launching into the reason for our visit. The guy wasn't much for small talk. "We're doing some new things with the Rangers that have never been done before. I want you to understand that it's very important to me that the Rangers get priority support."

Ordinarily the Rangers, a flexible, highly trained, and rapid light infantry specializing in surprise and stealth, would operate as commandos, sneaking into villages, taking out the bad guys, and moving on. But, General McChrystal said, that approach just intimidated ordinary Afghans and resulted in little actionable intelligence. This time, they were going to go openly from village to village in the Afghan mountains, guided by native scouts, courting elders, establishing relationships, and seeing what intelligence they could draw out that way.

The strategy was to see if they could flush these guys out with the Ranger Recon mission and native scouts, and then send assault teams in to nail them where they tried to move next. General McChrystal wanted to keep the enemy hopping from safe haven to safe haven, with assault teams of Rangers or SEALs ready to either grab them in transit or nail them at their next stop.

A little like jumping in the water and making enough noise that you scare the fish out of their nooks and crannies. You get 'em as they flee the scene.

Plus he wanted my case officers and their locally recruited Afghan scouts embedded with the troops to open doors for the Rangers and get the flow of information going. Our case officers would also run clandestine assets and look to recruit new ones in areas outside of the Rangers' advance of movement. Then info from the indigenous scouts and assets could help the Rangers guide our combat forces into the right targets.

I was kind of skeptical. American commandos being used in a form of outreach? Yet I did understand the concept of stirring up the pot in one place and then jumping ahead to nab the bad guy somewhere else, so I was certainly willing to give it a try. I'd heard good things about General McChrystal.

"Can you work with us on this?" asked General McChrystal.

I looked at General McChrystal and Colonel Keller. "Absolutely." It was clear to me that the Rangers were extremely important to General McChrystal, and our work with them would take precedence.

We got rolling. The Safe House had recruited a source from a province near the Pakistan-Afghan border in the Hindu Kush Mountains. Great guy. Tall (for an Afghan), good humored, talkative, and sneaky. One problem we had faced in recent days was trying to deal with guys who were former Taliban. That fella had not, as far as we could discern, been in their ranks and appeared to have sat out the conflict between the Taliban and the Northern Alliance in the decade-long fighting that broke out after the Russians bailed out of the country. With the help of the rest of the house, it had taken ████████ ██ ████████ He was going to provide great intel on the goings-on in his province and northeastern Afghanistan, but he could also be a nice mobile guide for Winter Strike.

He had been boxed (polygraphed) to make sure he was working our side of the street and had passed, although previous experience told us you could never be 100 percent sure of these guys. He was good for now, but there would be more vetting to come.

His new mission was to lead the Rangers through the mountains and to obtain actionable intel on known and suspected HVTs. We believed—hoped?—that he could help smooth things over as the Rangers moved through the villages to flush the bad guys out so they could be killed or captured . . . hopefully captured. Our source would introduce the Rangers all around and vouch for them.

Our source accepted the mission, a sign that he was either

brave—or dumb—enough to endure some hardship and take some risk in working with us.

I helped set him up and outfit him so he would meld into ██████ ████████████████████████████████ the DIA team of operators who were embedded with the Army Ranger Regimental Recon unit.

The Ranger's senior intelligence officer, Ranger 2, helped me to track down a set of desert camo from the Rangers. The guy seemed to get a real kick out of being given a uniform. He still wore a full black beard, but then again so did two of our case officers who were going forward on the mission. We gave him so much kit he needed a pack, so I loaned him my Army-issued olive drab ALICE (All-purpose Lightweight Individual Carrying Equipment) backpack (which I never got back).

There was a moment of panic when he sat in the convoy to depart from Bagram with the Rangers. We had overlooked one very key, necessary item for him to blend in with the Rangers—otherwise the whole mission would have been in jeopardy: super-cool sunglasses to wear so he could look like the other "operators."

It just so happened I had bought an extra pair of action-guy Bolle sunglasses. I ran the quarter mile to my tent and back to retrieve the brand-new glasses still in the box. Our source beamed like a ten-year-old getting his first BB gun when I handed them to him through the window of the truck that was just moments from departing Bagram.

Granted, even on a cursory examination, he would never pass for American, but in this role and outfit, he would function as a kind of scout for the Americans. He would help make the appropriate contact with village elders in order to get a friendly reception and to clear a path for enhanced intelligence gathering.

He gave me a big grin and a thumbs-up from the truck as he was dispatched with the Ranger Recon on their mission. We'd been tipped that the senior bad guys were hanging out in the villages north of Asadabad, a city of about 50,000 only five miles from the Pakistani border. Remote, mountainous . . . and an easy escape into a welcoming next-door nation. Al-Zawahiri, Hekmatyar—that ilk. Maybe our

warlord, with his connections, could find out what village the bad
guys were hiding in. Then, with these lieutenants in custody, maybe
they could lead us to our top targets.

White Toyota Tacoma 4x4s, loaded with storm troopers, driving
through the mountains struck me as kind of conspicuous, but there
were no other vehicles in the U.S. military inventory that could drive
those pencil-thin, single-lane mountain roads above 12,000 feet. As
the convoy went along, they would fan out through the valleys and
into villages to cover a lot of territory.

Just as we got rolling, the CIA entered the picture, and everything
went sideways.

• 19 •

ABORT MISSION

OUR source spotted them at the Forward Operating Base in Asadabad when he arrived there with the Rangers' Recon unit: two Afghan strangers from a different tribe in native dress from Kabul, hanging around with the Rangers on the base.

He went bat shit.

The CIA had recruited two assets in Kabul who didn't even know the mountains, but never mind that friggin' inconvenient fact. When the Ranger Recon team that our case officers and warlord scout were traveling with stopped at the Ranger Forward Operating Base in Asadabad, we discovered that the CIA scouts had somehow gotten the Ranger combat company there to go with their source of intel instead of our warlord's.

In this country, tribal rivalry trumps everything, and it could be very bad news for this guy if he was recognized by the Afghan CIA assets. They would have shot him. Afghans have made the shoot-first-ask-questions-later cliché into a national creed.

Which meant that the operation, with a qualified scout who knew the mountains, with great local contacts within them, was thrown under the bus so that two Afghan CIA assets, who weren't even from the area, could "lead" the Rangers into the winter safe havens of the senior al Qaeda and HIG leadership that our warlord knew so well.

Hours of phone calls between myself and various Klingons yielded nothing but disingenuous "Gee, Tony, I don't know what happened." Even the CIA rep to 1099 told me he'd been "caught off guard" by the situation.

Yeah, right.

We had to pull our warlord before the CIA's assets ran into him. Although he had seen them, they hadn't spied him—yet—because he stayed at a distance and was in a Ranger uniform. Because of that, he was indistinguishable from the Rangers at a distance. "We have to get our scout out," I told Colonel Keller, "and it has to be immediately."

He looked at me as if I had a third eye growing from my forehead. "We can't. We planned for your guy to guide the Rangers."

"CIA has co-opted the Ranger company you forward-based in Asadabad. They have decided to go with the two scouts the CIA sent forward. Our guy's in trouble."

Colonel Keller was annoyed.

"Have you spoken to the Ranger 2?" he asked. ████████████
██

"Sir, I just came from there," I said. "There is nothing he can do at this point."

"Before you do anything, Tony, let me make a call and get to the bottom of this," he said.

"No problem," I lied. My blood pressure had reached Olympian heights.

Colonel Keller made several calls and finally ended up talking to the Ranger element forward. I was sitting with my feet up on a desk and my chair back on two legs, when Colonel Keller finally looked over at me.

"They want to stick with the CIA assets." He wasn't thrilled. "So there is nothing your guy can do?" Colonel Keller was an intelligence guy, but more of a generalist. He didn't get HUMINT operations very well—the slow and delicate work of burrowing into the human psyche until you unearth vulnerabilities that can be exploited to your advantage. Still he at least realized the warlord needed to be handled carefully. Getting him machine-gunned by a rival tribe during his first week on the job was not good business. Tribal rivalries go back thousands of years, and they are not to be trifled with. "No," I said. "As much as we hate to throw away a week of planning and coordination, there is nothing we can do. We need to protect our warlord's identity from them. He can be used to shut the back door, using his personal army, as the Rangers push through the mountains."

"The old man is not going to like this," Colonel Keller warned, referring to General McChrystal.

"Sir, I understand," I said, "but there is nothing we can do. Your guys have decided to go with the CIA and, unless you overrule them, our guy is out."

It took twenty-four hours, a helicopter, and an extremely cooperative 3rd Army military intelligence captain I borrowed to extract the warlord while we hammered out a new mission.

I wanted to just pull out the whole Defense HUMINT team— three case officers and a debriefer—but Colonel Keller nixed that. They were the main battle effort. The team had to stay with the Ranger Recon unit. It still needed intel.

With no native scout on hand, my DIA team of case officers would have to go into the villages and do it themselves.

Using highly trained, national-level assets in a tactical mission, I knew Clarendon would soon be screaming about it. And, for once, they'd be screaming about the right thing. This was a misuse of resources—eating up the time of four American officers and keeping them from doing what they should be doing, running current assets, and looking to recruit new ones in areas outside of the Rangers' advance of movement. And, most important, our case officers, except for Asad, would have to rely on translators; chatting up the natives would be kinda difficult. I lost the argument, though. The case officers' new mission was hammered out.

Still, someone had to deliver it to them. The team's sat phones couldn't go secure, so I couldn't phone them. I went in to see the Ranger G2. ███████████████. He smirked when I asked him what transport was available to get me up to the front to link up with my guys—the smirk turned to a smile, then to a grin. "We've got an air assault going out in an hour," he said with some irony in his voice. "You're going to be on it."

It was the only way to get to the team. A Ranger assault team had arranged a staging area in the mountains to hook up with the 10th Mountain before sweeping through a village north of Asadabad that the CIA guys had assured them held Hekmatyar's top lieutenants. My team could meet me at the staging area, and I'd give them their new mission and supplies and head off on the air assault.

What a pleasant way to spend an evening: hook up with a few friends, chat about current events, and hope that the snipers were very bad shots in the middle of the night.

Lovely.

Since there was no way back from there, I would have to accompany the Ranger assault team and the 10th Mountain on their assault on the village as they sought to scoop up the bad guys the CIA had assured them were there.

Going into combat for the first time wasn't my favorite option. I was a spook, not a door-kicker. We usually move in and out before the bullets and the bombs have a chance to go off, but it was the only way to get to the team.

I phoned Mr. Pink, our code name for the forward team leader, and let him know I was on the way with new orders and gave them the arrival time of the assault force at the staging area. They were nearby with the larger Ranger Recon team with which they had traveled onto the mountain and could meet me there. Mr. Pink, however, was disbelieving. He asked me to repeat the last transmission.

"Yeah, you heard me right," I said. "I'll be there in about four hours. Look for me on the LZ. I will be flashing a blue light. Come grab me. We will not have much time to chat. I'll have cash and new mission orders."

Then I kicked it into overdrive.

I had just forty-five minutes before the convoy left for the aircraft. I had already been on the phone to Randy for the better part of the afternoon, and he knew I was going to lose the battle with Colonel Keller, so as soon as I got word of my going on the air assault to link up with the team, I called him and asked him to bring the cash out. Randy had already warmed up the cars, and they were ready to leave the house.

To make it in time, which he did, he had to be doing 100 miles per hour the whole way. He had pulled $10K in cash, in hundreds and twenties, out of the house's safe and stuck it into a black plastic bag just slightly bigger than a bowling ball. The team would use this money as "payments" to loosen lips and buy goodwill from the Afghan villagers. Considering what the average Afghan made in a year, the funds should go a long way. Randy had the foresight to put candy and other sweets into the bag for the team to use with kids. Nice move.

Normally I would have put on a real uniform; I had a DCU assault uniform for us to accompany combat forces into shit like this, but no chance for combat gear this time. This was going to be a come-as-you-are event for me.

Weapons. I already had my 13-round M-11 SIG on my hip. Racing to my tent, I grabbed my M-4 with optics out from under my cot. Randy had given it to me from a special stash of weapons he received for another secret mission. I grabbed a black army issue fleece, Nomex green/gray gloves, along with my body armor and my ammo vest.

Helmet. Where was my helmet? I dug through my stuff. Damn. No sign of it. Soft cap it was . . .

Then it was out of the tent and a dead run to the Ranger tent.

"Where do I go?" I said, wiping sweat off my brow as I approached Ranger 2.

He motioned to a young soldier.

"Sergeant Harold will get you to the vehicle. Go!"

The sergeant walked briskly toward the opposite end of the Death Star complex. I saw Randy and Maj. Chris Medford look at me as I sped by. I couldn't quite make out their expressions. Envy? Fear? Better you than me, brother? A case officer rarely goes off on a real firefight.

"Good luck, Tony," Randy shouted.

"Thanks," I said between breaths, hoping I'd be back to have coffee with them the next morning.

Once outside in the dark, the young sergeant motioned me to a Toyota with the motor already running.

"Sir, you'll be riding out with the regimental commander. Please hop in the back."

Wow . . . Col. James Nixon himself was leading this assault. Pretty cool.

Too bad his intel was probably shit.

I stuffed myself into the back of the 75th Ranger Regiment commander's vehicle. My breathing had just returned to normal when Colonel Nixon walked up to the vehicle and sat down in the front passenger seat.

"Who is in my vehicle with me tonight?" he called back, unable to make out who was sitting behind him.

"Sir. Major Shaffer—DIA—going out to link up with my team forward."

The other NCO said his name and duty, a senior E-7 going on the air assault as a communications guy.

"Great," Colonel Nixon replied. "Let's go," and the driver moved out, leading the convoy of Rangers from the 1099 compound to the airfield.

Soon I was standing in the northern flight line, in the queue to walk out to the designated 47, the giant Chinook chopper used by the Night Stalkers, 160th Special Operations Aviation Regiment (Airborne), the special operations unit of the army that provides aviation support for Special Operations Forces. The Chinooks used by the Night Stalkers were made for night missions, with dual rotors and extra gear and air-refueling capacity. I was informed by one of the 160th's guys there that I was to go on the CSAR—Combat Search and Rescue—for all intents and purposes the medical/first responder chopper.

As I waited, the NCO in charge of the manifestation approached me.

"Maj. Shaffer, sir?"

"Yeah, here," I replied, standing in the thin evening Bagram air. The sky was pitch-black above, with only a few low-level lights throwing highlights on the hangar and choppers.

"Could you do us a favor?"

"Sure, be happy to do so," I said, wondering what favor I could do a bunch of armed commandos getting ready for an air assault.

He wrote the name of a Ranger from the recon unit that had headed out in the Toyotas on the top of a five-pound red plastic container of Folgers coffee in thick, black Magic Marker, and handed me the container. "Can you deliver this to him up front?"

"No problem," I said. It wasn't exactly what I had expected. "But how am I going to find him?"

The NCO just grinned. "Oh, he'll find you."

So, with an M-4 slung across my front, $10,000 cash in one hand, and the coffee in the other, I moved off toward the bird along with everyone else, marching out single file to our respective aircraft.

I was greeted by an air force combat controller, the U.S. Air Force's most highly skilled commandos. "Sir, you will be on our bird. Have you had any medical training?"

"Only what I have gotten from being in the army."

He stopped and spoke into his radio for a second and looked up at me.

"No problem. We may call upon you to help us out should we have a helicopter go down. Are you willing to help?"

"Absolutely," I responded. God. I'd probably kill more guys than I'd save with my army training.

"Stand by here for a second. We need to run you through a drill."

As the other helicopters completed loading, I was walked with the combat controllers through some motions of where they'd want me to be if we had to go down and secure a crash site and assist the survivors. In this situation, rank meant nothing. If you were there, you would help, and you would help in any way you could.

Off we went, with me having the best, and only, seat in the house: a gray folding chair set directly in the center of the chopper, just behind the gunners.

After the flight and the landing, a mystery Ranger approached me out of the dark for the coffee and I met with my pissed-off team— ███ ███████████████████ —and promised to somehow pull them out so they could work with the SEALs. Along with working with the Rangers, we had been developing intelligence to assist a SEAL on an upcoming raid on a suspected ███ senior lieutenant in a village to the north. ████████████████████████████████ ████████████████████████████████ ███████████████ Although they had to get out of this Ranger mission they would need someone ██████████████ who would direct them to the suspected compound containing the ███ senior lieutenant. Then I climbed back aboard the CSAR bird for the next stop: the assault.

We set down just outside the village and moved out of the CSAR, leaving Mr. White, who had accompanied me out of the field when we met there, on the chopper since he hadn't been trained or rehearsed. I left my seat and stepped between the folks—about a dozen—who were now sitting on the floor in the Chinook as I followed one of the CSAR guys out the back, once again into the hot rotor downdraft that made the transition into the below-freezing air more stark.

I assumed I'd be helping the CSAR guys out with something—no words were exchanged—so I followed. Just as we had walked outside of the rotor wash, I could make out in the ambient light a mountain ridge about 200 meters northwest of us, with a village of grayish buildings in four or five chaotic rows embedded in it. The Rangers had gotten there earlier while the CSAR was waiting for me to talk to my team in the field. I couldn't tell if the Rangers were firing; they were in the village. If there were casualties, I assumed they would move them to our landing zone for evacuation.

I had moved halfway up a tan berm that looked to be next to a road. As I did, I could see the steam from my breath as I exhaled with renewed exertion under my body armor.

The CSAR troop was about to say something to me. Then things went into Twilight Zone mode in a hurry.

UNDER FIRE

AGAIN, that distinctive hacking of Kalashnikovs. Bullets whizzed and pinged by us. The sudden violence startled us all. What was going on? I had assumed this was the "safe" side of the village. We had landed here to pick up any wounded Rangers or detainees, out of the line of fire.

I froze, trying to get my bearings, but I was pulled back by one of the combat controllers. "Get down!" he shouted. I fell back, flat on my ass. So much for grace under fire. I could just make out the CSAR team going into a crouch.

Somehow, time seemed to slow down. *Maybe my luck has run out*, I thought. I'd already had a near miss with that ambush in Bagram. I'd been mortared a couple of times. I'd survived dozens of convoys back and forth between Kabul and Bagram, with gun battles and IEDs.

No time to think. I low-crawled up to the top of the berm. The Chinook was behind us maybe 80 meters, apparently below the line of fire coming off a nearby ridge across the road from us. Bullets slammed into the dirt that shielded us—for now. I judged whoever they were to be about 100 meters away. Too close to us for the attack helos still loitering nearby in the air to get a good bead on them without risking hitting us, and the Minnie guns on the 47 behind us did not have the right angle. The Rangers and 10th Mountain were on the other side of the mountain in the village proper, within the rows of buildings that lined the far ridge. I had no freakin' clue of what I was supposed to do. Yeah, I was a soldier deep down inside and more than able to fight, but I wasn't part of the assault team.

"Do you want me to return fire?" I shouted to the nearest CSAR guy.

"Hell, yes!" he shouted back as he fired back toward the target.

I didn't have night goggles, so I tried to catch a glimpse of their muzzle flash and then fire in that general direction, making sure not to hit our guys. There is a difference between the sounds of an AK-47 and an M-16, still, in the heat of battle, it was hard to figure out where the bullets were coming from. So I rose to one knee, keeping low, and aimed at the light on the ridge, getting off two to three rounds every five seconds and ducking back down. I could feel the bullets hitting the dirt in the berm in front of me. Oh, this is friggin' fun, I thought.

The shooting went on until the Rangers had secured the village and were headed in our direction—at least, that was the impression I got from the radio chatter I could pick up on the CSAR guys' headsets when they were close enough to overhear.

One of the combat controllers tapped me on the shoulder and motioned for me to come with him. I could now hear suppressive fire on the far side of the perimeter coming from the Rangers or 10th Mountain guys now moving our way, until everything stopped. There was just this eerie silence. All I could hear was the whoosh of the helicopter blades behind me.

We loaded back into the CSAR. Before I was able to sit down, I would feel the MH-47 lift off with a vengeance. I could understand why. Small-arms fire close in to helicopters is never a good thing, and it was clear that the village was not as secure—or safe—as you'd want for landing helos.

I later learned that there were no HVTs found in the village, and it was never clear who was shooting at us: the Taliban, the HIG, or military-aged men who feared being captured simply because they were at the wrong place at the wrong time.

The bottom line, though: The CIA "scouts" didn't do anything except nearly get us shot. The enemy, if there were any, had gotten away. The "scouts" had given the Rangers inaccurate information on where to set up blocking positions. So the bad guys had escaped toward us, who were on the CSAR.

I was thoroughly pissed off and bone tired as the CSAR began its winding flight to a refuel point.

Since I hadn't been briefed on the flight plan, I didn't know where we were going for refuel until we arrived at the base. So it was even more of a surprise to see we were flying along a river with a long bridge across it. On the bridge were rows of modern electric lights. This was not Afghanistan. It couldn't be. There was no power grid in Afghanistan. We were in Pakistan.

We set down, and they performed a "hot" refueling in which the motors continue to run and the fuel is carefully pumped into the aircraft.

I was beyond freezing at this point. It was a winding three-hour ride back while I fumed. I had to get our guys out of this freakin' disaster of a mission before they got killed. They would be more of use with the SEALs.

I could just make out the first dim light of dawn as the Chinook's tires touched down on the flight line at Bagram. There was no one around, so Mr. White and I had to walk about a mile from the tarmac to the 1099 compound.

We arrived back at Bagram at the crack of dawn, and I went right back to work. Mr. White told me they'd already done a lot of work with the SEAL team, giving me a lot of good information to enhance my argument with Colonel Keller to pull my team out and swing them over to the SEALs' mission.

I also had to talk to General McChrystal and get him to agree to pull our guys out of the Ranger mission.

I started with Colonel Keller. He was not an overly joyful camper.

"The old man isn't going to like this," said Colonel Keller. "He is adamant that the Rangers get all of the support."

"Sir, I understand, but this isn't working," I argued. "If we keep them forward, you would be missing an opportunity to work with the SEALs and go after Hekmatyar and his lieutenants."

Colonel Keller persisted. "General McChrystal is going to want to know what we're going to do and the chances of success."

"I've already talked to the SEALs," I said. "We can't assist them right now because the guys who would direct the team of Afghan assets can't talk to them from out in the field."

"Tony, you heard the old man," Colonel Keller said. "The Rangers are the main effort."

"We have done everything we can to support you and the Rangers," I shot back. "We understand they are the main effort, but the moment the forward Ranger element in Asadabad signed up with the CIA, that screwed it up for everybody. And you saw the failure that came out of that raid on the village based on their information."

Colonel Keller relented on my last point. "All right, Tony, I'm going to let you talk to him. You've got to be very clear on what the value added is going to be to move your case officers over to the SEALs—and he will expect results."

I went back and grabbed Mr. White, telling him he was going to have to spell out in excruciating detail exactly what he could do to help the SEALs in their upcoming raid. Pulling out the rest of the team depended on that. He got it.

Colonel Keller, Mr. White, and I met with General McChrystal in his small and Spartan office that was in a small subtent just off the main floor of the Death Star. As I came in, he and Colonel Keller were talking about the growing IED problem that had already taken out two Rangers.

"We've been able to obtain an EA-6 to start doing counter-IED missions before our guys walk through the valleys," Colonel Keller was telling him. "They should be able to set the things off in advance."

An EA-6 Prowler is a navy electronic warfare aircraft. Since the Taliban were using radio-detonated IEDs, 1099 had been sending an EA-6 flying low and fast over the route of a march, emitting on all known frequencies used by the Taliban. That would detonate the IEDs ahead of the troops. It became a very effective counter IED technique that resulted in no more deaths from IED during the winter operation.

General McChrystal appeared pleased with what Colonel Keller had told him.

"Excellent," he said. "At least *that's* good news."

Then he turned his attention to us and got tight-lipped and tense. I could tell he was already pissed. Combat operations had not netted anything so far, and two Rangers had been killed.

Mr. White was with me, but he did his best to look inconspicuous. I ended up doing all the talking.

"Sir, Maj. Shaffer needs to talk to you about the problem we're having with his guys who are embedded with the Rangers," Colonel Keller said.

General McChrystal looked me square in the eyes. "Major Shaffer, I've already told you that the Rangers are our main effort in the current combat operations. I'm not keen on removing you from the Rangers. You know that."

"I'm fully aware of that, sir," I said. While I'd been the bearer of bad news to general officers more than a dozen times in my career, it never got easier. I knew I had only a few minutes. "But it ain't working." I explained how the CIA had stepped on us and forced us to remove our warlord from the area.

General McChrystal looked even more unhappy. "I don't know why you had to remove him."

He was a tough cookie. "General," I said, "there were two reasons. First, he is a valuable asset—a source with his own militia that can shut the back door on the Taliban trying to leave the battle space in the current operations. We don't want to lose him. Second, sending my guys out to go village to village with the Rangers will not net us any long-term leads or create any goodwill with the local populace. In fact, people are intimidated by the Rangers. No matter how friendly our guys are, or how well they talk to the village elders, there is still this reality that they are with troops who are there to conduct combat operations—to kill people. It's just not a good combination."

General McChrystal was listening carefully. "Major Shaffer, what are you proposing?"

"Sir, I've been talking to the SEAL team, and they're planning a raid on a suspected compound of Hekmatyar in the mountains about 50 klicks from last night's operation, and they are about three days away from execution. If we pull my guys out of the Rangers today, we can get them back to Kabul, have them tasked, and dispatch one of our Afghan asset recon teams ahead of the SEALs to get real-time situational awareness on the target site."

General McChrystal sat back, his arms crossed. "I don't like this," he said bluntly.

His gaze was like steel. "I don't like this at all, but you can pull them out. But I'm telling you, I want to see results."

"Thank you, sir," I said, moving rapidly out of the room, before General McChrystal had a chance to change his mind. Colonel Keller and Mr. White left with me. I was relieved I could keep my word to my team and get them off the Ranger mission, but I knew we had better damn well deliver with the SEALs.

I walked outside the building to get a clear shot to the satellite and called Mr. Pink to give him the good news. He immediately passed the news to the rest of the team. They were relieved as hell. Apparently the day's activities at the front with the Rangers had not gone well. I told them to get to a known landing zone, tell me where it was, and we would get them a helo immediately.

After two hours of coordination and leveraging the folks I knew in the air force element of the 160th Aviation Regiment, the team landed at Bagram just as daylight was fading to the west.

They were grateful I'd pulled it off and got them out of the field. I got them cold water, promised them hot chow, and brought them to the meeting with the SEALs. The idea was to get through the planning meeting and get them back to Kabul, even though it was getting dark, so they could contact their assets and get them moving to the village with the suspected Hekmatyar compound. They needed to have the enemy on target for at least twelve hours.

The targeted village was about 10 kilometers north of the village that was the target of the air assault. The SEALs had ID'd what they believed to be a Hekmatyar senior lieutenant in the village and wanted help to confirm the particular compound where they were staying. The thinking was clear: roll up Hekmatyar's lieutenant, who was thought to be helping protect bin Laden and his inner circle, then the quicker we can get to bin Laden to kill or capture him.

Unlike the Rangers' village-to-village searches, the SEALs had a more covert mission to conduct precision raids on leadership targets. Get in and get out. No hanging around.

We believed that working with the SEALs was a better use of our limited resources. We could get a recon team of Afghan assets into an area, where they could blend in, ahead of the SEALs. We had several teams of tribesmen who could come and go at will. For the SEALs, we had to know exactly what was going on, including which building the bad guys were in, so we didn't nail the wrong house and hit civilians.

I made a quick excursion to the Rangers' tent to make sure there were no hard feelings. No sense pissing off a bunch of commandos. The Rangers' J2 was gracious and said his guys forward had screwed the pooch by committing to work with the CIA, not realizing that he had worked on giving us the mission.

At the SEALs' tent, we went quickly over the operation. We would send one recon team into the village. They would arrive within thirty-six hours and then, within twenty-four hours, the SEALs would pay their visit. We got a handle on the warlord to make sure he was safe and could set up blocking positions north and west of the village to prevent the enemy from escaping. The SEALs wanted me to go on the raid, and even furnished me with one of their tan uniforms, but I felt it was best to be on the ground in Bagram.

At the end of the meeting, we went outside, where night was descending and the wind was blowing in short gusts. To the west, a violet hue glowed as the sun set.

"It's going to be tough to get our guys to that location," Randy said. "It's really bad territory."

"We can do it."

"I think so, but the case officers are new," said Randy, referring to Mr. Pink and Mr. White. "Jim Brady had an excellent rapport with the assets, and the case officers are just learning how to work with them."

"I understand," I said. "You're really going to have to help them."

I went back over to Colonel Keller and told him we were good to go on the SEALs' mission. He emphasized again how the old man was very concerned about pulling us off the Rangers' mission. He said we needed to talk more about how to better support the Rangers next time. I promised to do that after this mission with the SEALs. The only way to fix the situation with the Rangers, I told him, was for him to work with the CIA chief of station to make sure there was a clear delineation of responsibilities.

This damned SEAL mission had better work, or my ass was in a sling. ███████████████████████████████████ "Thanks for getting us out of there. You came through for us."

"It was the right thing to do," I said.

He grinned at me. "It's like you're a Jedi knight. Somehow, you get things done."

"You guys did a hell of a job out there," I said.

Sean slapped me on the back and headed for the truck for the dangerous night convoy back to the Safe House.

I smiled as they drove off into the night. Time for a cigar.

I hadn't slept for two days and was at the outer limit of exhaustion, but I decided I had to go back to the 180 tent and check on e-mail and what had come in from Clarendon. I had not seen Kate or had time for a cigar for nearly three days. I had a sudden longing to see her, even though I was just about asleep in my boots.

She was her usual witty self, and it was a luxury just to sit and be quiet and listen as I pulled on my stogie. I asked her to come out to the Safe House with us for the planning meeting the next day.

"It'll be good to spend time with you."

✦ 21 ✦

"ALPHA TEAM, GO"

IN the SEALs Tactical Operations Center in the Task Force 1099 compound, the assault team was in its final walk-through in real time for its assault on the Hekmatyar compound—as soon as our assets confirmed where it was and whether the right people were present.

On my trip to the house, I'd coordinated the specifics with Mr. Pink and Mr. White, ███████████████████████████████ to support the SEAL assault. And, oh yeah, I'd finally collected a quality massage from Kate and gotten some extended sleep in a real bed. I felt almost human again.

While in Kabul, I detoured the convoy from its route to make a stop at Blue, the Western-style concession store located on the outskirts of the Kabul airport that sold all manner of Western luxuries—everything from Jack Daniel's to the latest PlayStation. It had all the Western luxuries that were forbidden to the devout Muslim, and signs posted in the store said as much.

I had an order to pick up two dozen steaks for the 10th Mountain Intel NCOs. Blue sold the most outstanding, thick-and-juicy Australian T-bones, and everybody would buy them on a regular basis. We would always buy the 10th Mountain Intel NCOs a few more than they ordered to show our appreciation for the help they gave us, and I always liked to pick up some for the ████ folks, who never got the appreciation they deserved.

I had spent thirty-six hours integrating our HUMINT intelligence-collection into the SEALs' planning. I knew if there were any problems with the mission because of us, I'd have to answer for it to General McChrystal.

Mr. Pink, Mr. White, and I had each been issued two sets of SEAL assault uniforms. Unlike the Rangers, the SEALs appeared to have an unlimited supply of kit, and they wanted all of the team—including me and my guys—to wear the same uniform.

At that time the SEALs were in their tan uniforms. They had blood-type markers—black writing on tan with Velcro backing that went on the top left arm. There was no rank insignia, only Velcro-secured patches with two-letter insignia denoting who was doing what on the team similar to those noting blood type on the top of the sleeve.

They'd pulled their weapons out, broken them down, and re-oiled them. Some carried M-4s with scopes and silencers or smaller MP-5s with silencers. A sniper, who would stay on a helo, had an M-14 in case the enemy decided to bolt the compound and he could get a bead on them from up above.

The SEALs were prepped to go in quietly—at first. Choppering in on five MH-6 Little Birds, they would land out of town and proceed in on foot to surprise the enemy. No use coming in accompanied by a brass band and lots of shooting—the bad guys would just escape and melt into the village.

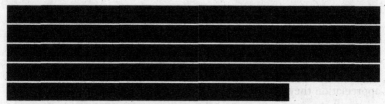

They had located the Hekmatyar compound. A small one—pretty typical—in the midst of about eighteen other compounds in the village. It was a remote burg, in the mountains about 10,000 feet up, where no one in the current war had conducted combat operations. The challenge was to get in—and out—safely.

The question was: Was Hekmatyar himself there? At the very least, we knew that one of his senior lieutenants was.

At 2100, there had been little movement in and out of the house since 1600. Our assets were watching it closely. They didn't know when the assault would go down—we didn't trust them *that* much—but they'd been told to plan to stick around for another twenty-four hours.

"We'd like one last report from your guys before we hit," the SEAL commander told me. "Is that possible?"

"What time do you want the update?" I asked.

"Wheels up at twenty-three hundred hours. We'd like an update while we're in the air," he said.

"Around midnight?" I asked.

"Would be good, but later than that if possible," he said.

"How about oh one hundred or oh two hundred?" I asked. They were expected to hit their target about 0300.

There was already a Predator above, sending down images, and those were appearing on a large screen in the main Tactical Operations Center of the Death Star.

We had maps showing approaches to the village, where the helos would drop off the SEALs. The overwatch helo with the sniper would hang off to the side for the first twenty minutes while the guys made their way to the village on foot.

Start was delayed slightly while they made sure the moon was over the mountains. At 0100, we had our usual global teleconference at the Top Secret/SCI level. Admiral Eric Olson, ████████████ was on, along with the Counterterrorism Center at Langley, ████████ ████ CENTCOM HQs from MacDill Air Force, and Special Operations Command HQs, also at MacDill.

Colonel Keller reported in on our SEAL operation. He noted that DoD HUMINT had provided key information for the planning of the raid. McChrystal shot me a warning look. I smiled. Winking would have been too over the top.

Back at the SEAL TOC, I dialed the house on the Iridium.

"Individuals walking in and out of the house twice during the evening, but none of the targets of interest," Randy told me. Good news. A mass exodus of vehicles would signify they'd gotten wind of something.

"Anything else?" I asked.

"That's the best we can do," said Randy.

"That's all they can ask of us," I responded. I told him to tell his assets to stay put after the raid so they could check out the village chatter.

I signed off with Randy and went back to the TOC and gave the senior intel guy the news. Swallowing cup after cup of coffee, I tried to kill time by talking to Colonel Keller about retooling the scout project. I was also trying to keep my mind off the upcoming raid. Once again, lives were on the line based on our intel. I was confident it was quality stuff, but life can take some left turns at times. I just hoped this moment wasn't one of them.

We were getting updates from a helicopter via the team leader on board.

At 0200, I walked back to the SEAL tent. They had gotten their helos into the valley and expected to have SEALs on the ground about 0220. The challenge was to drop them off close enough so they could get there quickly, but far enough away so that the sound of the helos didn't wake everybody up.

The SEALs would start their walk-in to the village at 0245, and the raid was at 0300. I went back out and called Randy one more time to make sure nothing had changed. Randy said they hadn't called. I took that as positive news. I hoped.

The SEAL recon element was up in the mountains looking down on the compound, setting up blocking positions.

Back at Bagram, in the SEAL HQ tent, there was near silence. The room was filled with a group of men with a great deal of stress on their faces. I decided to move out and leave them be. There was nothing more I could do from here on. The intel was in, the operators were moving into place, so I decided to go into the main TOC and join Colonel Keller to watch the raid.

Just as I moved toward the door, I heard the command.

"Team Alpha, go." The SEAL team leader's voice in the helo came in clear over the radio, over a low, but distinctive, hum. The speaker chirped a couple of times with static.

I decide to loiter to hear the outcome—and hoped it would be good, both for the sake of the HUMINT collection effort and my own ass with McChrystal.

There were multiple transmissions—conversations all going on at once—nothing I could really discern. Then an eerie silence.

Well, that probably meant someone got killed. More undecipherable, overlapping voices, and then another break.

"Clear," came the last call.

The team leader radioed in that they had secured the compound without killing anybody, capturing six individuals. Three were suspected Hekmatyar lieutenants. There seemed to be a collective sigh and smiles all through the room. I started to move toward the door and felt good that we had played some small role in the effort. . . .

"In the wall," we heard.

Just as I moved to go to the door, an excited voice broke in from one of the helicopters.

"They've got a runner. He's now observable."

The runner had taken a back way out of the compound and headed for the mountains.

Somebody had escaped. But who? In the TOC, the intel guys

were starting to formulate questions for the team leader in the helo to get a spot rep on who exactly they had captured.

Who do they think got out? The team leader relayed the question to the guys on the ground.

A few minutes went by, and then we heard the team leader's voice.

"We don't have the target. The prime target is not here."

"The runner," said the SEAL commander in the TOC. "Do you have the runner in your sights?"

"Yeah, we got him," came back the answer. "We see him."

"Can you take him out?"

A brief pause.

"Yeah, he can. He's got a clear shot."

"Is there any chance the ground team can capture him?"

A brief delay.

"No, we don't think so. He's got too much of a lead."

Everyone looked around the room.

"Take him out," said the SEAL commander in the TOC.

"Roger."

A thirty-second delay.

"OK, he's down."

"Is he still alive?"

"Can't tell. We'll have someone to him in less than ten minutes."

The TOC SEAL commander looked pissed.

"What the . . . ? Why is it going to take ten minutes?"

"We're still trying to secure the compound, sir. Give us a minute."

It only took them five minutes to reach the guy.

"OK. We're there."

"What do you got?"

"It's him. It's the guy we were after. He's dead."

"Do you need us to do site exploitation with the FBI team later today?" I asked.

"Stand by," said the SEAL team leader on the helo.

A minute went by.

"Affirmative. If they want to bring the guys out of Jalalabad to do the exploitation, that's fine. We'll maintain security until then. How soon can they be here?"

The commander looked at me.

"Depends on your aviation," I said. "When you guys can get them out there. Let's go talk to Keller."

"Fair enough," he said.

I breathed a sigh of relief. While they hadn't gotten Hekmatyar, they had taken out one of the senior guys and rolled up a couple of junior lieutenants, so at least the change of mission would alleviate General McChrystal's concern about refocusing the resources.

The FBI got to the site by late the next day and found material that provided critical info about additional safe havens relating to Hekmatyar and bin Laden. The problem was, it was all stuff on the Pakistan side of the border.

We were back to *that* again. Pakistan.

"THEY'RE REALLY PISSED AT YOU"

DECEMBER, like a cold banshee from the iciest parts of the surrounding mountains arrived, yet leaving Bagram to go back to the States was bittersweet. Even after extending twice, my six-month tour was now up.

As the days ticked down, I spent long hours running along Disney Boulevard (named after a fallen soldier, Jason Disney, not the amusement-park company). My knee was still swollen and sore from my awkward landing coming off that helo in ▮▮▮, but I needed those runs to clear my head.

As I passed the 1099 compound and the 180 headquarters, I thought about how I would miss this place that I had become so familiar with. Part of me didn't want to leave the Spartan conditions of Bagram because, in some ways, it was so "pure"—as much as chaos and savagery can be pure. Performing my mission in Afghanistan was the culmination of twenty years of training and working. It was the nexus of everything I had been taught and everything I had been born to do. In a way, it had all come together: the right people at the right place at the right time in a desperate battle based sometimes on flawed policy decisions.

Hell, there had even been several times when I was the happiest I'd ever been in my life and, at those times, there was not a place on the planet where I would rather have been. I was doing service for the people I worked with. I believed that when they asked me to get a mission accomplished, I did it. I wasn't seeking glory or fame; I just wanted to get my freakin' job done.

I believed there was a clear path forward to victory. It wasn't out of arrogance but out of clarity. Anyone could have seen it. I wanted to grab bin Laden, and I believed we could if we were allowed to do cross-border operations. I wasn't the only one who thought that. Back at the 180 HQ, I briefed Colonel Ritchie, on my departure.

"Do you have to go?" he asked.

"I don't want to, but I have to," I said. "This was originally a ninety-day tour, and I've already extended twice. If I could stay, I would, but it's programmed in." My replacement was already in the cue and set to arrive.

"I'd like you to come back as soon as possible," he said.

"I'll ask," I told him.

In a message that day to Bruce Gains, the desk officer for Afghanistan for Defense intelligence, I told him I'd like to return and asked him what he thought. I liked Bruce. He could stay calm and make decisions when things went haywire, and he had an encyclopedic memory. Bruce told me he also wanted me to go back and that his boss, Col. Greg, Bruce also thought it best that I return.

I ran convoys right up until I left. I figured if the bad guys hadn't gotten me yet, well, they might get me, but I'd take my chances. I worked with 1099 on its upcoming spring mission, Operation Shadow Matrix. I think the command recognized that its tools and techniques needed to be refined. Winter Strike had routed the enemy out of their winter havens, but it appeared many who hadn't already fled to Pakistan had done so this winter.

Everyone needed to take a step back and rethink the tactics. I agreed to think about the scout program and how to better use indigenous Afghan scouts in the upcoming operation.

I also was asked by my boss, Bill Wilson, to try to capture the methodology that we had either stumbled on, or figured out, for integrating intelligence capability into combat operations. General Lloyd Austin, new commander of 180, had sent a note of appreciation to Defense HUMINT congratulating us on the success of the integration effort. I knew that would piss off DIA because the top bureaucracy didn't want to see me succeed.

The going-away party for me was subdued—just a small cookout with what remained of the group I had worked with. Brad borrowed the CIA tent, and there was a band playing that night from the USO—Varicose and His Itchy Veins or something like that. We all stood around and yapped. I had a nonalcoholic beer, while the others in the group, the nonmilitary types, shared a bottle of wine.

The LTC had been dismantled because of fights between the senior intelligence officer and the senior operations officer of Task Force 180. It had been reduced to nothing more than a small cell of analysts that would put together very detailed, very lengthy reports that would be received with enthusiasm by senior leadership, who would pick it up once, look at the cover, and put it down, never to pick it up again. The information would be useless to anyone since it would not be timely or actionable.

The original team that I served with from summer to early winter—Colonel Negro, Dave Christenson, John Kirkland, Tim Loudermilk, Bill Wilson, Lisa Werman, and John Hayes—had departed. Although in some cases, the replacements were outstanding, a more conventional, conservative thinking was taking hold. There was a return to a more conventional approach—nothing cross border—that focused on securing locations rather than going after the enemy. Essentially, it was a defensive, rather than an offensive, posture.

Aside from the challenges I was leaving behind in Afghanistan, I had some upcoming issues in my personal life. Rina and I had agreed to spend some time together over the holidays and see if anything was still there. Rina. She was such a free spirit. She'd had her doubts about settling down. When it came to kids, I wanted more; she wasn't sure. Despite that, we decided to try our relationship again. She had put together a dynamite trip to New York City: to hang out in China-town for a few days, then on to a remote bed-and-breakfast in up-state New York afterward. One-on-one time would do us good . . . or bad . . . one way or another, time would serve as a catalyst to answer the question of our future.

Then there was Kate. We spent my last night in Afghanistan to-gether at the Safe House. No sleep. No sex. We just lay awake and held each other. Just as the first gray rays of light crept to the top of the window, came the unforgettable, haunting call to prayer from the mosque across the street from the House. Both of us knew this was coming to an end, and that real life was about to return.

I felt changed, from the inside out. I was finally able to accept myself for who I was. Maybe it was because I'd never known my real dad that I had kept trying to prove I was a man with high-risk behaviors—always thinking that if I survived, I must be worthy and a good guy. The ghosts that had chased me and pushed me to "prove" my worth were gone. Maybe it was the first time I felt complex. I was more flexible—and less fearful—dealing with life.

I went through the CIA pipeline to get back to the States, flying on a Blackwater-chartered flight from Kabul to ██████████████ DoD case officers were allowed to travel there to decompress during our tour, but I'd never taken them up on it. There were troops in Af-ghanistan for a full year. If I was there only six months, why should I get R&R and not them? Didn't make much sense.

As I looked out the window of the Bombardier turboprop aircraft, my mind still going at 100 miles an hour, I kept thinking about Dark Heart. If I went back to Afghanistan, I might be able to influence events so that they led more in that direction in '04. ███████████ ████████████████████████████████████ Always a strange disorientation at first to answer again to my real name, no matter how many times I made the switch.

Bruce Gains walked me down to navy Capt. Mike Anderson's office. He was about to become the chief of DH03, the Pacific division of Defense HUMINT, which included the Mideast. Gregarious and friendly, Captain Anderson was becoming a skilled inside operator in DIA. He knew how to work the system, though he'd come out of NSA and didn't have a history with the bureaucracy within Defense intel. He'd seen the request from Colonel Ritchie and recommended that I be sent back to Afghanistan out of cycle. Colonel Becker, who was being replaced by Anderson, seconded that idea. That was a shocker; Colonel Becker was usually one of my adversaries at DIA and had even originally opposed my deployment.

Before going back, however, Captain Anderson wanted me to work on the desk for a couple of months because Ward was being transferred to another unit down at Fort Belvoir. I agreed, as long as it was a temporary assignment and I could get back to Afghanistan for the spring surge.

Before starting my temporary assignment, I took three weeks off to decompress. Rina and I took the trip to New York. I thought about the war and Kate. She was so young and so certain about where she wanted to go with her life. I had turned into her mentor rather than her lover—probably a better role for a long-term relationship and one surely to be less dramatic.

Rina and I began to be comfortable about being real with each other and were upfront about the relationships we'd had. I told her about Kate, and she told me about the romance she'd developed but had ended. We decided there would be no pressure this time around. We would enjoy the moment and see what came of it. Yet I had this feeling of hope, of being accepted for who I was without regard for the past or the future. I made the same effort with Rina.

On the train ride to New York City, we sat across from Tony Snow and his family. A former speechwriter for President Bush, he was just starting his new radio show on Fox News Radio. We talked about the war. I told him I'd refused to shake Geraldo Rivera's hand when I ran into him at Bagram as he came out of a Porta-John. "Smart move," Tony had remarked, "at a number of levels."

When I got back to Clarendon, things started to get weird.

Captain Anderson called me into his office. Something seemed different.

"I know you want to go back, and I know they want you back, but DIA leadership is very concerned about the Inspector General issues."

I was under investigation by the DIA IG, although for issues that were so minor that I couldn't understand why an IG had even gotten involved.

"I know what the IG issues are," I told him. "They're bullshit."

"I agree, they're bullshit," Captain Anderson said, "but there's something else."

I couldn't think of what the hell else there could be.

"What do you mean, there's something else?" I asked.

He wouldn't tell me. "There's something else," he repeated.

Now I was getting ticked off. "I don't have the right to know what that issue is?"

"Yes, you do, but they aren't talking to me, either. But they're really pissed at you."

I figured he knew but wouldn't tell me.

"By the way," he added, "they're unhappy that you got the Bronze Star."

That blew me away. I'd earned that damned thing.

"You've got to be kidding me," I said.

"Nope, I'm not," he said. "They're trying to figure out a way to pull it back."

"They can't do that," I shot back.

Captain Anderson said their position was that any award given to someone serving in a DIA billet overseas should be processed through DIA.

"Captain, I know you're navy, but that's not how the army award system works," I snapped. I pointed out that, by regulation, anybody can nominate anyone for an award, and the army can choose to issue it based on the merit of the nomination.

"And, further, DIA can't issue Bronze Stars," I said. "They're not a combated command."

Captain Anderson, who was from the navy, said he wasn't familiar with that army regulation. "With all due respect, sir, what they're telling you isn't correct," I added.

Captain Anderson tried again.

"I think they're looking at it as a policy issue," he said. "DIA wants to control any awards."

"It ain't gonna happen," I said. "DIA doesn't have that kind of authority. Plus, as you may recall, sir, Bill Wilson was awarded a Bronze Star by Task Force 180 six months ago. Are they going to try to pull his Bronze Star?"

Captain Anderson sighed deeply. He seemed to be staring over my shoulder.

"This isn't about the Bronze Star," he said after a short silence. "This is about you."

Oh, great, I thought. The love fest between me and DIA continues.

Captain Anderson tried to reassure me. "I want you to go back," he said. "There is no doubt that you are fully capable and competent to return to your duties and continue the work you were doing. I do need you to help Chris Boston get up to speed on the desk. Can you do that?"

U.S. Air Force Colonel Chris Boston had been pulled from out of retirement just after the war in Afghanistan had started. He was one of thousands of military personnel brought back after the September 11 attacks. He was a highly experienced case officer who had spent decades doing human intelligence, most of that spent working issues relating to Afghanistan and Pakistan. He was assigned to be the first Defense attaché in the newly established American Embassy in January 2002. He had conducted a successful tour there for about eighteen months.

"Absolutely," I told him, "but I want to be back in Afghanistan before the spring offensive."

"I understand," Captain Anderson said.

███

████████████████████ Colonel Boston and I instantly hit it off. He told me early on that there had been a high-side (top secret) by-name request for me by the Rangers. They wanted me to be integrated with their task force in the spring surge. Since I wasn't a Ranger, it was the ultimate vote of confidence.

I tried then to follow up on other business left undone from my first tour. I called the 9/11 Commission, as Philip Zelikow had asked me to do back when I made my presentation to him in Afghanistan.

I didn't have a good feeling dialing that phone. Nothing good was going to come of this, I remember thinking. Nothing good. I knew DIA was going to be pissed off that I had talked to the commission in the first place about the problems it had put in front of me on Able Danger, even though I'd gotten approval from the army to discuss it with the commission. It had the potential for making the DIA controversy over my Bronze Star look like a kindergarten spat. Still, I felt it was the right thing to do—to make sure that Able Danger issues were fully disclosed to the commission.

I did inform Colonel Boston before I called and told him I'd go through official channels to notify DIA that the commission wanted to talk to me. I wasn't trying to hide it.

One of Zelikow's deputies answered the phone. ████████████
███
████████████████████████████—that Dr. Zelikow had asked me to call him after I returned from deployment.

"I remember you," he said. "I met you. I'll talk to Dr. Zelikow and find out when he wants you to come in."

I told him they needed to formally request this through DIA. He said he understood and would get back to me after talking to Dr. Zelikow.

I also told him I had copies of the Able Danger documents with me. I had tracked them down in Clarendon and put them at my desk: two boxes of material, a leather briefcase where I kept the most sensitive documents, three large charts—including the one with the photo of Mohamed Atta—and some smaller charts rolled up in a tube. Along with the cover plan (the documents that conceal the true purpose of the papers) and copies of legal documents, I had a complete copy of the essential papers on Able Danger.

One of the most crucial documents was the operational plan signed by Gen. Hugh Shelton, then chairman of the Joint Chiefs of Staff. In it, the operational objectives of Able Danger and the operational techniques and the technologies and methodologies were laid out in significant detail. I also had records of our dealings with NSA on its database and on the MIDB (military intelligence database).

I'd been around long enough to know it was important to have a complete paper trail on the creation and implementation of a program. I also knew my set of documents would tell commission members everything they needed to know about Able Danger, short of getting the raw data. I told Zelikow's assistant I was willing to bring it all over if he wanted it.

"That would be great," Zelikow's assistant said. "Let me talk to Dr. Zelikow, and we'll let you know when he wants you to come in." And that was that.

I had no way of knowing what I'd just unleashed.

I jumped back into my duties, helping Chris Boston oversee the Kabul Safe House and support Task Force 1099, including mission analysis for what was designated Operation Shadow Matrix, the operational nickname of the spring surge, which was three times bigger than Mountain Viper. I got a copy of the Concept of Operations for the mission and started doing the same sort of analysis I had done for Mountain Viper—looking at the operational objectives and trying to match Defense HUMINT capability and resources to the mission requirements so we could completely integrate ourselves into the mission.

Captain Anderson asked me to put together an Afghan operations center that would serve as a war room here in the States to support the surge. We were planning to send ███████████████ in country to serve in all forward areas supporting all combat operations, including the Rangers ███████████████████████████ They would manage our existing assets and work ████████████████ to develop new ones. The idea was to develop the Defense HUMINT footprint: Everywhere our forces were, we would be there to support combat operations. Our indigenous spies would supply us with information. We would also serve in leadership targeting as well—not the way it was done by the LTC, but some new format yet to be determined.

My job stateside was to get this operation up and going before I headed back in country. I also saw this as my opportunity to resurrect Dark Heart at some point. I assumed senior leadership wasn't dumb; they'd see the light and figure out sooner or later that they needed to pursue the bad guys into Pakistan. By working at the senior operations level back in Afghanistan, I'd be able to bring them around to a Dark Heart–type operation, maybe after the spring surge.

Some trouble on the ground came up: My replacement in Afghanistan turned out to be a glory-seeking cowboy. He was a competent guy, but he decided he was going to personally hunt down bin Laden and the other HVTs by attaching himself to any combat team or element that was outside the wire rather than doing his job of being a leader and managing the planning processes with 180 and 1099.

Sure, I'd gone outside the wire to run ██████ convoys, but I'd stayed focused on my main responsibilities. I didn't go galloping through the countryside looking for bad guys under every rock and pile of camel dung.

Although Hank sure did. He was always gone from Bagram, so no one was running the shop. The complaints started to roll in. Also, Colonel Ritchie had been transferred to Kabul to work for General Barno, leaving a lieutenant colonel in charge who was more interested in running after bin Laden with Hank than in running the shop. The two egged each other on. It was like watching a great Steven Seagal movie—without the action, the plot, or the successes.

The quality and frequency of reports dropped dramatically, and we got only silence on every inquiry made on any issue relating to planning for the spring surge. I mean nada. So it soon became clear that, whatever problems DIA leadership had with me, there was no one else in the wings who could go back in and put the train back on the track.

I had tasked Hank to do the ground mission analysis, figuring out staging areas for our people and material coming into country—weapons, ammo, radios, tactical gear for setting up camp, GPS systems, but I ended up doing it from a desk in Clarendon, and I was damned unhappy about it.

I tried to stay on top of the 9/11 Commission. After about a week, when I hadn't heard back from Zelikow, I called his office again, but his assistant's tone was different this time. More distant.

"We don't need you to come in," he told me. "We have all the information we need on Able Danger."

That was a shocker. Where had they gotten the documents? I thought I was the only one with a complete set. Oh well. I shrugged it off. Maybe they had what they needed from Eileen Preisser or Scott Phillpott.

I found out later that wasn't the case at all, but at the time, I took Zelikow's assistant's word for it. Frankly, I was kind of relieved. I wouldn't have to deal with DIA leadership on this and end up getting accused of going outside the box again. Maybe somebody else had taken the burden off me and dropped the dime on the agencies and people who'd screwed Able Danger.

So I focused on Afghanistan. I spent the next three weeks getting oriented and selecting a team to lay the groundwork for the surge on my next deployment. In all, I was figuring out beans to bullets, computers to tactics. For the first time, I was issued a top-secret cryptographic phone that allowed me to talk to anyone who had an STU II (secure phone) at the highest classification level. The technology had not been available during my first tour. I had to figure out how to plug the full spectrum of capabilities and resources that Defense intelligence had into the larger battle plan to support Special Operations and conventional forces.

My stay would be open-ended; I also had to go in and fix what Hank the Cowboy had broken by getting the reports flowing and the HUMINT operations cell functioning properly again.

By this time, Randy had moved on from his assignment to run the Safe House, and his replacement had made a clumsy attempt to clean up the atmosphere at the Safe House—no more French cable!—which pissed off the team there and accomplished nothing. But, what the hell. People come and people go. I still had to work with them.

Captain Anderson called me in one day. The news wasn't good.

"I'm getting a huge amount of resistance from the fourteenth floor about sending you forward," he said. The fourteenth floor was DIA's senior leadership.

I tried to shrug it off. "Let me go talk to them."

He shook his head. "Won't do any good."

"So, sir, what do you want me to do?"

"I need you to go lead the advance team," said Anderson. "You are my scout. You are the only one who can do this, but I want to tell you that, this time, they are really pissed off at you."

I caught up with Bill Huntington, DIA deputy director of operations, in the elevator one day and asked him for some DIA "challenge" coins—tokens of appreciation to be given out for a job well done—to take back with me. I'd given out the last fifteen to folks in country, and they had been effective awards. Huntington told me he'd get me some.

"By the way," I said casually, "I understand the Rangers have done a by-name request for me to go forward. Are you going to approve it?"

Huntington was coy. He tried to smile, his chubby red cheeks reminding me of a mirthless Santa Claus. "Your name is one of several on the list."

"I understand that," I said, "but I believe I'm at the top of the list."

He exited the elevator without a word.

SECOND VOYAGE

I was finally given a green light in late January to go back to Bagram, and I returned in early February as OIC of an eight-member advanced operations (ADVON) team. Our job would be to prepare for the ███████ ██ ██ ██████████████████████████████████████ I also had to fix the screwups that had occurred since I had left.

I took some ribbing from my team because I was coming back with two full sets of fleece and GORE-TEX, and I had made sure that everyone who was going with me was equally equipped, because I knew how harsh Afghanistan could get in the winter. The highs would barely break freezing during the day, and there would be plenty of freezing rain and snow.

We brought two full pallets of weapons and gear, including dozens of M-4s and M-11s for the HUMINT teams, ammunition, top-secret crypto keys, and a computer system. We flew to Bagram on a C-17 from Dover Air Force Base in Delaware nonstop with two in-air refuelings. I sat across from a pallet of Alaskan King crab meant for the troops' Friday night seafood feast, and a pallet of M-16 5.56mm ammo. It was even more uncomfortable than my first trip into Bagram. Eighteen hours, and if you had to go, you basically pissed down a hole in the side of the plane.

All of us managed to hold it.

My plan was to get everything up and going, get the HUMINT team in place in late March, and then go forward with the Rangers, as they had requested.

I had a strong suspicion I had been selected for promotion to lieutenant colonel by the army. DIA had no control over that because I was on active duty for the army—and the army has its own way of doing business. So while I had no way of knowing 100 percent for sure, I had "good paper"—a spotless record with high block evaluations—going into the selection board that was held the prior October. The promotion list would be out soon, and I had felt very confident that I was on the promotion list. So when the list came out in January I wasn't all that surprised . . . but I knew it would take time for the actual promotion to be effective since I and everyone else on the list would require congressional approval before it took effect (all commissioned officers in the military require U.S. Senate confirmation).

This passage was different. It was more than just a longer flight. The first time, I had gone over alone into the unknown and thought of it as an adventure. This time, I knew—or thought I knew—what I was getting into. I spent the long hours in flight sleeping, meditating, and thinking about my personal life. Rina and I had reconciled, and things were over between Kate and me—something we both had known before I had left. She had fed me helpful information about Hank while I was stateside. We were both pros, so I wasn't worried about that, but we could have our awkward moments. I also thought about Alexander. He was past the juice box stage now, but he was still—naturally—worried about his dad going back into a combat zone. I had seen him every weekend while he was at home, and he was growing up quickly.

I also contemplated the job ahead of me: In Mountain Viper last fall, we had broken the back of the Taliban in their attempt to retake ground in Afghanistan, but they'd learned from that and were adapting. They'd retreated into the mountains and into Pakistan. We had tried to go after them in the mountains with Winter Strike. We'd stirred up the hornet's nest and shoved some of them out of their winter havens. It hadn't killed them, but it had routed them and put them on the move. Now, Shadow Matrix was designed to hunt them down and kill them. Operations were going to be all along the border: Khowst, Asadabad, Kandahar, Jalalabad. The 25th Infantry Division was moving in to replace the 10th Mountain. Troop size was almost doubling, from 10,000 to about 20,000. The tide was turning.

In the stiff seat of the C-17, I shifted uncomfortably. Suddenly I felt weary, bone tired. Headed back to a war zone to . . . what . . . do it all over again? Without access to Pakistan, we were going to play this game again and again. Push them back, only to see them surge forward again. Push them back. Surge forward. Push. Surge.

Like playing Ping-Pong against a wall. The harder you slam the ball against the wall, the faster it comes back.

We could end up doing this for years. Decades, maybe. Sometimes we got so caught up thinking about the enemy's suicidal tendencies—their willingness to die on the battlefield for their cause—that we forgot what a shrewd and persistent adversary they were.

Things were going downhill. I could see it. The Taliban could see it, too—and it was to their benefit.

It wasn't that we didn't have the intelligence. We did, but our initiatives couldn't seem to get off the ground enough to deliver a lethal blow to these guys. We kept making the same mistakes over and over again. Push them back. Trust the Paks. With that strategy, any tactical gains made by any commander would be short-lived and easily reversed.

Leadership—the White House, Rumsfeld, top brass at the Pentagon—just didn't get it. They were focused on Iraq. They weren't listening. You could see that: Rumsfeld was showing up in Kabul every few months and declaring that combat was over. I had to believe that people were passing the right information up the chain. Whether he got it, I don't know. His deputies sure didn't get it. The Taliban didn't recognize international borders. The Paks were in bed with the Taliban. The intelligence was irrefutable. Believing otherwise was a failure of leadership at the highest level. For any educated human being to somehow ignore the intelligence and battle facts was almost criminally negligent.

People like me wanted to fix it. Good commanders like General McChrystal wanted to fix it. Without leadership at the highest level, however, we were doomed to keep repeating our mistakes, like in the movie *Groundhog Day*, where Bill Murray is doomed to keep repeating the same day until he learns. Only this time, there were no laughs—and people died.

I had put the issues in Clarendon in the back of my mind, but it was clear that it had followed me to Bagram. My first night back, I had dinner in the mess hall with Jack Foster, a former deputy of mine on other missions who now held the job I had held during Winter Strike as HUMINT chief Task Force 1099. "Listen, Tony," he said bluntly. "Something's going on and I don't know what the hell it is."

Oh, wonderful, I thought. The creepy stuff continues.

Clarendon had gotten a by-name request for me signed by Colonel Keller, Jack told me. Jack knew that because he was the one who had drafted the request. Regardless of that the fourteenth floor had delayed and hemmed and hawed and finally said that Task Force 1099 couldn't use me through the spring. They could rely on me only while I was running the ADVON, and I could only stay through April. No reason was given. That had made Jack suspicious. Usually the ███████ ████████████████████████████ got whatever they wanted. ███████ element that has been tasked consistently to be on the cutting edge of war. It wasn't a security issue because DIA would have taken me off duty immediately. That's what made it even more suspicious. Jack couldn't get to the bottom of it.

So while Jack and I recognized the strangeness coming from Clarendon to be important, we were halfway around the world from them and we had to deal with the war in Bagram.

The first thing I did was track down Hank the Cowboy and give him hell. I'm not sure it helped much. I do not, as a rule, yell. Also I hardly ever use rank to "lock people's heels"—but in the case of Hank, I did both.

He insisted he was doing the right thing by going out to track down HVTs. I pointed out that he'd been doing such a lousy job that I was going to have to essentially take over his shop just to get everything back on track. He said that was fine by him. He wanted to keep running around hunting bad guys.

So I had to reconstitute the ████████████ program, which Hank had singlehandedly shut down, pissing off ████████████ ███ in one boneheaded move.

At the Safe House, Randy's replacement was putting up a fight about sending his case officers out into the field. ████████████ ██ ██ He didn't want them to be anyplace dangerous. It got ugly. He lost and the case officers went forward.

In the meantime, Jack was trying to get to the bottom of the situation with Clarendon. He kept telling them what a great job I was doing. I wasn't sure that was helping matters a hell of a lot.

One day Jack came to my computer grinning.

"I really pissed them off this time," he said.

"What do you mean?" I asked. That was usually my job. I felt jealous.

He gestured toward his computer. "C'mon over and look at this."

He showed me an e-mail he'd sent back to Clarendon. It was a photo of me getting the Bronze Star.

"Oh my God, Jack," I said. "You must have spun them right out of the room."

Jack laughed. "Oh yeah, I did. I won't show you the responses. They were pretty pointed."

A bigger issue at the time, though, was getting ready for Shadow Matrix. General Barno was adamant about the issue of American troops crossing the border in Pakistan for any operations. He said that American and Pakistani forces were cooperating to create a "hammer and anvil" strategy, in which forces on one side of the border would drive al Qaeda members across the border to troops waiting on the other side, a tactic that was supposed to crush the al Qaeda elements between the Pakistani and the coalition forces. He now restricted everyone from even going into Pakistan in hot pursuit. To do it, you had to get approval from top Afghani and Pakistani leaders. Well, a hell of a lot of good that did when you were closing in on bad guys. We knew they would disappear as soon as they hit Pakistan.

I heard that General McChrystal was opposed to this policy, but he couldn't budge General Barno, either. Not that he wasn't trying, but Barno had authority since he was commander of forces in Afghanistan. Along with the border ops, General McChrystal was also stationing snipers at very long ranges to aim at border hot spots. It gave me hope that at least some people in the military got the picture.

You see, the way I figure it, there are soldiers and there are warriors in the military. Soldiers do everything by the book. They just follow orders. Warriors . . . well, warriors understand that their job is to win. Their primary objective is to adapt and achieve victory over the enemy by adjusting and changing their tactics and procedures as necessary to stay one step ahead of them. I figured General McChrystal, like General Vines, was a warrior. He was trying to win the war. He lived like a warrior, he had the warrior ethos, and that carried over to everything that he did.

On the other hand, I saw General Barno as a soldier—a bureaucrat in uniform. He did everything by the book. He was toeing the party line and didn't want anything to go wrong on his watch.

The Taliban were on the attack again, but they were smart enough not to take us head-on. Instead, they were now moving to asymmetric warfare methods—hitting soft targets and trying to use our strength against us. There was a string of attacks on foreign and Afghan aid workers, including one 40 miles northeast of Kabul in February that killed five Afghan workers and wounded two others. The shooters had jeered at the aid workers for "living in luxury while our friends are in prison in Cuba."

Then Rumsfeld showed up in Kabul and appeared to be seriously delusional. He and Karzai claimed that the Taliban were no danger to the country.

"I've not seen any indication that the Taliban pose any military threat to the security of Afghanistan," Rumsfeld told reporters.

Wow, I remember thinking. *We must have just spent the last eight months chasing ghosts. . . .*

Karzai had drunk the Kool-Aid, too.

"The Taliban doesn't exist anymore," he claimed. "They're defeated. They're gone."

Yeah, right.

It was clear that the United States was conducting foreign policy by wishful thinking. Wish it and it would happen. Our intelligence was telling us they were coming back. We knew they were going to come again, but U.S. and Afghan officials were trying to wish them away.

Good freakin' luck.

At another level, though, the U.S. military was involved in some bad stuff. For weeks, Jack Foster had been bugging me to come over ███████████████████████████████ to show me how they'd converted the former ████████████████ HQ ████████████ clearly set up for the "enhanced interrogation" program, and offered me a tour.

I knew what he was trying to do, and so I kept putting him off. I had known that there was a "special" system for handling HVT prisoners that the Pentagon leadership didn't want going to the BCP. They also had to be kept from the FBI since the agents who weren't told that an "enhanced interrogation" program had been authorized at the highest level of the U.S. government were legally required to report any prison abuses they witnessed. The interrogation program, ███████████████████ was authorized, but a lot of us felt it wasn't appropriate and just wasn't right. We also all knew that the CIA had a separate secret prison at Bagram. We just stayed away from it.

The 1099 facility was an "enhanced interrogation program," Jack told me. "You ought to come over and see it."

I just kept putting him off because I knew this was more than a tour. Jack wanted me to get involved. Finally I said I'd take a look.

I was blown away—and not in a good way—by what I saw. The building had been completely gutted. Rooms had been converted into holding cells or open areas, framed in wood and steel, that Jack told me were for interrogation. These were nothing like the interrogation areas I was familiar with, which were small rooms with a small table and three chairs (for the interrogator, the translator, and the detainee) and a window for observers. These interrogation areas, it was clear, had holding points for a prisoner's arms and legs. They were designed for prisoners to be shackled and held in stress positions to maximize discomfort and pain.

Standing in the giant facility, I could feel a sense of tension in the air—palpable and raw—like walking on a beach before a hurricane is about to hit.

I had a reputation for rushing in and taking missions that others viewed as too politically risky, but I always weighed the potential good that a successful mission would bring to the country against the risk of undertaking it. Here, there was no potential good. From my perspective—and I had run some of the blackest operations in the last decade of the twentieth century—this would only be bad.

At the end of the tour Jack, clearly proud of his work in planning and setting up the facility, smiled at me. "What do you think?" he asked.

My stomach was in a knot. "It's quite a change to the building," I said lamely. Jesus. This was bad juju. I wanted nothing to do with it.

Jack leaned forward eagerly. "You know," he gestured at the interrogation areas, "you could help me with this."

"Jack, don't ever bring me back here," I snapped. "I have no desire to get involved in this." I turned around and walked out. I thought back to the interrogation that John Kirkland and I had conducted of the American citizen. We'd questioned him by using our own format and techniques. We'd broken him without using any methods that weren't approved by the army. No funny stuff.

Let me be clear here. I'm not saying torture should never be used. I'd torture someone if, say, I believed they had information that would prevent a nuclear weapon from going off or would likely prevent a massive loss of life. Albeit those kinds of situations are exceedingly rare. In fact, they usually only occur in the movies, not in real life. In the vast majority of cases, I don't believe torture works—nor should it be used.

The intent here by DoD was to "regularize" enhanced interrogation. Turn it into a cottage industry. It was just not a good idea, and the "results" do not justify the means, since there is no clear evidence torture ever directly contributed to saving a single life.

I headed back to the compound to focus on planning missions that I believed would net us *real* intelligence information.

It was only later, after all the publicity, that I realized the full scope of what was going on. I'd been led into the top-secret interrogation "system" authorized by my boss at the time, Secretary of Defense Donald Rumsfeld, as well as Stephen Cambone, undersecretary of defense for intelligence, permitting highly coercive interrogation techniques on detained personnel in Afghanistan. It was later moved to Iraq, according to investigative reporter Seymour Hersh, where the methods were used against Iraqi prisoners at Abu Ghraib prison.

UNSAFE AT ANY SPEED

WEEKS later, I was still feeling uneasy about what I'd seen at the new prison. What the hell was going on here?

This second tour of Afghanistan was taking on the feel of a bad *Twilight Zone* episode. I could just hear Rod Serling speaking in the wings: "Little did Tony Shaffer know that he was no longer in the U.S. Army. He had slipped into . . . the Twilight Zone."

One morning in early March, I got an e-mail in my secret-level box from George Anderson, who oversaw the Defense HUMINT collections operations in Iraq, asking me to give him a call. Interesting, I thought. George and I had worked together supporting a black special-mission unit that had gone well, and I respected him, but why would he be contacting me now?

George had recently been involved in a decision to combine the Afghan and Iraqi case officers into a single task force. George wasn't happy about it and, personally, I felt it would have been smarter to combine Afghanistan and Pakistan desks. That wasn't what the brass wanted. The feeling was that there was a lot of redundancy, with staffs in Afghanistan and Iraq involved in active combat zones, and efficiencies could be achieved by combining the management of the two units.

I called George on the secure phone. He came right to the point. "I know you weren't in favor of combining the two task forces, but now that it's been done, I'd like you to come over and be the operations officer for the combined Afghan-Iraq task force."

I was surprised. I had no experience in Iraq, but George told me I had a reputation for getting things done and, since I had already commanded an operating base, I had the leadership experience. I would have an overall staff of about forty people, with about a dozen direct reports. Most would be from Iraq. The job would involve supervising everything from money spent to ensuring everyone was trained, to issuing them gear and material; then, once the guys were on the ground, monitoring all activities and giving guidance and support. Word out of Iraq was that things weren't going well. Defense HUMINT had played a major role in trying to help the Special Forces find those weapons of mass destruction that President Bush had promised.

That had gone badly, of course.

I thought about it for a couple of days and talked it over with some folks whose opinions I respected. I had planned, after I returned stateside, to spend the remainder of my recall to active duty as an instructor at the farm, I had been approached about it and had passed my interview to become one. It would mean long hours of role-playing for the trainees, reading and grading reports, but it would be a reprieve. There would be no politics or intrigue from HQ to deal with—just the pure duty of training new kids.

After concluding that Bill's offer was a good one, I e-mailed him that I would take the Iraq-Afghanistan job as long as I could stay until May or June in Afghanistan and finish up my mission there. My active duty would have to be extended two years. I was fine with that because I felt this was the right war to be fighting. It was clear to me that we could well lose our victory there, and I wanted to stay with the mission.

George wrote back, welcoming me aboard and saying he would talk to my Reserve officer about getting my orders extended. I was pleased. I had a plan that would keep me doing something useful but not too dangerous.

Next came a call from Mike Anderson. He had bad news: Somebody was complaining that I was running unsafe convoys. I was stunned. I had been running convoys through some tough stuff for months. I clicked through my mind: no loss of life or material, no one injured, no damage to vehicles. My Bronze Star had even cited me for running convoys. What the hell was going on?

"What's this based on?" I demanded.

I could tell that Captain Anderson was uncomfortable. "Well, they felt unsafe."

"Who felt unsafe?" I asked. Turned out "they" were two individuals from the Safe House. I groaned. "What did they complain about?"

"They complained you were running an unsafe convoy."

I was getting frustrated. "How was it unsafe?"

"Well, they couldn't say."

This was bullshit. "Captain, you do understand how we run convoys here, right?"

Captain Anderson was getting exasperated, too. "I know how convoys are run, but they felt you were running them in an unsafe manner."

"Captain, *all* convoys are fundamentally unsafe," I said. "You know how we run them—at what would be considered unsafe speeds, even through traffic. But we have unarmored vehicles here, and that's the way it's done for security and survivability. Sir, you know that. You also know I've run over forty combat convoys."

I could almost feel Captain Anderson pulling at his collar. He didn't like this conversation at all.

"Chris, I understand that, but they still complained."

"What exactly am I supposed to do about it?" I said. "This is bullshit. Total bullshit. What exactly are you asking me to do? Unless you can define for me what 'unsafe' is, I don't know what to do."

"Well, I don't know, either." Captain Anderson shifted gears. His voice got lower and more urgent. "Tony, it seems to me that they're gunning for you. They want to have something on you."

"Who's 'they,' sir? What's going on?"

"I can't get into that," Anderson said, "but they're pretty unhappy with you. It's one more thing that they're going to try to use against you."

"What do you want me to do?" I asked.

"You need to quit driving," Anderson said. It was clear he was trying to help me out.

"That's kinda hard to do," I said. "I'm one of the few who is qualified to drive." By this time, my voice was raised, and I could feel everyone in the SCIF looking at me, including a sergeant with ████████

"I'm not telling you not to go on convoys. Just don't drive." He was trying to warn me. "Tony they're looking for something on you. They are looking to kill you."

"I got it," I said as reality started to sink in. There was something unseen here.

"I'm serious," said Captain Anderson. "They're really gunning for you. You need to take this seriously."

"I got it," I said and hung up. I sat back and put my hands on my forehead.

"What are you going to do?" asked the sergeant. He'd heard enough to figure out what was going on.

"I don't know," I said. What the hell had I done?

"That's bullshit," the ████████ sergeant said. "You've run convoys the same for the past six months. Are you going to stop driving?"

I thought for a moment. "Hell, no. If they're going to fire me over driving convoys, there's no hope."

I continued driving convoys. There were no problems—and no more complaints. I made sure that those on the missions were folks who were loyal to me.

Shortly after that, at the end of March, I got a terse e-mail from

George Anderson. It was about the Iraq-Afghanistan job. "Tony, I'm sorry. I can't offer you the job. Best wishes."

And that was that.

What the hell? I felt helpless. I just couldn't put my finger on anything I had done to draw this level of angst from DIA leadership. This went beyond their usual annoyance with me. It haunted me to the point of distraction.

I tried to shrug it off and keep going, but I was damned confused. Something was going on back in Clarendon, which involved me, but nobody was clueing me in.

First, there were the warnings from Anderson when I was in Washington, and from Jack Foster when I had returned here. Then I had gotten this unbelievable call about my driving. Then this job offer had mysteriously been pulled back.

On top of that, I had refused to provide to the Pakistanis the intel we had on Wana serving as the Taliban and al Qaeda base of operations, but someone on the U.S. side had passed it to them. I suspected either General Barno or his staff.

Apparently, there had been a demand then that the Paks take action—and they did. Kind of.

Amid much fanfare, several thousand Pakistani army troops had attacked heavily fortified compounds just outside Wana. It looked at first like they'd surrounded al Qaeda fighters and possibly al-Zawahiri, but suddenly, whoever was there just happened to melt away. Most, if not all, of the al Qaeda–allied foreign militants fighting alongside local tribesmen escaped. Goddamnit, I thought. We had it right. We had suspected a Tier 1 HVT—someone at the level of al-Zawahiri—because of the patterns of activity ███████████████ in Wana. If we were right about Wana, I was betting we were also right about the identification of Quetta and Peshawar as the other two key safe havens. The Paks had let him escape. Probably deliberately.

I tried to focus on my job. ADVON was wrapping up, but I wanted to stay and go forward with the Rangers, as they had requested. Jack

Foster offered to send a note to Phil Trent, the DoD HUMINT operations chief in Clarendon, seeking to extend my stay—an offer that I gratefully accepted.

As Foster told me later, Trent told him that was fine, that he could have whomever he wanted.

By the way, Trent asked, who is Tony Shaffer, Trent was a senior operations guy, so he was above the level where he kept track of ████████████████████████████████████

Get him on a plane, Trent told him. I want him back here within a week.

At about the same time, I walked into the SCIF to find a message that Anderson had called me. He had asked for me to call him on the Iridium immediately.

I went outside the tent for some privacy and phoned him.

"Sir, what's up?"

He got right to the point. "Tony, I think you need to get back here as soon as possible. When will you have things wrapped up?"

I thought it through, trying to keep my mind off the odd stuff of the last several weeks. "We've got the progress review on the status of ADVON, the handoff of our activities to the main body, and then we have a briefing to General Ennis at the end of next week when he comes in for a visit. I could come back after that." (General Ennis was the global head of DIA HUMINT and Trent's boss.)

"Right after that, I need you to get on a plane," Anderson said.

"What about the spring surge?" I asked.

"Tony," Anderson said, "you need to get on a plane and come back."

So much for the Rangers, I thought.

"OK," I said. "I got it. As soon as I finish briefing Ennis."

This was strange. They were allowing me to brief General Ennis. So whatever was going on had nothing to do with security or my leadership abilities.

I got my staff together, and we organized our PowerPoint presentation. As we do in the military, we color-coded our progress:

red—stalled; amber—broken; and green—on track. I gave my presentation, proud that everything was green except the telecommunications issues. I'd had to fire the guy who was doing that because of his lack of expertise, but, aside from that, all of my stated operations objectives were met, and General Ennis seemed pleased. He didn't hint at any problem, and I had the impression he didn't know I'd been called back.

It took two days to catch a flight out. I ended up coming back with Mitch, a member of my ADVON team. We were finally able to hop a flight on a C-17 bound for Davis-Monthan Air Force Base in Arizona—another nonstop flight with air refueling. Jack had introduced me to the Delta medics, and they gave me Vioxx, a painkiller, for my knee, and Ambien so I could sleep through the flight. I accepted both.

From Arizona, we caught a C-17 to Charleston Air Force Base, where we picked up a rental car there and headed home. As we hit the Beltway in the Washington area, I reminded myself that I'd done nothing wrong.

Still, I wondered just what the hell I was facing.

• 25 •

DARKNESS FALLS

IT was Friday night, well after close of business, by the time I got to my home, ██████████████████████████████ I could get into the ████████████████████ Whatever the Inspector General had come up with, it couldn't be much. I'd always played it straight. Yes, I pushed the envelope and behaved obnoxiously at times to paper-pushing bureaucrats, but they can't fire you for finding ways to get your job done.

In fact, I'd been told by one of the senior staff who was aware of the investigation's results that they were just going to fire a shot over my bow now that my two protectors—DIA Director Lt. Gen. Pat Hughes and DIA Director for Operations Maj. Gen. Bob Harding—were gone. I figured the worst they could do to me was a letter of reprimand.

First thing Monday morning, I headed over to DIA headquarters, leaving my equipment, including four Iridium phones with a top-secret crypto key, at home. I figured I'd turn them in later. As usual, when I got to Clarendon, I called upstairs to the cover staff and told

them ██
██

One of the sergeants said he'd be right down. I had done this dozens of times over the years, so I knew the routine. The sergeant would
bring down my DIA badge and swipe me in, and ███████████████
██
██
██
██
███████████

Then the sergeant showed up, a big manila envelope tucked under
his arm. ████████████████████████████████ He avoided my
eyes.

"Sir, we have to go to the sixth floor," he said. "You have to see
Colonel Sadler."

That was a bad sign. Colonel John Sadler was the executive officer
to deputy director of HUMINT operations for DIA. I remembered
that Huntington had been the one who'd predicted in that meeting
when I was an Iraq war intelligence planner that U.S. Armed Forces
would be greeted with children throwing flowers at their feet. Well,
that hadn't happened. He didn't like me much but, more important, he
didn't ordinarily have ███████████████

"Where's Captain Anderson?" I asked immediately. He would
have to know about this.

"Sir, Captain Anderson is not here." Another bad sign. Anderson
was my boss. If there was just going to be a letter of reprimand, Captain Anderson would have had to be in on it.

I knew something else was up.

The sergeant swiped me in, but kept my ID. We got onto the elevator, where we ran into Dan Orlando, senior operations officer for
DH01, which was Europe. Orlando greeted me jovially.

"Hey, Tony, are you back or are you going?" I was still wearing my
rugged Afghanistan getup.

"I just got back," I said briefly, glancing at the sergeant. He looked down. ████████████████████████████

"I hear you've been doing great stuff in Afghanistan," Orlando said.

"I thought so, too, but I get the impression that I'm still not ringing the bell for some folks around here," I said.

Orlando shot the sergeant and me a puzzled look. "Well, good luck," he said as he got off the elevator at the third floor.

"I have a feeling I'm going to need it," I said, looking at the sergeant again, who continued to eyeball the floor.

In silence, we rode the elevator to the sixth floor and got off, heading for the executive offices where Colonel Sadler's office was. The sergeant stayed right at my elbow. We walked into the small waiting area, but no one was there except for the admin guy, a captain, sitting at his desk.

"Let Colonel Sadler know that Tony Shaffer is here," the sergeant said.

The captain nodded. "Colonel Sadler isn't here right now," he said. "Go ahead and wait in his office."

There was no one in Colonel Sadler's office. I contemplated taking my jacket off, but decided to keep it on and sat down at the table opposite Colonel Sadler's desk. Might as well be comfortable, I thought. We waited ten minutes. I tried to make some chitchat with the sergeant, but he just gave me an uncomfortable nod. He was not diggin' this one bit.

Then Colonel Sadler burst into the room with three other people. He seemed almost bubbly. I stood up.

"Major Shaffer," he said.

"Colonel," I responded.

"Do you know why you're here today?" he asked, retreating behind his desk.

I couldn't resist. "To give you decorating advice for your office?"

He was clearly caught off guard by my comment. I could see anger start to flash, but he stopped, gave me a humorless smile, and turned to the sergeant. "Go ahead and give him back his documents."

The sergeant handed me the manila envelope and then started to give me my DIA badge.

"Except for the badge," Colonel Sadler added.

What the hell was going on?

Colonel Sadler picked up a sheet of paper and proceeded to read aloud from it.

"Don't interrupt me until I'm done," he ordered me. It was the IG's findings. "The DIA has found three serious items . . ."

As he spoke, I looked around the room at the other people. I knew everyone except one guy—drawn, gaunt, and leathery, who remained by the door. He reminded me of the *X-Files*' Cancer Man. He never said a word or changed his expression.

I recognized a guy from Huntington's office, one of his personal staff, and another guy from DAC—DIA's counterintelligence and security activity office. He handled security clearances.

It was then I knew they were about to do something about my clearance.

Colonel Sadler droned on. "Undue award of the Defense Meritorious Service Medal." DIA was claiming I'd received a major award unlawfully—despite the fact that the award was for my documented work on Able Danger and other leadership roles.

"Misuse of a government telephone" adding up to $67. I had periodically programmed my government phone to my personal cell phone for a 25-cent charge for every call forwarded. This added up to $67.

"Filing a false voucher" for $180. I attended army training at Fort Dix that was required for my expected promotion to lieutenant colonel, but DIA was claiming it was a false claim because I was only authorized to attend the Command and General Staff School at "no expense to the government."

Total alleged loss to the government: less than $300. Wow, and I was worried that they had actually found something serious.

Colonel Sadler finished up. I was being reassigned to Fort McNair pending disciplinary action.

Then he came to his real point.

"On this day," he read, "your security clearance is suspended."

I was so surprised that I smiled.

They were suspending my security clearance over *this*?

Colonel Sadler looked up. "Do you have any questions?"

I stared at him.

"You've *got* to be kidding," I said.

Colonel Sadler stared back. "Good luck, Major Shaffer. You will need it," he said tonelessly, and turned around a folder to face me with some papers to sign.

With that, I was escorted out of the building.

After all the warnings I'd gotten in Afghanistan, I knew to expect something, but I had no idea this body blow was coming. It was clear they had decided to aim not over my head, but right for it. Decapitate me from my career.

It was all over. My career, and my days as a clandestine officer, were finished. There was no doubt, even if the accusations didn't match the severity of the punishment.

I walked into the courtyard next to the Clarendon Metro station thinking over the consequences. Around me, the drone of the Monday morning rush-hour traffic was increasing and people were rushing out of the Metro, headed for the start of a new workweek.

This was a death sentence. Real tough to take for a guy who always wanted to be a spook. I couldn't imagine doing anything else in the world.

I headed for my car and gave myself to the moment. It was a bright spring day, and the wind's chill bounced off my GORE-TEX jacket. This was OK, I told myself. This was happening for a reason. This all meant something. Perhaps this day would end on a low note, but the story wouldn't end, and I believed somehow, someway, this was meant to happen and would lead me to another dangerous and challenging adventure. I was right.

EPILOGUE

I spent the next three months in limbo, then left active duty and resumed my position as a DIA civilian employee in June 2004. I was placed on paid administrative leave while the security clearance suspension wound its way through the system—a process that could take years. So I settled in for the long haul. It took the better part of two years before they finally fired me.

I remained serving in the Army Reserves. The army took no adverse action against me and promoted me to lieutenant colonel in February 2005. I remain a reserve lieutenant colonel to this day. I am now assigned to a U.S. Army Reserve Division, which I serve as a primary staff officer with three different key areas of responsibility: Assistant Chief of Staff for Information Management as well as the command's Anti-Terrorism Officer and its Public Affairs Officer. I never could stick to doing one job at a time.

No one could understand why DIA was taking such an extreme action over minor allegations that the army refused to even accept as valid, and it took almost two years before I figured out DIA's vendetta. Finally, with the help of my attorney and friend Mark Zaid and others, the picture started to take form.

The first realization came in May 2005 when, as an army reservist on active duty, I was attached to Deep Blue, the U.S. Navy's counterterrorism think tank at the Pentagon, where I was working to re-create the Able Danger capability. ██████████████

I was sent by the navy to Capitol Hill to request money to fund the project. I took a chart with me that showed some of the previous results of Able Danger and was asked by the navy to provide Congressman Curt Weldon, vice chairman of the House Armed Services Committee, a full background on the original Able Danger.

I gave Representative Weldon pretty much the same briefing I gave Philip Zelikow at Bagram in October 2003, and Representative Weldon was equally stunned at my information. He then asked me whether I knew that there was no information in the commission report about Able Danger. I said I assumed that, because of its sensitive nature, it was in the classified annex of the 9/11 Report.

Congressman Weldon looked me square in the eye and told me, "Colonel Shaffer, there is no classified annex."

Now I knew that something was wrong. How could a major effort driven by the top management of the Department of Defense focused on conducting offensive operations against al Qaeda—an operation that had discovered Mohamed Atta—a full year before the 9/11 attacks not be mentioned at all?

Congressman Weldon's chief of staff, Russ Caso, was the first to figure out DIA's reason for coming after me. It was not about the $300 I was accused of misusing. It all came from my disclosure of the existence of Able Danger to the 9/11 Commission.

In August 2006, I ended up going public with my revelations about Able Danger—the unclassified part—and the fact that it had not been included in the 9/11 report. It caused a media sensation. To quote one of my favorite characters of science fiction, Agent Mulder of *The X-Files*, I became "the key figure in an ongoing government charade." The Defense Intelligence Agency moved to have my security clearance permanently revoked, and senior DoD leadership engaged in what is called a "whisper campaign" to discredit me.

To do that, they went as far back as they could—back through every statement I ever made as part of my clearance process. They even found my admission in 1987 to taking U.S. government Skilcraft pens from the American Embassy in Lisbon and sharing them with friends in high school at the age of fourteen. Yes, they were digging deep for anything, but they could find nothing of substance.

The entire weight of DoD leadership came down on me—with the exception of the army. God bless the U.S. Army. When I had gone to the Hill to ask for money for the navy, I called back to my boss on the army staff to ask for direction because I was being asked hard questions about Able Danger. I was told, "Tony, tell them the truth." And I did.

DoD denied the request that I testify in September 2005 in front of the Senate Judiciary Committee, claiming that the Judiciary Committee "had no standing" to investigate DoD passing or not passing information to the FBI. Instead I sat, silently, wearing my army uniform in the chamber while the hearings were held.

I eventually testified twice, both times in February 2006, to the House Armed Services Committee and the House Government Reform Committee in open and closed sessions. I concluded in my testimony that the Able Danger project might have prevented 9/11—and in closed (top-secret) session, I outlined exactly my judgment in great detail based on the larger work, which is still unknown to the public.

After multiple denials, DoD was eventually forced to confirm that Able Danger did exist, and to confirm that it was an offensive operation designed to identify and attack al Qaeda in a preemptive manner, two years before the 9/11 attacks. General Hugh Shelton publicly confirmed the existence of the operation and that he had come up with the idea and tasked it to General Pete Schoomaker, then commander of the U.S. Special Operations Command (SOCOM).

Despite this admission, DoD refused to admit that Atta's photo or information was contained in the data despite the fact that, by late August 2006, six people within DoD confirmed the Atta identification. Still, DoD refused to accept their confirmation and, instead, redoubled efforts to discredit and fire me.

Congress requested that the DoD Inspector General investigate

Able Danger, but that was kind of like having the fox investigate why chickens were missing from the henhouse. What resulted was a complete sham report. The IG report concluded that while there were multiple witnesses, there was no credible evidence that Atta was found. While it found 10,000 Able Danger–related documents during the investigation, it claimed that nothing was found to support my claims and the claims of other witnesses. Yet not one of these 10,000 documents—95 percent of which are unclassified—was ever released to the public.

One of the key conclusions to the DoD IG report on Able Danger was aimed directly at me. I was called a "marginally qualified intelligence officer" in an effort to discredit my credibility and the fact that I was the most accurate, consistent witness. Given my twenty years of training and experience, I would say that is patently untrue and a sign that their larger investigation was equally lacking in accurate content and veracity. The report—and the Senate Intelligence Committee report that followed in November 2005—were both whitewashes of the facts, and contained no discernable truth that I could tell.

Eventually the truth does come out, and little by little it has.

Maj. Gen. Geoffrey Lambert, the SOCOM operations officer under Schoomaker from 1998 to 2000, who also was the supervisor of the Able Danger team, recently confirmed in a book called *Horse Soldiers* the three key points of my testimony to the 9/11 Commission and to Congress. The view from the military lawyers, General Lambert says, was simple: If we don't pass intelligence to the FBI, it cannot be used and therefore, if it is not used, nothing can go wrong to potentially put SOCOM in a bad light.

So that is it. You know the rest of the story—and how, in the middle of combat in Afghanistan, I unknowingly sowed the seeds of my own career's demise. I revealed embarrassing mistakes made by Defense Intelligence and by multiple senior leaders in DoD in mismanaging pre-9/11 intelligence information and then trying to cover up their incompetence from the 9/11 Commission.

Fast-forward to today. My work continues to focus on global

security—a different path from my work at Defense Intelligence. As a senior fellow and director of external communications for the Center for Advanced Defense Studies, I perform as the center's spokesman and expert on intelligence-gathering operations and transnational terrorist threats. A key area of my work is Afghanistan and, because of its inexorable historic and cultural link, Pakistan.

I frequently appear on television and radio as an expert and analyst on the full spectrum of military and intelligence issues, and I work as a consultant for multiple organizations that perform support to the Department of Defense.

As for my personal life, Rina and I were married in 2006, and our son Ryan was born later that year. My son Alexander is now in high school. He continues to excel in Boy Scouts and is working to achieve the rank of Eagle Scout.

It's been said that you never know the value of light until you've walked through the darkness. Well, I've walked through more darkness than I ever expected, and now stand in the light of a new day, but the daylight I find myself in is no safer or secure than the one I left—and that is why I continue to do the work that I do.

HOW TO WIN IN AFGHANISTAN

Right now we appear to be barreling down the same path as the British did twice, the Soviets did once, and others as far back as Alexander have done. All ended with disastrous outcomes.

We have to abandon the current policy.

The constant minor adjustments to theme and style are akin to shuffling the deck chairs on the *Titanic*. We continue to do the same thing over and over, and expect to achieve different results. In Alcoholics Anonymous, we call this insanity.

Talking tactics—for example, whether Provisional Reconstruction Teams (PRTs) are the right way to go—is useless. Tactics do not matter if your strategy is flawed, but that is the path we are currently on.

We can win in Afghanistan, but the emphasis here is "we."

We (the United States) will never win this war in the conventional military sense. We must also abandon this notion.

The victory must be one that resembles the conclusion of World War II—with all participants sharing in the success. This victory should include the warlords, the people and tribes of Afghanistan, the people of Pakistan, and our NATO/ISAF allies. Let's not forget, "we," the United States, did not win in Afghanistan in 2001. It was the Northern Alliance, with some operational support from us that resulted in that victory. We must accept this—embrace this—and move back to focus on how to get "us," the United States, out of the middle.

In the larger context of the international "we," we cannot think of winning in Afghanistan without winning in Pakistan. To win in each country requires careful strategic considerations and actions, and a complete departure from the current, clearly failing, strategy.

Here are my thoughts on how to achieve victory:

ESTABLISH A TRUE COMBINED FORCES COMMAND

To win in Afghanistan without winning in Pakistan is not possible. After all, the Pashtu tribe saddles the border, and there is no such thing as an Afghan-Pakistan border for either the Taliban or al Qaeda—or what remains of it—as well as for the Pashtun people who inhabit the area. There is only the land that the indigenous Pashtun population—including the native members of the Taliban—has known for thousands of years. We also know that the Taliban "intel net" stretches from Bagram all the way into the interior of Pakistan. We need to understand these facts, and accept that the Taliban have created a "shadow government" that now touches the lives of virtually every Afghan in one way or another. Then we need to adjust our strategy around this understanding.

We must create the "Supreme Headquarters Allied Expeditionary Forces—Afghanistan-Pakistan," and name an Allied Forces commander who would have command and control over all military forces, including Afghan and Pakistani forces, on *both* sides of the Afghanistan-Pakistan border. We need to have one commander who can conduct operations on both sides in real time, with unity of command and control. We must have the military equivalent of a hammer and anvil.

Radical? Yes. Huge issues of sovereignty and national pride of all the nations involved will have to be addressed and managed, just as they were during World War II when everyone had to swallow their pride and focus on the common adversary. The bottom line here is this: We need a commander who can exercise supreme authority, just as we did when the supreme commander was created during World War II; all countries within the Supreme Headquarters Allied Expeditionary Forces—Europe (SHAEF) performed under Dwight D. Eisenhower. That is what it will take to win here. Granted, this is only the military fight. It doesn't include the civil fight—the hearts-and-minds fight—but it's a start.

Eisenhower would not have been successful in Europe if he was told, "You can conduct all the operations you want in France—but leave Germany to the Russians." For that matter, General Douglas Mac-Arthur would not have been successful in the Pacific if he was told to go only as far as the Solomon Islands and leave the rest to the British.

Once unity of command is established, we will require a much smaller operational force footprint. Combat units will be able, due to the fact that truly synchronized operations can occur on both sides of the border, to focus on achievable objectives. I believe we could cut U.S. troop strengths in half through gains in efficiency and by enabling our Afghan and Pakistani allies to work in synchronization under the guidance of a supreme commander.

We can make this "SHAEF—Afghanistan-Pakistan" of a limited time duration (perhaps two years with options to renew), and limit the scope of operations (to only the Federally Administered Tribal Areas). No matter, it has to be a real military force, with real teeth, able to conduct combined missions.

We must change the very fabric of the types and numbers of combat forces engaged in the conflict—more on this later.

APPOINT A LEADER WHO IS A COMBINATION OF
ULYSSES S. GRANT AND DWIGHT D. EISENHOWER

Someone who is respected by both sides, Afghan and Pakistani, a man who is permitted to run both sides of the border as a unified command—and who is out to win.

Let's examine these two different leadership types for a moment within the context of their eras.

General Grant was dogged in his pursuit and containment of his adversary, as well as committed to finishing the Civil War with a victory. The Civil War was one that could well have ended without a Northern victory; there was talk (and it was the South's military objective) of a negotiated peace in which the South would have remained an independent country. Grant was selected not because of his pedigree or his politics, but because he could win—and he did.

As for General Eisenhower, his brilliance was in being a master organizer, diplomat, and politician. He understood the concept of cooperation and was able to organize the Allied forces to focus on a single purpose: defeat of the Germans.

Will General David Petraeus be given this authority? Is he the right leader to perform this mission and achieve positive results? Could he be the hybrid of Eisenhower and Grant if the border can go away and he can be given the authority to win? I'd like to believe so.

CREATE AN INTERNAL OPERATIONAL POLICY FRAMEWORK—THE INTERNAL DEFENSE AND DEVELOPMENT (IDAD) PROGRAM

Take lessons from General Creighton Abram's IDAD program from the Vietnam era, whose goal was to eliminate the Vietcong in South Vietnam. The problem then—as now—was that the back door was not closed, so there was an endless resupply of insurgents coming in to replenish the Vietcong from North Vietnam since Laos and Cambodia remained safe havens for the insurgents. (Sound familiar?) The IDAD would create a framework for local units to work in their region, but coordinate in an interlocking and synchronized way, and this would have to be done *without* regard to the international border. Units would have to work in full synchronization at the local level. In Vietnam, this format was not fully successful because the spigot of insurgents was not turned off. This time, we need to turn off the spigot.

We must look at enhancing our relationships with the leadership of the thirty-four provinces of Afghanistan. We cannot count on, or become part of (in perception or reality) the central Afghan government— we are not President Karzai and he is not us.

We can (and should) reduce our operational footprint back to 2003–2004 levels, and focus our efforts at the local level, using Special Forces elements (from all nations), and step away from the use of conventional forces. Yes, their activities should be centrally coordinated, but one of the problems we have been up against is the misguided attempts to foist upon the country a central government that cannot function due to both cultural issues and corruption.

Special Forces teams are best suited for this type of warfare. They can run clinics and conduct training during the day, and advise and assist the Afghans (and Pakistanis under a supreme allied command) in conducting military operations at night. We need to put the war effort squarely back onto the shoulders of the Afghans (and the Pakistanis on their side of the border), and limit our role to surgical military strikes focused on specific terrorist targets. We must replace conventional forces with true special operations forces who understand how to conduct the full spectrum of operations at the local level. We must not take on the appearance of an army of occupation.

We should train, advise, and equip the Afghan Army, Air Force, and National Police (and the same on the Pakistani side of the border if necessary), but we should not do their job for them. The best way to address this is by decentralized execution by small units. We do not need a dozen general officers in Afghanistan with layers of bureaucracy; we need one corps level commander, with smart colonels, and the appropriately trained special operations soldiers, to help bring regional stability.

CONTROL THE BORDER

This must also be done at the local level, from Afghan border policemen to Pakistani border policemen. We must help both countries create a professional, uncorrupted force. Again, think strategically, but encourage and guide action locally. This may mean strategic teams working directly with border units, but we need to advise and assist— and make them do the work. Border guards on both sides of the border should talk daily, see each other, and work together to control the territory against insurgents.

FOCUS ON A PROGRAM TO REDUCE ALL VIOLENCE
IN THE LIVES OF THE CITIZENS—EVEN
GOVERNMENT VIOLENCE

Make sure that every act of violence on our part is backed up by good intelligence and an understanding of the expected outcome—best case and worst case. As we all know, some commanders are too willing to accept "collateral damage" in their directed attack. Would any commander make such brash decisions if he were ordering an air strike on insurgents operating within his hometown in the United States? I think not.

With the correct unified command and control as the overarching strategy, and with an emphasis on fixing things at the local level without regard to the border, we can help shape the future toward the elimination of violence. This reduction in violence against the civilian population must occur on both sides of the Afghan-Pakistan border.

The Predator drone program in its current focus is not bringing us closer to victory, and is helping to create a whole new generation of radicals who will likely turn to terrorism as a method of revenge. The use of deadly force, especially when you are shooting through a straw at targets half a planet away, must be applied with precision, not at random. When we take out one terrorist, and kill three civilians in the process, you have only added to the problem. By this killing of innocents you have now created the potential for twelve terrorists (the family members of both the terrorist you killed and the newly created radicals who will self-recruit based on the killing of their family member).

RADICALLY RETHINK OUR ANALYTICAL APPROACH

We need to comprehend and evaluate our adversary through his eyes—not ours. We must understand our enemy to defeat our enemy. He certainly seems to have our number.

We continue to use a twenty-first century lexicon with Western conceptual overlays in dealing with this region of tribes and families.

Constant mistakes are made because we put Western cultural filters on top of a tenth-century situation and react with Western tendencies that often antagonize the very people we are trying to help. Why has the $25 million reward for the capture of Osama bin Laden remained uncollected? Because the people who protect him and support him have no concept of $25 million. It means nothing to them. This is what is called a "clue" in the intelligence business.

We do better when we deal with cultures similar to ours. At the Center for Advanced Defense Studies, I teach a class on World War II and use Operation Body Guard as an example of brilliant deception that was successful because of a clear understanding of the German mind-set and culture. Operation Body Guard was designed to keep the Germans from finding out that the Normandy beaches, not Pas de Calais, were to be the D-day point of attack. Pas de Calais was the location Hitler judged would be the place, and that bad judgment was reinforced through double agents, false radio broadcasts, and a general manipulation of the perceptions of the Germans.

That was the key to the success of both Body Guard, and the path it made to the D-day invasion: We understood the Germans, and we could manipulate them because their culture and method of filtering information was not dissimilar from the Allies.

No such luck in today's war. We are dealing with an adversary who lives in a tribal culture that has not changed much since the tenth century. We have to accept the adversary for what he is, trapped in that mind-set in which international borders are not recognized and much of what he sees is filtered through religious extremism.

Let's not forget that this is *not* a battle against an organized army. This is to win the soul of a people, some of whom have been seduced by the siren call of a faction of a religion that will kill anyone, even other devout followers, simply because they do not share the same radical view. We need to understand the mechanisms the radicals use and break the cycle by replacing it with something that will draw them into the mainstream of their belief system. Simply creating "conditions for success" with enhanced security and economic progress is not enough. We have to become involved in helping to shape and improve the message of the true Muslim faith.

CHANGE OUR LOGISTICAL FOOTPRINT

It is far too large and tends to alienate the very people we are trying to help. Western culture offends the local population. Let us be realistic and examine the real "thorns" that do not give us any operational advantage and wind up serving as cultural blemishes. We do not need to have Burger Kings on our bases. We do not need to build America in Afghanistan; we end up putting creature comforts in places that net us nothing.

Don't get me wrong. Our troops deserve the best. I did not enjoy living in a tent in Bagram for six months, but it kept me focused and it made me want to get the job done and get home—not hang out at the base Starbucks and talk about how great the food is at the new Romeo's Pizza.

FOLLOW THE MONEY

Much warfare can be conducted at the basic level without money, and it has been that way for thousands of years. However, the enemy cannot conduct operations against a modern military, like that of the Pakistanis or the United States, without technology. Basic material, such as telephones, guns, and logistical support, are necessities. Target these necessities, and follow where the money comes from and goes to. We have not done this well, and since the drug trade has not been greatly affected, we need to understand how the money is moved and spent by the Taliban.

ESTABLISH A REAL PEACE PROCESS

The most important thing we must do to win the conflict in Afghanistan is to find a path to reduce the violent conflict to a level of social competition—and to do this we must learn from the Northern Ireland Peace Process. We are naïve and setting ourselves up for failure to believe we can resolve the current Afghani issues within an 18–24 month period. I also believe if we walk away now, our problems will not only follow us home, they will be made worse by our inattention.

President Karzai recently proposed that senior members of the Taliban be exiled. This is the wrong answer. The Black Taliban (the most committed) must be allowed to return to the political process of the country in some form, or else the process is doomed before it starts. Exiling them will only permit them to fundraise and plot terrorist attacks, and ultimately, violent revolution that would lead to their return to power.

We must focus on methods to reduce the current regional war/insurgency to the level of sporadic conflict and then ultimately transmute violent conflict into civil and sustainable competition conducted through the political process. This is why Northern Ireland is an excellent example to study. The peace process there began to take hold in 1992–1993, with serious political negotiations for the next decade. There were setbacks and terrorist attacks during this period, but the process proceeded.

One of the most direct parallels between Afghanistan/Pakistan and Northern Ireland is that the Republic of Ireland was the safe haven and source of terrorists' material and logistical support. Pakistan is now playing the same role for Afghanistan. In Northern Ireland, the Omagh bombing of August 15, 1998, became one of the most decisive points in the conflict. It resulted in 29 deaths and 220 injuries. In this horrific attack nine children, a woman pregnant with twins, and people from multiple Christian faiths were murdered. Afterward, the Republic of Ireland stopped terrorist organizations from using its land as a safe haven and ensured that terrorists could not receive material support. The loss of that safe haven was a crucial point in their progress on the path to the present peace. Similarly, the elimination of safe havens in Pakistan is a critical step toward forcing the Taliban into real negotiations and into a sustainable political process.

Northern Ireland is prospering and both sides—the loyalists and the republicans—live in peace. Belfast is now a center for economic development. Yes, there are still periodic terrorism incidents (the Real IRA conducted an attack in March 2010 against MI5 that caused no casualties and only material damage), but the process has worked and is working.

In addition to the "carrot" of economic development, there is still the "stick" of force. There are still police garrisons around the city (mostly toned down in the cityscape), and the ability of the authorities to call in overwhelming military force that can be deployed within a four hour period.

Former enemies now live side by side in peace. I heard an account of how two of these men, from opposite sides, will not talk to each other as they pass in the halls of the Northern Ireland Assembly—but they no longer work to kill each other, either.

We need to look at how this path from "conflict to competition" worked and how we can apply it. "Victory" in Afghanistan will need to look a whole lot like what we see in Northern Ireland, and less like Iraq.

ADDRESS THE ROOT CAUSE OF REGIONAL INSTABILITY: THE PAKISTANI-INDIAN COLD WAR

The real reason the ISI and the Pakistani army will only go so far in supporting the United States and ISAF efforts in Afghanistan has nothing to do with Afghanistan, and everything to do with their perception of security, and their need to ensure that the Indians do not gain advantage through Afghanistan. The Taliban have been used as an active extension of national will by elements of the ISI and Pakistani army, much like Hezbollah has been used by the Iranians as an extension of their national power. We must accept the Pakistani perception of their self-interest and security as being focused on its regional nuclear competitor, India, and work from there.

The primary focus of the U.S. diplomatic effort must be to reduce tensions between Pakistan and India. There are ways that the United

States can participate and ensure regional stability by direct engagement and real reforms that would allow for a lowering of tensions between the two countries. America must create incentives for the Pakistani government (and the ISI and army) to stop its support of the Taliban. As long as the ISI and Pakistani army continue to provide material support to the Taliban, Afghanistan will not be secure. The Taliban is a tapestry of organizations and there is no single "point" within its structure that could be targeted to affect the whole of the structure, however, if you are able to cut off funding, logistics, and operational support, they will eventually fade in their effectiveness and be forced into a political process.

By extension of this logic, as long as the Taliban exists in fragments and are not fully controlled by the Pakistani government, there is the likelihood that they will continue to pursue their attacks against Pakistani targets and even pursue stealing nuclear weapons (as they and al Qaeda have stated as one of their operational objectives). It is clear that should the Taliban obtain a nuclear weapon and are able to find the expertise needed to move it and explode it, there is little doubt they would do so. The United States or an ISAF member nation would be the target of such a device.

THE PRICE OF FAILURE

The consequences of our failure in Afghanistan and throughout the region would be massive. It would take several things going catastrophically wrong—perhaps not right away, but within three to five years of our troops departing. The degrees of consequence will vary, but ultimately, the price of failure will be another 9/11 attack or series of attacks that will dwarf the original in destructive effect and loss of life by orders of magnitude.

First, the central government of Afghanistan could lose whatever tenuous control it has of the country. The army and national police would quickly fail and become completely ineffective in maintaining civil order in any form. While the Taliban may not be able to take control of the country, they will be strong enough to keep the entire country destabilized and ensure that their allies, such as al Qaeda, can resurge into the country.

Second, with the ability to move with impunity within Afghanistan and through the Swat Valley in northwest Pakistan, there would be a rapid increase of jihadist strength and audacity, and they would move on the Pakistani central government. If economic conditions remain poor in Pakistan, the chances of a successful coup or other radical and violent change of elected government would occur, and the Pakistani army would attempt to come to the rescue, as it has several times before, to stabilize the central government, and by extension, the entire country. In this case, in this post-U.S. occupation of Afghanistan, they would not have sufficient forces to take control. That is because the leadership ranks of the army, formerly filled by Punjabi officers, would not be able to sustain control even of the Punjabi because minorities now make up a larger proportion of the Pakistani army and do not have the same commitment to stability. The army, too, would fall into chaos.

The security measures around the Pakistani nuclear arsenal would continue to degrade, and eventually, one or more of the country's nuclear weapons would be obtained by one of the radical elements. This weapon would be moved, via a network of conspirators, out of Pakistan and to one of a dozen potential targets. Yes, there would be massive efforts to find and contain these weapons, but if even one makes it to a Western target, there is a potential for huge property damage and thousands killed.

Many feel that this view is alarmist and that this scenario could never take place.

Nevertheless, many believed that the Shah of Iran would never fall and that Iran would always remain an ally of the United States. History proves that with the right leadership and circumstances, radical groups can be successful in taking control of nation states. There is no reason to believe that Pakistan is somehow immune from radical change because there are radical elements operating there—and operating, even now, with great effectiveness.

We must be vigilant and realistic, and craft a path to victory. If we don't, we will, as a nation, suffer the consequences. We need to make the correct choices *now* to shape the future. These are costs that neither we, nor our children, should have to bear.

INDEX